McDonnell Douglas
F~4K and F~4M
Phantom II

McDonnell Douglas
F~4K and F~4M
Phantom II
MICHAEL BURNS

OSPREY AIR COMBAT

Published in 1984 by Osprey Publishing Limited
12–14 Long Acre, London WC2E 9LP
Member company of the George Philip Group
© Michael Burns 1984

Sole distributors for the USA

Osceola, Wisconsin 54020, USA

British Library Cataloguing in Publication Data

Burns, Michael
    McDonnell Douglas F-4K and F-4M Phantom II.—(Osprey air
    combat series)
    1. Great Britain. Royal Air Force—History 2. Phantom
    (Fighter planes) 3. Great Britain Royal Navy Fleet Air Arm—
    History 4. Phantom (Fighter planes)
    I. Title
    358.4'3'0941   UG1242.F5
    ISBN 0-85045-564-2

Editor Dennis Baldry
Designed by Roger Daniels
Printed in Spain

*To the aircrew who fly the Phantom in our defence and the
servicemen and servicewomen who keep their aircraft
operational.*

Contents

Chapter 1
Genesis of the Phantom II

By 1953 the McDonnell Aircraft Corporation had an excellent record. Founded in 1939 at Lambert Field, St Louis, Missouri, McDonnell's reputation as a leading jet fighter designer had been established in the immediate postwar years with two successive twin-engined fighters for the US Navy: the FH-1 Phantom, the USN's first all-jet powered carrier aircraft, and the F2H Banshee. In 1950 the USN ordered their successor, the single-engined McDonnell F3H Demon. Then in May 1953 McDonnell won its first USAF production contract, for the twin-engined F-101A Voodoo. McDonnell's future success seemed assured.

In mid-1953 the F3H was encountering development problems, and foreseeing future trends and the imminence of advanced supersonic fighters, McDonnell initiated low priority, company funded design work to develop a long range, supersonic, all-weather, twin-engined successor to the F3H, provisionally designated F3H-G/H. The USN had already announced a requirement for a first generation supersonic air superiority fighter, but had also indicated its preference for the Vought XF8FU-1 Crusader by approving development in May 1953. The USN's Request for Proposals was not formally issued until September 1953. Eight proposals were submitted, including McDonnell's, but the XF8FU-1 was selected and thus McDonnell lost this important contract.

However, the Navy's Bureau of Aeronautics was impressed by McDonnell's ability and encouraged the company to redirect its design studies towards an attack fighter to meet anticipated USN needs. This was a new departure for McDonnell, but the company was already noted for bold and intelligent approaches to subjects. Indeed, McDonnell had already started an intensive

'market research programme', seeking opinions from interested bodies to establish the form that the next generation of carrier-borne air superiority and attack fighters might take.

McDonnell reworked the F3H-G/H. The resulting design proposal was a large, twin-engined, single-seat aircraft with a flat, broad chord, thin, high lift delta wing. The flat tailplane was mounted high on the fin. Notwithstanding the considerable size of its wing and tail areas, and its general bulk, the aircraft's maneouvrability promised to be unprecedented, at least among carrier fighters. It would also be fast. It was proposed to use two Wright J65 turbojets (licence-built Armstrong-Siddeley Sapphires), judged capable of permitting Mach 1.5 at high altitude, and the proposed variable intake ducts would improve on this figure. The fighter was heavily armed, with four 20 mm cannon in the lower nose, and one belly and ten wing stores pylons. Provision was made for a large nose-mounted radar, the AN/APQ-50 being proposed. While its ancestry in the F3H-2 Demon could be seen, the embryo Phantom II could already be discerned.

McDonnell built a company funded mock-up and in August 1954 formally presented the design proposal to the Bureau of Aeronautics. The USN issued a Letter of Intent on 18 October 1954 covering the planned procurement of two prototype long-range, twin-engined, all-weather, supersonic attack aircraft under the designation YAH-1, plus one static airframe for tests. However, the USN stipulated that a number of changes be made, including the adoption of the more powerful and larger General Electric J79 afterburning turbojet then under development, although to speed the programme the prototypes were to use J65s.

On 26 May 1955, the USN fundamentally changed the specifications and sought a long-range, high-altitude, all-weather, all-missile armed carrier-borne supersonic interceptor. McDonnell revamped the design and on 23 June 1955 the designation was formally changed to F4H-1 – McDonnell's (H) fourth fighter for the USN. Detail specifications for the new aircraft were finalized and the USN issued Contract No a(s) 55-272 on 25 July 1955, covering two XF4H-1s and five pre-production YF4H-1s, thus effectively accepting the design, the McDonnell Model 98.

The F4H-1 had a thin, low wing, with no anhedral and a quarter chord sweep of 45°, the outer panels folding upwards. The tailplane had slight anhedral and the fuselage was area-ruled. Two J79s were mounted side-by-side in the lower mid-fuselage, fed by fixed-geometry cheek intakes and exhausting below the tail. Twin J79s would make the F4H-1 the USN's first Mach 2 aircraft. Gone were the YAH-1's four 20 mm cannon and all but the centreline pylon. The armament was to be six AIM-7 Sparrow III AAMs then under development by Raytheon and based on the Sparrow I used by the F3H-2M. Two were to be carried on wing pylons, and two under the rear

and two under the forward fuselage on retractable rails. Later, four were carried semi-recessed in the lower fuselage and ejection launched, an innovative compromise which saved internal space and minimized drag. The F4H was thus to be the USN's first purpose-designed all-missile armed fighter, which accorded with late 1950s philosophies.

For all-weather Mach 1.5 missile interception, sophisticated avionics were required and the nose-mounted Westinghouse AN/APQ-72 AI radar was selected. To handle the heavy cockpit workloads a radar intercept officer (RIO) cum navigator was necessary. However, McDonnell prepared single-seat and tandem two-seat configurations because the USN was vacillating. Between 17 and 23 September 1955, McDonnell built a mock-up of a two-seat F4H-1, which representatives of the USN inspected enthusiastically. Within two days the USN had decided upon the two-seat version, a capital reason for the design's longevity.

The centre wing structure of the Phantom II is based upon a torque box, which carries the major loads and forms the structural backbone of the aircraft. This is an F-4B

Wind-tunnel tests revealed serious stability problems, and several design corrections were made. The conventional 45° wing sweep incurred several aerodynamic penalties, including wing tip stall at high and low speeds with high angles of attack. These were cured by increasing the chord of the outer panels 10 per cent by extending the leading-edge to produce a dog-tooth, which increased the area and lift co-efficient, thereby decreasing stalling speed. To improve lateral stability in the simplest fashion, the outer panels were given 12° dihedral, equivalent to 3° overall wing dihedral. A one-piece, all-moving, slab stabilator was introduced with 23° 15' anhedral to clear wing downwash, but mounted above the jet efflux to clear turbulence. Variable-geometry engine air intakes – the first installed on a fighter – were fitted, automatically controlled by an air data computer activated by air pressure/temperature to permit optimum engine performance throughout the speed range and at all altitudes. Supersonic nozzles were fitted to the J79s.

After satisfactory wind-tunnel tests, the XF4H-1 design was frozen in August 1956. McDonnell received orders for a further sixteen YF4H-1s on 19 December 1956, bringing the total order to 23. Initial structural release, marking the start of construction, was authorized on 31 December 1956. As the FH-1 Phantom was no longer in service, the F4H was christened Phantom II.

The first XF4H-1 was completed in April 1958. XJ79 development had progressed better than expected and it was decided to install J79s in the prototypes too, although the specified version, the J79-GE-8, was not yet available. The first prototype made its first evaluation flight on 27 May 1958 from Lambert-St Louis Municipal Airport – McDonnell's home field – flown by McDonnell's chief test pilot, Robert C. Little, and powered by J79-GE-3As lent by the USAF. Manufacturer's and USN test programmes commenced at Edwards AFB and Naval Air Test Center (NATC), Patuxent River, Maryland. Performance was exceptional, and few problems were encountered, but the angle of the air intakes was changed. Test flying revealed that handling under certain conditions was actually better with Sparrows fitted than without.

In competitive evaluation during 1958 against the new Chance Vought F8FU-3 Crusader III, the F4H-1 was judged superior and was selected as the USN's next standard all-weather interceptor. On 28 September 1959, Contract No a(s) 60-0134 was issued covering a total of 72 J79-GE-8-powered production F4H-1s.

Changes were progressively incorporated during the research and development and evaluation flying carried out by the 23 pre-production YF4H-1s. Both canopies were redesigned and the nose was refined in detail. The introduction of

F-4B forward fuselage illustrating four reasons for the Phantom II's success: two seats, endowing flexibility and survivability; variable-geometry intakes to give good engine exploitation at all heights and speeds; twin engine safety and power; and an adaptable nose

boundary layer control (BLC) through engine compressor air blown over forward and aft flap sections considerably improved carrier operability. All these changes were incorporated in the first definitive production batch.

Concurrently, the USN conducted an intensive evaluation programme. Initial carrier suitability trials were conducted with the sixth F4H-1 aboard USS *Independence* in February 1960, and later in the year a series of operations from one of the USN's smallest carriers, USS *Intrepid*, proved the Phantom II's flexibility. The USN increased its order to a total of 192 in October 1960.

The F4H-1 was designated as a carrier-borne air defence and tactical strike (attack) fighter for the USN and USMC, carrying four AIM-9 Sidewinders on wing pylons in addition to the AIM-7s or up to 16,000 lb (7,257 kg) of stores on one centreline and four wing hard points. The first definitive production aircraft flew on 25 March 1961. Thereafter the pre-production model and the first 24 production aircraft were re-designated F4H-1F, the F suffix indicating non-standard engines, the J79-GE-2 or 2A. Production F4H-1 deliveries began in June 1961.

Bearing out the performance estimates, the flight trials demonstrated that the Phantom II was an outstanding and versatile warplane with excellent development potential. McDonnell began giving consideration to purchasers other than the USN and USMC early in the development programme. More markets would increase McDonnell sales and benefit sub-contractors, while reducing the aircraft's unit cost and permitting development of new versions that would make the Phantom II an even more attractive and marketable product.

As a result of discussions in 1959 at Edwards AFB and NATC, McDonnell decided that the most effective way, short of a war, to bring the Phantom II to the attention of military and naval air staffs and their politicians was a record breaking campaign. Although records may only reflect combat capability, they do demonstrate absolute performance and certainly capture interest. McDonnell pursued and broke successively every record open to the Phantom II. Moreover, the record attempt Phantoms were basically unmodified USN aircraft. No other aircraft had broken such a diversity of records. The record breaking campaign, undertaken between December 1959 and March 1962, demonstrated exactly what it was intended to: that the Phantom II was without equal.

The Phantom II clearly had the potential to attract a wide market and overseas sales attracted McDonnell, although the company had little experience in this area. Obvious targets were nations with aircraft carriers, principally the UK and France, but including Canada, Australia, Brazil, the Netherlands and Argentina. Markets for land-based variants included nations with large or vulnerable air space to defend, including the UK, Canada, Australia and West Germany. Politically influenced choices lay in nations which were covered by Military Aid Programs or were allied to the USA. McDonnell were also aware of the problems facing the British and French aviation industries and the marginal economics of other nations' aviation industries.

US military missions would assist McDonnell's representatives in marketing operations, the record-breaking programme would reinforce the message, and taking the product to the potential customer, such as Project *Short Look* flight demonstration in Europe, was planned to have direct appeal, as the Phantom II's sensational debut at the 1961 Paris Air Show proved. Invitations to test fly it could also be extended.

McDonnell could offer an attractive package to potential customers. Fixed price arrangements, with credit facilities at low interest rates provided by the US Government for multi-year procurement and delivery, offset against the placement of US Government purchase orders and by sub-contract with the customer's aviation industry could readily be offered. USN and USAF training, servicing, supply and support facilities could be made available. In the event of losses, even through war, replacements could be readily supplied from American stocks. The US aviation industry, dependent upon mass production and low unit costs, could now supply a product at least equal to any competitor in service (or under development) to any nation at least as quickly at a competitive price, and backed by good after-sales service. This comprehensive product support would be difficult for any customer's aviation industry to match.

The benefits to McDonnell were obvious. The development of role-optimized and multi-role models would in turn stimulate demand; the customers would pay for development work; mass production to meet demand would reduce or maintain unit cost to levels unattainable by small nations or aircraft concerns; and the whole programme would keep McDonnell occupied and prospering for a long time, along with several airframe, avionics and weapons companies. The benefits to the US Government were less tangible, but equally real. The Phantom II could become a part of foreign policy in terms of military aid to ensure the stability and ability to defend themselves of various friendly, treaty-bound or client nations. The development of multi-role capabilities, quantity production and low unit costs were financially, practically and militarily attractive to a Government which had assumed a wide ranging role in world affairs and a critical burden in the balance of power, and supported multi-billion dollar defence programmes. Spreading programme costs abroad and the revenue from overseas sales would be welcome.

McDonnell tackled prime targets first, and prepared project studies on Phantom IIs for the British Royal Navy, Canada, and France. It would be extremely practical if the Canadians bought the Phantom, especially because of the integrated North American air defence system, while a Royal Navy Phantom II would be an excellent advertisement. Neither Canada nor France bought the Phantom II, but the British were interested, tentatively, from very early on.

On 9 December 1959, launching its British marketing programme, McDonnell published Report 7233 entitled *Carrier Suitability of F4H-1 Airplane on British Carriers*. A fundamental factor was that British carriers were smaller than US Navy carriers, and thus a Phantom for the Royal Navy would require higher lift and greater power.

In April 1960, a McDonnell mission arrived in London. The British were attempting to sort out their military aircraft programmes in the aftermath of the cancellations brought about by Mr Duncan Sandys' obsessional all-missile all-nuclear defence policy announced in 1957. An existing aircraft with proven performance which was cheaper than a UK equivalent might have a chance. The RN was McDonnell's primary target, as the Phantom II was a carrier aircraft. It would be an ideal replacement for the Sea Vixen and possibly the Scimitar. On 8 April 1960, the first direct Royal Navy contact was made with the Vice-Chief of Naval Staff at the Admiralty, Admiral Sir Walter T Couchman.

McDonnell were also aware of the tenuous futures of the UK's aero-engine manufacturers, who were in the process of merging to secure the few major contracts available. Co-operation with a

UK aero-engine company was sound tactically. They were also aware of the current British aircraft and aero-engine programmes. On 11 April 1960, the McDonnell representatives met Ronald Harker, the Military and Aircraft Industry International Liaison Manager of Rolls-Royce, at his Conduit Street, London office to discuss the use of RB.168 in the Phantom – the Spey. Rolls-Royce were in the process of selling the Admiralty a military version of their civil Spey for the Buccaneer, partly in the hope that the RAF would then buy the Buccaneer as their Canberra replacement instead of TSR-2, development of which had been authorized in July 1959.

The RAF recognized that the new Lightning was not ideal as a fighter, and that the Hunter would need replacing in the ground attack role. With multi-role developments of the Phantom II already under consideration, McDonnell felt confident enough to meet the Vice-Chief of the Air Staff, Air Chief Marshal Sir Edmund C Huddleston on 12 April 1960, to whom the representative quoted $2 million per aircraft. The McDonnell representatives also put their case to Norman Meeres, the Under Secretary for Aircraft at the Ministry of Aviation, on 12 April 1960. RAF interest was limited, and no positive response was made until nearly four years later.

On 14 April 1960, Captain Nigel Bailey, the Director of Naval Air Warfare at the Admiralty, visited McDonnell's plant at St Louis for discussions on Phantom II. On 26 July 1960, Cdr P C S Chilton became the first British pilot, and the seventy-third in total, to fly the F4H-1, an encouragingly positive move for McDonnell.

In July 1961, the twenty-first production F4H-1 landed at RNAS Yeovilton en route to the USA after a sensational debut at the Paris Air Show. It was the first Phantom in the UK, and RN personnel viewed it with awe. The message was being reinforced, although there had been no strong RN reaction since 1960.

On 12 April 1962, McDonnell Report 7233 Addendum I, *F-4 For The Royal Navy*, was released, one of several under this title. It included plans for trials of an F-4B aboard *Ark Royal* on 7 September 1962, using a dolly to lift its nose, but these did not take place. A further revision of Report 7233 was issued on 9 October 1962.

Meanwhile McDonnell had been pursuing another primary target, the USAF. A contract with the USAF, whose several commands required various specializations, would offer quantity production and the opportunities to develop the Phantom II as a multi-role land-based aircraft. The USAF was under pressure in the early 1960s from the Secretary of Defense, Mr Robert McNamara, to reduce expenditure through commonality of armed forces equipment. One

programme was the TFX for the USAF and USN, which resulted in the F-111. As the Phantom II had been selected by the USN as a major aircraft type, it was an obvious contender for USAF procurement. The USAF operated the McDonnell F-101 Voodoo, and a firm basis for communication already existed.

The USAF were suitably impressed by the F4H-1, and its capabilities were being reinforced by the record breaking campaign. The USAF evaluated the F4H-1 in 1961, primarily as a successor to Air Defense Command's F-106A Delta Dart interceptor. The trials demonstrated that the F4H-1 had a clear ascendancy not only over the F-106A, but over every other combat aircraft in the USAF. In March 1962 the Department of Defense announced that two versions of the F4H-1 were to be bought for the TAF, PAF and USAFE: the F-110A air superiority, interdiction, counter-air and close air support fighter, and the RF-110A unarmed, multi-sensor, all-weather, day/night, high/low reconnaissance aircraft. This was an extremely important advance for McDonnell, promoting the development of the Phantom II's full multi-role capability. A photo-reconnaissance version had been proposed to the USN in 1959 and now USN interest had returned.

On 18 September 1962 the tri-service standardized designation system became effective. The familiar F-4 was applied to the Phantom II, the USN and USMC F4H-1F and F4H-1 and the USAF's F-110A and RF-110A becoming the F-4A, F-4B, F-4C and RF-4C respectively. Under the new designations, the USAF authorized production of the RF-4C and F-4C on 31 December 1962 and 8 February 1963 respectively.

The British Government's new Defence Minister, Mr Peter Thornycroft met McNamara in the USA between 9 and 12 September 1962 for 'useful talks' on weapons development. But on his return to London, Thornycroft stressed that the talks had concerned joint research on parts of weapon systems, but did not cover 'the development of a complete weapon in the country of the other'. The UK already had an agreement with the USA providing for the exchange of technical information on defence matters, and the USA was assisting in funding the BS.100 vectored-thrust engine for the UK's V/STOL fighter project, the Hawker P.1154. But Thornycroft's statement clearly excluded the development of a British version of the Phantom in the USA.

On 2 January 1963, McDonnell Report EW 348, *Fixed Extended Nose Gear For Flight Test on F-4B*, was released, which included new plans for Phantom trials aboard *Ark Royal* in April 1963. These, like the earlier trials, did not take place, but carrier deck trials with an F-4B in such a

Perhaps the ultimate Phantom: the lethal electronic warfare F-4G, of which 119 were converted from F-4Es for the USAF. This F-4G (c/n 3932, USAF 97254) carries the Texas Instruments High Speed Anti-Radar Missile (HARM), AGM-88A

configuration were conducted satisfactorily aboard USS *Forrestal* on 11 April 1963, and trials were also carried out on field facilities at NATC.

On 20 February 1963, it was announced that the Hawker P.1154 V/STOL would be the Hunter's successor in RAF service. On 30 July 1963 the British Government stated that a version of the P.1154 was being developed for the RN as a successor to the Sea Vixen. There was now no room for the Phantom II in the RN, or so it appeared, while the RAF (scheduled to replace Canberra with TSR-2 and Hunter with P.1154), had given McDonnell no encouragement. But McDonnell kept listening; Britannia was a contrary lady, going through an uncertain time.

The Phantom II is an exceptional example of the tactical fighters which have taken over many of the offensive tasks previously assigned to bombers. Its speed and power, large warload, ruggedness, reliability and versatility made it the most sought

after combat aircraft in the Western world for a decade and a half. It has served with the US Navy, Marine Corps and Air Force, and with ten foreign nations, and was a major weapon in the Vietnam War.

The Phantom II was one of the largest military aircraft programmes since World War II, and enjoyed the largest run of any supersonic Western fighter. When production ended in March 1979, McDonnell had built, assembled and test flown 5,057 at St Louis. In addition, 16, the last batch, were built for Iran but neither assembled nor delivered owing to the Islamic revolution, eleven were supplied as components to Japan, and 127 were licence-built in Japan.

The Phantom II provided US workers with an estimated one million man years of employment, and thousands of hours for British, German and Japanese workers. The value to McDonnell Douglas exceeded $10 billion after deducting engines and components purchased by the US and other Governments under separate contracts and supplied to McDonnell. The estimated total value of the entire Phantom II programme exceeded $20 billion, international sales amounting to $6 billion.

Chapter 2
'The Most Attractive Solution...'

Apart from the sheer excellence of the Phantom II, the major reason McDonnell were able to make such progress in interesting the Royal Navy was that, in the early 1960s, British military aircraft procurement programmes were confused, compromised and unstable. Drastic reductions in defence expenditure had been demanded by the Conservative Prime Minister, Mr Harold MacMillan, for the late 1950s and 1960s. In pursuit of this, Mr Duncan Sandys' Defence Review of 1957 asserted that offensive and defensive missiles would replace manned bombers and fighters, and that the balance of nuclear deterrence would render large conventional forces unnecessary. Most aircraft programmes were cut.

Carrier-borne air power, required to fulfill Britain's many overseas commitments, escaped Sandys lightly. The Buccaneer survived as a naval strike fighter, and a Mark 2 version, powered by the new Rolls-Royce RB.168.1 turbofan, was ordered for service into the 1970s. The RN were relying on the Sea Vixen all-weather, all-missile interceptor for fleet defence, and the Scimitar for strike/air defence up to the mid/late 1960s, but programmes to find their successors would have to begin in the early 1960s.

The Royal Air Force bore the brunt of the cuts. The UK nuclear deterrent, the RAF's V-bomber force, would be replaced by nuclear-powered submarines carrying Polaris ICBMs in the 1960s. Nevertheless, the air defence of the UK was organized primarily to protect the V-bomber force bases from attack, and the Lightning interceptor programme survived the 1957 Review, albeit in emasculated form as an 'interim' replacement for the RAF's Javelin fighters from the early-mid 1960s. The RAF would essentially become a tactical air force: the Service developed a policy of mobile tactical air power based on the short-take-off TSR-2 strike/attack aircraft, the supersonic V/STOL P.1154 in the fighter/close support roles, and the STOL AW.681 tactical transport.

Conceived by Sir Sidney Camm, the Hawker P.1154 represented a revolution in fighter design. A supersonic development of the subsonic experimental V/STOL P.1127, the P.1154 was to use the Bristol-Siddeley BS.100 vectored-thrust turbofan, with plenum chamber burning (PCB), developed with the aid of US funds. It had an estimated performance of Mach 2 at altitude and Mach 1.2 at sea level. Although designed as a successor to the Hawker Hunter, it was put forward for a NATO requirement (NMBR-3) issued in mid-1961, for a sophisticated V/STOL tactical strike fighter; NATO sales would keep the unit cost low. P.1154's principal competitor emerged as the Dassault Mirage III-V with eight Rolls-Royce RB.162 lift engines. But when the USA withdrew its support from NMBR-3, NATO withdrew the requirement in mid-1962. France and Britain proceeded independently.

The Air Staff regarded NMBR-3 as largely irrelevant to RAF requirements, but was interested in P.1154 as a Hunter replacement. The Admiralty, for whom NMBR-3 was wholly irrelevant, had been developing a requirement for a Sea Vixen replacement. But in mid-1962 the Air Staff and the Admiralty, at Defence Staff level, began to draft a joint requirement for an aircraft similar in concept to P.1154. In standardizing, it was hoped to save money on procurement and support, like the USN/USAF with TFX (F-111). In practical terms, the P.1154 was the only suitable aircraft the British aviation industry could develop in the time available.

Requirements conflicted widely. The RAF required a single-seat strike aircraft with supersonic dash capability and sophisticated terrain-following radar to replace the Hunter. The RN required a two-seat carrier-borne all-weather interceptor/Fleet defence fighter with an advanced AAM weapon system, long range and sustained supersonic high altitude capability. Reconciliation posed serious problems. Moreover, the Services demanded extremely tight schedules, proposing the first prototype flight for mid-1965 and entry into service by January 1968. HSA drew up proposals, based on the BS.100PCB, in August 1962, and began drafting a final development plan late in 1962. To meet the schedules, the latter had to be submitted in March 1963 and a development contract issued a few months later.

The Air Ministry was worried by the cost of P.1154, the time-scale of development, and the single-engine safety factor. The Admiralty was also critical of the BS.100: in the event of engine failure there was no safety margin, vital for over-sea operations, while the range and endurance were inadequate for the RN, but the weight of additional fuel would make catapult launching essential, ruining the concept.

Rolls-Royce had neglected its military development contracts. Having failed to convince HSA to adopt lift engines for P.1154, it had relinquished rights in the RB.162 to France. The company lacked orders and thus its financial and job situation was acute; but Ronald Harker of

Rolls-Royce heard of the dissatisfactions over P.1154 and proposed a scheme using twin handed-Speys and cold ducting for P.1154. The Spey existed in civil form and was being developed for military use in the Buccaneer, and Rolls-Royce claimed that a vectored-thrust variant could be available and in production sooner than BS.100, which was still under development.

Developed for the BAC One-Eleven and Trident airliners, the design of the RB.168 Spey two-shaft, axial-flow turbofan was optimized around the arduous requirements of short/medium haul commercial operations, and emphasized simple handling, long overhaul and component lives, easy servicing, and low specific fuel consumption. Design began in September 1959 and the first static test was made in late December 1960. On 12 October 1961 flight tests of two Speys in a Vulcan commenced. Trident prototype trials began on 6 January 1962.

The RN already knew the Spey, having ordered it for the Buccaneer. They were interested in the

D.H. Sea Vixen FAW.2, with live Red Tops, from HMS Victorious, *about to be catapulted from USS* Oriskany *(CVA-34), in transit to Hong Kong, on 15 September 1966 during Operation* CROSSDECK. *The air defence fighter the RN sought to meet the foreseen maritime long-range stand-off threat required greater endurance and speed, and a more sophisticated radar-controlled missile weapons system*

twin-Spey concept, which offered twin-engine safety in addition to increased take-off thrust and better SFC, and hence range, while standardizing on a single engine type was attractive. The Spey developed for the Buccaneer S.2 to replace the S.1's Gyron Juniors, was the first military Spey. Designated RB.168.1 or Spey Mk 101, it was developed from the basic civil Mk 505 to meet the higher-duty requirements of the military rating. Design began in November 1960 – before the civil Spey had run on a bench. Following a prototype development contract placed only weeks after the first civil flight tests, bench tests commenced in December 1961. A production order was placed by the Admiralty in January 1962, and the first Spey Mk 101 Buccaneer S.2 was scheduled to fly in May 1963. The RN were therefore well acquainted with the Spey's capabilities.

The twin-Spey project was put to Hawkers in early January 1963. Both the Air Ministry and Sir Sidney Camm gave it consideration, but were not too enthusiastic. Despite BS.100's disadvantages, the twin-Spey would introduce fundamental problems, and delays in development. The American financial interest in BS.100 had also to be considered. Nevertheless, a Spey design study by Rolls-Royce was followed by a full project study of engine development, production and costs. Official evaluations of both BS.100 and Spey installations were begun, but in order to meet the time-scale required by the P.1154 schedule, a decision had to be taken before March 1963: BS.100 was selected. Rolls-Royce now doubted if they could develop the Spey to meet the specification demanded by P.1154, so in effect withdrew, but Rolls-Royce were offered the HS.681 engine contract (Medway). The Government, having forced them to amalgamate, was seeking to divide existing contracts fairly among the surviving aero-engine companies.

To meet the Services' schedules, the design of the RAF's P.1154 was frozen in February 1963 and, on 20 February, the Government's Defence White Paper announced the selection of the P.1154 as the Hunter's successor. Soon afterwards, when the joint RAF/RN requirements had finally stabilized, and the argument over the powerplant had abated, the P.1154 RN was frozen. On 30 July 1963, Mr Peter Thornycroft announced in the Commons that the RN and RAF had reached agreement at Joint Defence Staff level upon the characteristics of a common aircraft to replace both the Hunter and the Sea Vixen; based upon the P.1154 design already adopted for the RAF, he said it would 'greatly increase the flexibility of air power and provide opportunity for economies in its disposition.' The P.1154 was given the development go-ahead with a requirement for several hundred aircraft for the RN and RAF at total cost of £750 million.

While the argument over P.1154's powerplant ran its course, and even after P.1154's procurement had been announced, the Admiralty's interest in the aircraft waned. The RN criticized not only its lack of range and its powerplant, but the late date it would enter service, and the unit cost of £1.5 million. The RN therefore began to look for another suitable aircraft. The F-4 could fulfill the RN's requirements and by October the case for buying the Phantom II had been prepared. The fact that the RN was losing faith in the P.1154 had reached the US Naval Attaché in London and on 26 October 1963 he cabled the Chief of Naval Operations, USN, stating that there was 'renewed interest by the Royal Navy' in the F-4. This was confirmed on 31 October in a memorandum by McDonnell's Paris representative, Admiral C R 'Cat' Brown, USN, ret'd.

In October 1963 a party from McDonnell consisting of Admiral Brown, Charles Forsyth, and Mr Dickman, visited Ronald Harker at his Conduit Street office in London, to inform him that they believed that the RN was interested in buying the F-4 and not the P.1154, and that they thought that a Spey-powered F-4 would be more attractive to the RN than a J79-powered F-4. Harker was interested. It was imperative for Rolls-Royce's financial future to land a major military contract, essentially either P.1154 or AW.681. Although Rolls-Royce would probably get the AW.681 contract for the Medway engine, and were touting to win another Medway order – for the SAAB Viggen – they were anxious to win another major military contract for the Spey, apart from Buccaneer. If the P.1154RN was cancelled, Rolls-Royce could win a Spey contract for an F-4 for the RN. This might result in RAF interest in a Spey-powered P.1154, but more probably, with the P.1154 order reduced, the P.1154RAF would also be cancelled and an RAF Spey-powered F-4 be selected. This placed Rolls-Royce in a much better position.

The basic features sought by the RN for an F-4 Spey were similar to those they had needed in the Buccaneer Spey Mk 101: a robust, corrosion resistant engine, with high tolerance of intake disturbance produced by flight maneuvres, steam and bird ingestion, weapon firing, etc., at low level and during catapult launching. But the Mk 101 is incapable of powering the Buccaneer beyond Mach 1 (in level flight), and is not a fighter engine. Such an engine requires a reheat boost for take-off, acceleration, supersonic flight and combat. Rolls-Royce proposed a supersonic Spey: if they could conceive a vectored-thrust Spey, an augmented thrust Spey should not pose insuperable problems.

McDonnell did not need to be convinced of the Spey's merits or its suitability for the Phantom. McDonnell had approached Harker much earlier, in April 1960, with just such a proposal. On 4

May 1962 McDonnell published Report 8824 entitled *F4H J79/RB.168 Comparison*, working on the basis of the Spey Mk 101, and the US Department of Defense had given serious consideration to an augmented-thrust Spey-powered Phantom II for the TFX. McDonnell's Report was promising. Compared to the turbojet J79, the newer two-spool turbofan Spey would provide 'greater thrust to weight ratio and lower specific fuel consumption' with greater acceleration potential, more bleed air for BLC, more rapid engine response to throttle movements, higher thermal efficiency, and the ability to give maximum power for sustained high-speed performance. It was considered that the Spey 'is of about the same size as the J79 engine and could be installed in the F4H airframe without extensive modification. So equipped, the F4H would realize significant improvement both in performance and combat radius.' There were no practical engineering difficulties in converting the Spey to augmented thrust, and the by-pass principle would permit a greater thrust over a turbojet, mainly a result of the large volume of unburnt oxygen from the by-pass in the exhaust jet.

Despite the RN's interest and McDonnell's support, Rolls-Royce were cautious. They could not see how the RN could be interested in an F-4, let alone a Spey-powered F-4, after the decision had been made to buy the P.1154 so late. It took a party at the Savoy Hotel in London attended by Admiral Sir Frank Hopkins, Admiral Johnnie Ievers, and Capt 'Winkle' Brown (Deputy Director of Naval Air Warfare and responsible for operational requirements) from the RN, and Sir Denning Pearson, Chairman/MD, Adrian A Lombard, Director of Engineering, Cyril Lovesey, and Harker from Rolls-Royce to convince Rolls-Royce that the RN were very serious about procuring Spey-powered F-4s if the P.1154 was not satisfactory; and it was far from satisfactory.

But there were many problems to be overcome. The cost of a Spey-powered F-4 would be too high for it to compete with standard J79-powered F-4s in the export market and Britain would bear the full costs of development. Engine development costs were also rising, and the reheat Spey would be equally uncompetitive. The RAF was reluctant to have a Spey-powered F-4 – they did not need the performance advantage over the J79s and could buy more J79-powered F-4s at two-thirds the price. The full estimated performance of the civil Spey and the Mk 101 had yet to be realized. To have it in time, the reheat version would have to be based on an earlier design than might otherwise be preferable. Finally, there was strong competition from General Electric, who asserted that they could find more thrust in the J79.

Rolls-Royce now gave Spey-powered F-4 installation studies the highest priority. Technical brochures and cost figures were produced and a general sales case was made out describing the advantages over the J79. The RN was satisfied with the performance, provided engine handling was as good as that of the J79, that the cost was acceptable, and that maintenance access and engine changing would meet their stringent requirements. The RAF realized that if the P.1154RN was cancelled, as seemed probable, their P.1154 would become financially non-viable. They would then need the Phantom, but they were critical of the cost of Rolls-Royce power. General Electric seized upon this dissension to make renewed representations, but the Ministry of Aviation preferred the Spey, mainly because it was British and did not involve dollar expenditure, and accepted it had better performance than the J79.

McDonnell also gave the RN F-4 the highest priority, and kept pressure on the interested parties. They could draw upon the development programme of the USN's next model, the F-4J, to support their arguments, while the availability of the advanced, multi-mode pulse Doppler AN/AWG-10 radar system, which was replacing the earlier pulse systems in the F-4J, offered a considerable advance in radar capability to the RN. The extensible nose gear for the RN F-4, to improve its take-off performance from shorter RN catapults, had been tested and found satisfactory aboard USS *Forrestal* on 11 April 1963, and other high lift devices were soon to be tested for the F-4J. Therefore, McDonnell could present concrete proposals to the British. A memorandum of 21 November 1963 by Messrs Baldwin and Graff, *F-4B For Great Britain*, in essence a brief project study update, laid out the details of the McDonnell Model 98ET.

Events now moved rapidly. McDonnell Report 8696, *Phantom II For The Royal Navy*, essentially a project definition, was released to coincide with a visit by a British team to the USN on 2 and 3 January 1964 to discuss the F-4. On 23 January 1963, McDonnell confidently issued a 'new business request for estimates' to suppliers for the RN F-4, and the following day they released Report A453, *Phantom II For Great Britain*, simultaneously giving the pre-contract planning go ahead. Two days later, on 26 January, there was a visit to McDonnell by Joint Defence Staff, Ministry of Aviation, Royal Navy and Rolls-Royce Engineering delegates, led by Capt Eric 'Winkle' Brown, during which McDonnell was given the first indication of possible RAF interest in the F-4.

The Defence White Paper of 13 February 1964 did not mention the F-4 but did announce that 20 development and pre-production TSR-2 aircraft – 'one of the most potent and flexible instruments of military power yet devised', the Paper called it – had been ordered (30 production aircraft were ordered in late February). The TSR-2 was intended to replace the already obsolescing Canberra, and this order represented a significant stage in the RAF's re-equipment programme. But there had been important developments after the Paper had gone to press. During the debate on the Paper in the Commons on 26–27 February, Mr Thornycroft stated that studies of the possibilities of developing a common aircraft for the RN and RAF had suggested that such an aircraft would be 'too near the margin' to be viable. It was proposed to develop the simplest and most robust P.1154 possible, powered by BS.100, to go into full production as a replacement for the RAF's Hunter, and to cancel the P.1154RN entirely.

This left the RN without a replacement for the Sea Vixen. Thornycroft pointed out that only a limited number of aircraft would be required to replace the Sea Vixen 'which on any hypothesis would mean practically no export orders.' It would, he said, be possible to develop such an aircraft. However, 'undoubtedly the most attractive solution' was to purchase the McDonnell Phantom II powered by Rolls-Royce Spey engines in place of J79s. This solution, subject to appropriate negotiations, would be adopted.

Thornycroft made a further significant announcement during the debate. The HS.681 would be developed for the RAF, thus completing the RAF's tactical mobility requirements – and it would be powered by Rolls-Royce engines. This was a welcome boost for the British aviation industry. Rolls-Royce were well pleased with recent progress. The company had begun development of the augmented thrust Spey for the F-4, the RB.168-25R or Spey Mk 201, early in 1964, when the decision to adopt the F-4 was taken. But the final decision on adopting the Spey remained in abeyance, dependent upon cost, time scale of development, and performance, and was in doubt for some time before Thornycroft's announcement. To meet the required schedule, development was rapid, which led to problems and delayed the UK Phantom's entry into service. Even after development of the engine and airframe had begun there was revision; and the Labour Government which was elected in October 1964 reconsidered the whole project.

On 10 and 11 March 1964, Mr Julian Amery, Minister of Aviation since 1962, led a joint RN/Ministry of Aviation party on a visit to McDonnell, and between 28 and 30 April 1964 a Rolls-Royce VIP team visited St Louis. It included Mr A G Newton (now Rolls-Royce Ltd's Director of Engineering). On 11 May 1964, McDonnell published Report A789 entitled *Royal Navy Phantom II Program Plan*, the result of pre-contract planning by McDonnell, Rolls-Royce, the RN, and the Ministry of Aviation, the latter responsible for the execution of British defence research, development and production. It gave the

target dates for the programme go-ahead as 1 July 1964, the first flight as June 1966, and the first delivery as April 1967, ahead of that for the P.1154RN. Accordingly, the RN Phantom II programme (after UK Government approval) was given the go-ahead on 1 July 1964. The same day the UK Government confirmed an order for two pre-production YF-4K Spey-development flying aircraft, placing the order under modification of the USN's Specification Detail series, SD-513, as SD-513-1RN. By 1 September two production F-4K for systems trials had been added.

The UK thus became the first overseas customer to conclude an agreement for the purchase of the Phantom II, not as a result of a carefully planned re-equipment programme, but as a result of a sequence of events, decisions and misconceptions creating a gap in the RN's re-equipment programmes that could not be met by British airframe manufacturers. Shortly and almost inevitably, the same sequence – now compounded by the RN's Phantom II programme – led to a gap in the RAF's programmes. The RAF were already re-assessing the P.1154, and were tentatively considering the Phantom II. By abandoning the inappropriate P.1154 at an early stage, the RN were able to retrieve their re-equipment requirements rapidly. But they were doubly fortunate. The F-4 already existed and McDonnell had gone to considerable lengths to ensure that they were offering exactly the right product; the only other foreign competitor of merit was the Vought F-8E Crusader, which the French *Aéronavale* had procured, but this was an air superiority fighter, whereas the F-4 was multi-role. Although the F-4 was more expensive in the end and in service no sooner than projected for P.1154, it was more capable and (arguably) more flexible. The RN was also fortunate to have the Rolls-Royce RB.168, an engine which McDonnell had watched during its development, having foreseen likely RN interest.

The events of recent years had made it increasingly obvious that if British defence planning and procurement was to be realistic and realizable in future, more effective central control was required. There was also a parallel desire by the Government to control defence spending more closely. The creation of the Joint Defence Staff in 1958 had achieved neither end. On 16 July 1963 a paper entitled *Central Organisation For Defence* was published, announcing a fundamental change in the control of the British armed Services by the creation of the Ministry of Defence. The object was to 'improve the central control of defence policy' and to 'strike a proper balance between commitments, resources and the roles of the Services', whose 'separate identities will be preserved'. In other words, the new Ministry would operate upon an overall defence basis, rather than on a single Service basis. The Secretary of State for Defence would head the Service Boards and the Defence Council. The Ministry of Aviation would remain independent, but under the Secretary of State for Defence. The Ministry was formally created on 1 April 1964.

The Government could now apply consistent, co-ordinated and concentrated pressure upon the Services. Equally, lobbies within the armed forces and the aviation industry could seek to influence programmes which affected all three Services. The Admiralty under Mountbatten was particularly strong and was campaigning to have the Spey-Buccaneer adopted by the RAF in order to achieve commonality, share airframe and engine development costs and reduce unit price. The development of the F-4's Spey would maximize the investment in the Buccaneer's, but if the RAF also adopted the Spey-F-4, its development costs could also be shared. The case for the RN's F-4 was very strong. The case for the RAF's P.1154 was weakening.

Chapter 3
'A Wobble in Policy...'

The joint BJSM/MoA/RN team which visited St Louis on 26 January 1964 gave the first indication to McDonnell of possible RAF interest in the Phantom. When McDonnell had initially approached the RAF in 1960 there had been neither a land-based nor a ground-attack/strike model of the Phantom, and the RAF foresaw no need for buying a foreign aircraft to replace the Hunter. The RAF's requirements subsequently evolved towards a policy of mobile tactical air power with the P.1154 as the Hunter replacement in the fighter/close support role. This supersonic V/STOL tactical strike fighter promised flexibility and a limited need for vulnerable conventional runways. The possibility of the RAF buying the apparently inflexible air defence orientated Phantom with its requirements for long runways receded. When it became obvious that the RN were loosing interest in the naval P.1154 and were seriously interested in the F-4, the RAF clung tenaciously to the P.1154, but with the growing realization that if the RN were to withdraw the unit cost of the P.1154 would escalate, and the programme would become less attractive to the Government. The USAF's purchase of a multi-role F-4 at least made the F-4 more appropriate to RAF requirements but, whereas the RN stipulated that any British Phantom should have the Spey, the RAF rejected the Spey because the increase in performance over the standard J79 was not necessary and the higher cost was unacceptable. But when the RN did withdraw its support for the purchase of the P.1154, the various parties with interests in British aircraft procurement plans re-aligned. The next Government simply exploited the divisions and dictated its solution.

British military requirements are almost ancillary to why Britain ordered the F-4M for the RAF. The British General Election of 15 October 1964 returned a Labour Government to power led by Mr Harold Wilson. In his manifesto to the Labour Party at New Year 1964, Wilson had clearly stated that the Party did not see Britain continuing as a world power, but urged that Britain should now establish a balanced and just society based upon socialism. The implications were clear. They had far reaching effects on the British armed forces and aerospace industry.

Wilson's Government began a radical review of British defence policies, procurement and overseas commitments under the merciless lenses of 'cost-effectiveness' and 'rationalization'. As early as November 1964 the Air Staff were told that two projects out of the TSR-2, P.1154 and AW.681 would have to go: the Government had pre-judged the issues. Not only defence, but the entire British aircraft industry was under examination.

It was no secret that the Labour Government believed that the aerospace industry absorbed too great a percentage of the nation's research funds and personnel for too little return in income, particularly from abroad. The Government held that there were too many expensive projects to be sustained and too many companies competing for too few contracts, a view which differed little outwardly from that of the previous Conservative Government, but this administration was committed to collaborative projects with European industry. However politically motivated, the Government's strategy was arguably nearer the world of economic reality than the aerospace industry would admit. The UK's aerospace industry had enormous potential but disdained to play professional politics: to survive it would have to.

On 9 December 1964, Mr Roy Jenkins, the Minister of Aviation, announced in the House of Commons that a select committee had been formed under the chairmanship of Lord Plowden with wide terms of reference: 'To consider what should be the future place and organization of the aircraft industry in relation to the general economy of the country, taking into account the demands of national defence, export prospects, the comparable industries of other countries, and the relationship of the industry with Government activities in the aviation field; and to make recommendations on any steps and measures necessary.' This was a long overdue development.

Meanwhile, aircraft workers and the leaders of the main aviation groups discussed the future with members of the Government in mid-January 1965. Rumours of project cancellations leaked from the Cabinet, and the general mood was not helped by a newspaper report of pointed, but private comments by the Secretary of State for Defence, Mr Denis Healey, about the Government not being there to 'wet nurse retarded children' – the aviation industry. On 14 January, 10,000 aviation workers marched through London. Their main pleas were that the Government should neither cancel British orders nor order American aircraft. On 20 January, Jenkins allayed some fears by announcing in the Commons that despite severe doubts about its economic viability, Britain would continue with the Anglo-French Concorde project.

Uncertainty about Government policy created a profoundly agitated mood. On 2 February 1965, the Opposition moved a motion of 'no confidence' in the Government. The Opposition charged that the Government's apparent policies would have fundamental effects upon the aviation industry's structure, and would leave Britain without designers or technicians capable of developing sophisticated aircraft and forcing Britain to 'buy American at America's prices'.

Wilson riposted by moving an amendment to the motion deploring 'the irresponsibilities of the former Administration leading to the serious situation which confronts HM Government', and calling for 'remedial measures to strengthen the country's economy and security.' But the Opposition's challenge forced his hand. In the course of a long speech, he lucidly explained the substance and rationale of the Government's plans for the aircraft programmes and defence procurement. The motion of censure was rejected and the amendment was approved.

The main thrusts of Wilson's argument were that the Conservative Government's military aircraft procurement programmes were 'vastly expensive' and 'without cost control', that there was no certainty that any of the aircraft under development would provide the right capability, and that there were strong doubts whether any could be in service on schedule. Wilson stated:

The first duty of any Government of any party is to ensure that the nation's defences are adequate and effective and that the nation's security is fully defended

. . . (if this) could be guaranteed only by costs of this magnitude I should not hesitate to say so to the House. But the problem we face is not only, or even primarily, one of cost. It is a question of time-scale and the availability of necessary equipment.

The House will recall many statements and many changes of policy about the replacement of the RAF Hunter and the Royal Navy Sea Vixen. In July 1963 the P.1154 was going to meet both requirements. By November there was a wobble in policy. In February 1964 the last Government decided to buy the American Phantom aircraft as the Sea Vixen replacement. Meanwhile the P.1154 was to go on to provide a replacement for the Hunter when this was withdrawn . . .

. . . this is not a practicable proposition. It is not so much a question of cost, although the present estimate is heavy . . . The problem here is that on the present estimated requirement and latest realistic estimate of the remaining life of the Hunter aircraft, the P.1154 will not be in service in time to serve as a Hunter replacement . . . there is a time gap of some years which no Government can ask either its service chiefs or its servicemen to accept.

In these circumstances, on defence grounds alone, quite apart from the cost argument, it will be necessary to expand the late Government's purchasing programme for Phantoms and use this aircraft as a partial replacement for the Hunter. This is the only way of closing the time gap. They will have British engines and incorporate as many British components as possible. We are urgently examining the possibility of manufacturing or assembling these aircraft and making some of the parts in Britain.

Wilson did not dismiss V/STOL. He had termed the Phantom a 'partial' Hunter replacement: a developed P.1127 would take over the other tasks. But he did discard the HS.681 STOL tactical transport, and opt for the American C-130 Hercules. The RAF's concept of tactical mobility would now have to be radically revised. Wilson said:

We believe there is an urgent need for an operational version of the P.1127 . . . a contract will be placed for a limited development programme so that the RAF can have, by the time they need it, an aircraft which will be first in the field of vertical take-off for close support . . .

While the proposed HS.681 can be developed at high cost . . . its development was authorized so late that it cannot enter service at a date that will meet the real needs of the Forces . . . there will be no alternative to buying the American C-130s . . . There is also a considerable saving to the Exchequer.

Wilson then set out his assessment of parameters that would form the basis for a decision on TSR-2 – cost and capability. A decision could not be made 'at this stage'.

. . . it is still too early to say whether operationally it will succeed or not. To replace the TSR-2 with its nearest competitor, which would mean going to the United States (the TFX/F-111), would . . . save at least £250 million . . . (but) would require additional dollar expenditure which no Government would lightly undertake.

We are deeply concerned about the effect of any such decision on the aircraft industry, both in the immediate future and farther ahead . . . it is an agonizing decision.

Wilson also announced that modified Comets would be bought to replace the Shackleton maritime reconnaissance aircraft, and that discussions would be initiated immediately with the French Government and other European states about the collaborative development of a jet strike/trainer aircraft for the 1970s, both of which were welcome in terms of military requirements, but neither gave firm grounds for security for the British aerospace industry. If anything, they relegated the industry to the role of refurbisher of obsolete airframes and a politically controlled partner in an international project, while the decisions to buy the American Phantom and C-130 reduced the industry to the level of a sub-contractor to a major competitor – the US aerospace industry. Yet, it was a series of ill-conceived Governmental decisions which had produced the need for drastic measures, and the Services were given a coherent procurement policy and very capable aircraft. Wilson summed up his intentions for the British aviation industry thus:

. . . a healthy and balanced industry . . . which never again becomes virtually dependent for its existence on one highly costly venture of this type (TSR-2) . . . One of the basic problems . . . has been the growing research and development costs of developing a modern and sophisticated aircraft combined with the relatively small number required for our purposes. (The unit cost) is very high compared with what some other countries are able to achieve . . . joint production rather than separate and costly ventures must be the pattern for the future.

All these questions will be central to the work of the Plowden Committee, but meanwhile we are going ahead . . . with joint projects with our Continental partners. The future of the aircraft industry, the requirements of defence, the cost to the taxpayer, and the balance of payments are inextricably linked.

The combined effect of the decisions I have mentioned will enable us to save at least £300 million over the next ten years in terms of Government expenditure . . . The RAF will be guaranteed delivery at the right time of the aircraft it needs to discharge its operational role.

These announcements effectively ended the aviation industry's prolonged uncertainty, except in regard to TSR-2, although the shrewd guessed that the Government only awaited reasonable grounds and US dollar support before swinging the axe again. On 6 April 1965, the Government announced that TSR-2 had been cancelled and the F-111 would probably be ordered instead to replace Canberra in the conventional strike and reconnaissance roles from 1969.

On 9 February 1965, Healey and McNamara signed the F-4M Co-operative Logistics Agreement (with generous credit terms), and a similar agreement for the C-130E. Announcing the agreements in Washington the same day, a US Defense Department spokesman stated that they had been 'concluded in such a way as to minimize the UK's foreign exchange costs and with the aim of providing modern aircraft for the RAF at an early date', with the delivery of the Phantoms starting in two or three years time – the first in January 1967 – while the C-130E would enter service in late 1966. Special arrangements would be worked out for the Phantoms to be equipped with British-built Rolls-Royce engines, Martin-Baker ejection seats, and electronics equipment, and there would be 'a major US–UK co-production effort on the Phantom'. The RAF would receive equal priority with the US forces in production, development and supply arrangements. Credit facilities would include a seven-year loan at $4\frac{3}{4}$ per cent interest per annum for the purchase of the Phantom, effective from 9 February 1965. McDonnell gave the programme go-ahead date as April 1965.

The Government negotiated the extension of these terms to cover the RN's F-4K ordered by the previous administration. The US Government had been prepared to offset the dollar cost of the F-4M by placing substantial orders in Britain, including the purchase of VC10s for the USAF, none of which the inexperienced administration entertained although offset arrangements later formed the basis for the UK's F-111 purchase.

The Defence White Paper of 23 February 1965 stated that 'the Government remains free to decide the total size of its orders for the alternative American aircraft when its defence review is complete without increasing the unit cost if the size of the order is reduced.' It also stated that the RAF Phantoms would be capable of operating from aircraft carriers at sea 'thus increasing the flexibility of the force and perhaps making possible a reduction in its size'.

On 1 July 1965, the Ministry of Aviation stated that the Government had concluded arrangements with the USA to buy a first batch of F-4K and F-4Ms and C-130s. The C-130s would have Allison engines not Rolls-Royce Tynes as proposed earlier, but the decision on the Phantom's engines had still to be finalized.

On 4 August 1965 Healey announced at a Press conference that the Government was over half-way towards it objective of reducing defence expenditure by 1969–70 from over 7 per cent to 6 per cent of GNP (gross national product). The Government had reviewed the defence procurement programmes, and it was now reviewing Britain's overseas commitments. Defence savings made so far included £40 million on the interim aircraft which would have been necessary had Britain persevered with the P.1154 and HS.681; £75 million from changes in the RAF equipment programme by purchasing C-130s instead of HS.681s, possibly the F-111A instead of TSR-2, and purchasing Phantoms and P.1127 instead of P.1154; and £20 million through negotiating arrangements to purchase the RN's Phantoms on credit terms.

The arrangements for the Spey took several months to conclude, and the final official decision to adopt the Spey was not made until late 1965. Development of the Spey-F-4K by McDonnell and Rolls-Royce was already far advanced by then, but the decision had to be made on the basis of technical viability, delivery schedules and cost, for considerable development was required, estimated in May 1965 as costing £28.7 million for the engine and installation.

The decision was in abeyance when a crisis arose. Rolls-Royce had told Healey that engine unit cost was £137 thousand apiece, but the Ministry of Technology quoted £157 thousand. The available budget apparently could not stretch to an extra £40 thousand per aircraft: the Government would thus buy J79-powered F-4s.

Sir Denning Pearson, Chairman of Rolls-Royce, personally assured Healey that the company's price still held, and that the extra £20 thousand had been added by the Ministry as a contingency measure. The Spey contract, like all British F-4K/M contracts, was a fixed price contract, and the Government held Rolls-Royce to it. As a result, the cost of the engine had to be reduced by sacrificing performance at high Mach numbers by specifying inferior metal in the turbine blades. But it ensured that the Spey powered the UK Phantoms, and on 17 November 1965, Jenkins formally announced that it had been selected.

Although equipping the UK Phantoms with the Spey was politically useful for the Government, the impetus had come from the Royal Navy, Rolls-Royce and McDonnell. The RN wanted the higher performance, payload and range that it offered over the J79. Rolls-Royce needed a military contract to ensure a secure commercial future, and the Spey F-4 offered more security than the vectored-thrust Spey P.1154 project. McDonnell were pragmatic: they were more than willing to develop a new F-4 model for a paying customer, and if it took Speys to get the UK order, they could have Speys.

It was certainly better for the RAF, RN, MoD, HSA, Rolls-Royce and the Treasury that the P.1154 was cancelled in 1964–65 rather than at a later stage in development. The UK industry had been committed to four massive programmes, HS.681, P.1154, TSR-2 and Concorde, which involved the development of airframes, engines and equipment costing thousands of millions of

pounds and absorbing millions of manhours for an uncertain return. While they ensured work, reliance upon cost-spiralling programmes was dangerous in the increasingly difficult economic climate, especially as the costs on short production runs were becoming prohibitive. It was also doubtful that the UK industry could have supported all four projects. Moreover, the Labour Government was committed to abandoning the vestiges of colonialism, weakening economic ties with the Commonwealth, and entering the European Common Market. In pursuit of this, and not only on economic grounds, it was actively seeking collaboration on aircraft programmes with Continental partners, even if this meant sacrificing large parts of the UK aerospace industry. As a result three British programmes were cancelled. Concorde escaped because it was a collaborative venture and a civil aircraft, both of which pleased the Labour Government: it was certainly not the technological benefits which interested them. The Government's economic theory was sound, but if not short-sighted, it was deliberately blinkered.

Buying the F-4 was the only logical alternative to the P.1154: the Phantom II was simply the best aircraft available; a version was already under development for the RN; it was cheap; and the US would assist with credit. The F-4 was flexible, whereas the P.1154 was limited (paradoxically) by V/STOL. However, although it was highly probable that the P.1154 would have been late into service, the RAF Phantom was scheduled for service only slightly earlier, and the Phantom was itself late into service. The P.1154, with TSR-2 and HS.681, simply absorbed too much of the funds required for collaborative projects. Therefore, the F-4 replaced the P.1154, liberating sterling funds for collaboration.

In the *Battle of Britain 25th Anniversary Book 1965*, the Chief of the Air Staff, ACM Sir Charles Elsworthy wrote of the future of the RAF:

There was little to choose between TSR-2 and the F-111A in terms of military capability (in the strike role), and the latter is cheaper. ... We cannot afford to be left behind in any of the other important spheres of aircraft re-equipment. That is why the C-130 tactical transport and the Phantom fighter/close support aircraft are to be bought in place of the projected HS.681 and P.1154. ... We are determined that the Army's needs in the battle area shall not be neglected, and to complement the Phantom we plan to purchase the revolutionary V/STOL Kestrel (P.1127). The combination of F-111, Phantom and Kestrel would give us a complete range of options in the strike, reconnaissance and close support roles. For air defence we have the Lightning Mk 3 together with its new missiles, Red Top, and both the Phantom and F-111 have an air defence capability. . . .

Chapter 4
'On the Never-Never...'

In accordance with the agreement reached in February 1965, and as a result of concerted pressures on the Government by several associations, particularly the Electronic Engineering Association, it was agreed that manufacture of components, assemblies and equipment for the F-4K and F-4M would be open to British companies on a competitive tender basis against McDonnell's normal suppliers up to a target total of 50 per cent of the value of each aircraft. Similar arrangements were made for the Lockheed C-130.

There were a number of considerations which influenced the Government in stipulating a high British content. There was concern at the effects on employment in the British aviation industry, particularly at Shorts, and the long term effects on British design teams of cancelling large British programmes and placing substantial orders in America. It was a useful way of politically softening the blow, re-using elements of the TSR-2 programme, and re-focusing attention. There was also the requirement to ensure compatibility of equipment with other British aircraft. But the

basic consideration was the reduction of the foreign exchange content of the aircraft, thereby minimizing dollar expenditure with consequent beneficial effects upon the balance of payments and the Government's record.

The UK Government was therefore prepared to accept that most British tenders would be slightly higher than the American's. The British had the disadvantage of quoting for the manufacture of items new to them and for small quantities which rendered special tooling uneconomic, against American firms which had several years of experience behind them. However, the US Government helpfully waived the surcharges applied under the 'Buy American' Act to foreign equipment supplied to US defence companies in the cases of the F-4K and F-4M and C-130. The successful British tenders were in no case more than 20 per cent higher and in several cases were somewhat lower than the corresponding bids by established US suppliers. But the order quantities diminished over a period and so the proportional cost went up. The overall result was a more expensive Phantom. Moreover, manufacture under licence in Britain introduced delay, especially where new development work was necessary, as with Ferranti.

In this period the value of products which were being shipped abroad temporarily and not for sale to a foreign buyer, of which the Spey is an important example, were nevertheless included in HM Customs and Excise Overseas Trade Account export figures. Their value was subsequently

To emphasize the joint nature of the programme all the F-4K and M British-manufactured components and avionics were displayed at a ceremony at St Louis launching the first YF-4K on 27 June 1966

The Rolls-Royce Spey augmented thrust turbofan was the major British contribution to the F-4K and M: note the 'British-American Phantom II' logo on the display board on this Spey Mk 201 posed at St Louis in June 1966. (See back cover)

included in the import figures. In time, these transactions cancelled each other out, which helped Britain's balance of payments.

McDonnell, as the main contractor, and the Ministry of Aviation, responsible for defence research, development, and production, were instructed to work out the details of the British content on a compromise between the stipulated 50 per cent and cost and time, and to put the work out to tender. To satisfy these instructions many items would have to be built in the UK under licence from the original US manufacturer. The Patents Branch of MoD was responsible for royalties on licences, not the Contracts Branch, and were closely involved with negotiations.

True to dispersed mass production line principles, the F-4 airframe was divided into several sub-sections and assemblies. McDonnell normally subcontracted to other companies, including Aeronca, Beech, Brunswick, Cessna Aircraft, Douglas, Fairchild-Republic, Goodyear Aerospace, and Northrop. Bendix and Menasco Manufacturing supplied the main and nose undercarriages respectively, Cessna Aircraft supplied the missile racks and pylons, and Royal Jet the external fuel tanks for the F-4 series, in all cases including the K and M. McDonnell manufactured only 45 per cent of the airframe. Equipment was supplied from the various manufacturers to the customers specifications, and some procured by the customer, such as engines for the US F-4s, which were procured by the US Government and supplied to McDonnell.

McDonnell and the Ministry of Aviation considered and reviewed a total of 208 tenders. By early 1966, 28 British firms had received a total of 45 fixed price contracts to produce 10.5 per cent in value of each aircraft; airframe and equipment subcontracts accounted for 5.4 per cent and 5.1 per cent respectively. Ten of these firms were to supply British equipment to be fitted to the aircraft, while the others were to make US parts or sub-assemblies under licence for the construction of the aircraft. The contract with Rolls-Royce for the Spey alone accounted for 35.5 per cent of the value, bringing the total UK content to 46 per cent.

Fairchild-Republic manufactured the aft fuselage, fin, rudder and tail-cone assemblies, stabilator, and engine access doors for the F-4 series at Farmingdale, NY. The Warton Division of BAC, Short Brothers and Harland, and Scottish Aviation were three of the British companies which tendered for these components, plus the wing fixed inboard leading edges and outer sections and other items. Scottish Aviation did not proceed very far with any tender for Phantom sub-contract work, withdrawing because negotiations with Lockheed on sub-contract work for the RAF C-130K were at a very advanced stage, and subsequently were successfully completed, the company manufacturing major airframe components. BAC won a contract on a fixed price basis from McDonnell in early 1966 to produce the aft fuselage, fin, rudder and tail cone assemblies, the stabilator and the wing fixed inboard leading edge, and parts of the engine access doors. Much of this work involved fabrication in titanium. The Preston Division, which included the Warton and Salmesbury works, was responsible for UK sub-contracts. By mid-1966 jigging was well advanced at BAC's Strand Road, Preston factory. Production reached a rate of 10 units per month and the job was completely by 1969 with deliveries ahead of schedule. Following cancellation of HS.681, the Government had expressed its concern about the position of Shorts and had set up a body to investigate ways of replacing the lost work, possibly with sub-contracts on the American aircraft. Shorts won a contract to produce the left and right outer wing panels and their leading edge flaps, and had built the jigs and begun to gear up production by mid-1966. The alloys for these airframe contracts were supplied by British companies as 'common aeronautical materials' the end use of which would not necessarily be known to the suppliers.

US companies retained the contracts for the rest of the airframe. Beech manufactured the wing centre section trailing edge assemblies, the speed brakes, and the main undercarriage doors, Brunswick supplied the nose radome which was of a modified shape, and Goodyear Aerospace (USA) furnished the cockpit transparencies, for which the Aircraft and Special Products Division of Triplex Glass in the UK had unsuccessfully bid. The remainder of the airframe was manufactured by McDonnell.

The radar fire control system selected for the UK Phantom was the Westinghouse pulse-Doppler AN/AWG-10 which equipped the F-4J. To offset the high cost of AN/AWG-10, the British Government directed Ferranti to negotiate with Westinghouse Electric Corporation's Defense Group for a licence to produce it as the main UK contractor. A licence was signed covering the transfer of data to Ferranti and the UK MoD. Ferranti was also developing the INAS for the F-4M (based upon work done for TSR-2), to replace the Litton equipment installed on almost every other F-4 model. The total estimated unit cost of each INAS was about £23,660.

Marconi Avionics won four significant contracts, one of which was for Marconi Avionics Equipment fuel flow meters, produced by the Aircraft Engine Instruments Division (now renamed Powerplant Systems Division). The other contracts were for equipment to be produced under licence, the Military (now Combat) Aircraft

Aft fuselage section on BAC's Strand Road production line. At rear right is a completed upper structural assembly with fin afixed, while closer is a lower half, to the left of which are tail cone assemblies, with fuel vents

Controls Division producing the Bendix Corporation ASN-39 and ASN-46 navigation computers and the General Electric (USA) flight control (auto pilot) system, and the Aircraft Engine Instruments Division producing the Honeywell fuel gauge system.

The Ministry of Defence specified the Cossor SSR 1500 IFF Mk 10A Transponder and SSR 1503 Controller for the F-4K and M. This was the main Government Furnished Equipment (GFE) on the aircraft; the other British produced avionics equipment, whether or not specified by the UK Government directly, were procured by McDonnell rather than the MoD. Cossor, a Raytheon subsidiary, were also contracted to produce the test equipment for the UK's purchase of Raytheon AIM-7E-2 Sparrow III AAMs.

Delaney Gallay of Cricklewood won the contract to produce the aluminium heat exchangers, while Delaney Gallay of Biggleswade produced the titanium insulation blankets. Goodyear (USA) retained its position as the main contractor for F-4 wheels and brakes. Goodyear (UK) later negotiated a licence to manufacture the brakes, while Dunlop was involved in the brakes on small sub-contract machining work later. Dunlop manufactured the flight indicator retraction cylinder and the cylinder assemblies on a sub-contract basis with drawings supplied by Goodyear (USA), and manufactured the anti-skid braking system under licence from Hydro-wire (USA) using their drawings.

Martin-Baker were contracted to supply the Mk 5 cartridge-operated runway level/130 kt ejection seat, standard in the F-4A, B and C. The harnesses were the standard USN-type. Both the seats and harnesses were later replaced in service. Irvin (GB), under contract to UK/MoD, supplied their standard I24 ejection seat parachute and the brake parachute, the latter a 4.7 m flat diameter ring slot type equivalent in size to that used for USAF F-4s, but using British textiles.

Amongst those who tendered unsuccessfully or withdrew was Fairey Hydraulics, which considered the possibility of licence producing the flight control actuators, not supplied as part of GE's auto-pilot system for the F-4K and M, but the project was dropped and no other commitments were entertained.

The British manufacturers involved in the programme maintained service teams at McDonnell during the design, development, production and trials phases to provide technical support to McDonnell, and the Ministry of Technology (which superceded the Ministry of Aviation) had an office in St Louis for liaison which closed on 20 October 1970 at the end of the programme. For instance, Cossor were deeply involved with McDonnell in the installation and production flight trials aspects of the IFF SSR 1500 equipment, throughout which a Cossor engineer was resident in St Louis to provide full technical support to McDonnell, train their technical staff on the SSR 1500 and maintain liaison with other UK companies' service teams. Support to BAC in the UK was provided on an 'as required' basis from Cossor's Harlow facility. A number of the British sub-contracts involved development work upon basic US items, which also required liaison. Normal US Department of Defense quality assurance procedures were APPLIED AT St Louis, with a Ministry of Technology representative present. UK-manufacctured items were subject to the Ministry's normal inspection procedures.

Hawker Siddeley Aviation at Brough was nominated as 'aircraft weapons system sister design firm' and had a sizeable team at McDonnell to handle design queries and liaison. The agreement was approved on 28 September 1966, under which HSA would be responsible for the in-service support of the F-4K and M and for modifications to maintain their operational effectiveness throughout their service lives, treating them exactly as though they had been built at Brough. HSA became BAe Brough which continued in the same capacity, and built spares.

F-4K and M Status UK/UK Co-Production

This table represents the position in early 1966, and is therefore based upon 298 aircraft, and does not include age value. It is based on a cost per aircraft ('ship') of $2,685,700.

Description	UK tenders reviewed	UK tenders accepted	Ship set value ($)
Major Sub-contracts	8	5	249,471
CFE Common	118	20	24,834
GFE Common	28	6	76,570
F-4K/M Peculiar	19	3	3,660
UK Electronics	*5	*5	246,890
Minor Sub-contracts	30	6	9,014
MAC procured	208	45	601,425
UK GFAE (Spey)			940,000
Total UK Content			$1,541,425

*Customer Directed Procurement (ie Category 2)
CFE: Contractor Furnished Equipment (ie Category 1)
GFE: Government Furnished Equipment
GFAE: Government Furnished Aeronautical Equipment

An interesting assessment of the success of the UK co-production programme on the Phantom is provided by a report entitled *Productivity of the National Aircraft Effort* (HMSO London 1969) produced by a committee of inquiry appointed in March 1967 by the Minister of Technology, Tony Benn and the President of the SBAC, J T Lidbury, under the chairmanship of Mr St John Elstab, in accordance with the recommendations of the Plowden Committee. Chapter 7, 'Production Under Licence: Manufacture of Major Sub-Assemblies', paragraph 71, reads:

71. The quotations (the committee) have seen were fixed prices . . . Where we were able to compare manhours as well as costs, we found that although British costs were competitive and sometimes lower, unit manhours exceeded those of the corresponding American firm by anything from 20 per cent to more than 80 per cent. This was mainly attributable to the small production quantity required for the British order. To give some idea of the scale of difference, an American manufacturer had produced 2,500 oil cooling radiators at a rate of 50 per month. The British producer whose tender was accepted (Delaney Gallay) received an order for 110, at a rate of 10 per month. The American firms benefitted from prolonged learning while the British companies started from scratch. Furthermore, with the quantities and rates the former could justify the use of special machines or better fixtures and jigs. They could also sub-divide tasks, making each operatives' job simpler and more repetitive. If their price was to be economic British firms had to keep special tooling to a minimum, and place greater reliance on manual skill, with each operative handling several operations. The challenge which this presented stimulated some ingenious methods which enabled the British sub-contractors to equal and sometimes exceed the quality of the American products, though not usually at an appreciably lower cost.

The Reckoning

The Government's accounts had now to be worked out. On 28 February 1966 Healey described the costs for the F-4K/M, F-111K and C-130K procurement, the three aircraft being considered together, including supporting equipment, initial spares and the UK's share of US research and development costs. He stated in the Commons that, although no final decision had been taken on the exact size of orders for the F-4K and M, it was likely that the dollar cost would be £300 million of which £160 million would be paid before April 1970, the size of this figure reflecting the high UK content. The repayment terms to cover the three aircraft programme provided that the bulk of the repayments would be made in 1968–69, but spread evenly, with an interest rate of 4¾ per cent. Under the arrangement with the USA, the UK had the opportunity to enter into 'a co-operative logistics supply support agreement under which we enjoy

An aft fuselage section tail cone assembly, which will house the brake chute, under construction at BAC Strand Road. The structure forms the fairing behind and below the stabilator and rudder attachment points

the same production price and other benefits as the US Air Force in respect of supply of spare parts, modification kits, repair and overhaul services, and engineering support.' Later that day the Minister of Aviation, Mulley, indicated the Government was thinking in terms of a total order of 'about 200 Phantoms'. McDonnell were quoting 298.

Within a week the estimated costs had become firmer, with a sterling content. In a written reply to a question in the Commons on 4 March 1966, Healey gave the following estimated dollar and sterling cost to the UK for the three aircraft over a ten-year period:

F-4K/M   £590 million (£310 million in dollars; £280 million sterling)

F-111   £280 million (£240 million in dollars; £40 million sterling)

C-130   £210 million (£110 million in dollars; £100 million sterling)

These figures included spares and replacements, UK contributions to US research and development, running costs and all interest payable as a result of the credit payment terms. The relative sizes of the F-4K/M dollar and sterling payments reflected the fact that some 46 per cent of the aircraft would be of UK origin, while the high comparative dollar cost of the F-111 programme would be fully recovered by offset arrangements, a similar concept.

On 11 May 1966 the Military Aircraft (Loans) Act was given an unopposed second reading in the Commons and received the Royal Assent on 26 May 1966. The Act authorised the borrowing of sums totalling £430 million ($1,200 million) to meet the cost of purchasing the F-4K/M, F-111

Phantom Speys being built at Derby. The engine compressor units (ECUs), upright, front down, await the completed afterburner and nozzle system sections, in the left foreground. Speys are now built at East Kilbride, Strathclyde, but still tested at Derby

and C-130, in addition to £18 million ($52 million) which had already been drawn on the US Export-Import Bank under the terms of the 1965 Co-operative Agreement. White Papers published on 28 July and 29 September 1966 set out the arrangements which had been made with the US Export-Import Bank for credits of £12 million ($35 million) and £92.9 million ($260 million) to be drawn under the Act for the periods from 1 April to 30 June 1966 and 1 July 1966 to 30 June 1967 respectively. The terms of both loans were 4¾ per cent interest with repayments over seven years. Actual drawings from the bank in the second quarter of 1966 in respect of purchase of US military aircraft amounted to £18 million ($52

million) in April and £12 million ($36.7 million) in June; in the third quarter they amounted to £11 million ($31.7 million).

Unofficial but informed estimates were suggesting in mid-1966 that each F-4M would cost about £1.2 million and each F-4K about £1.15 million which, on an order of about 210, brought the total 'flyaway' value to some £300 million. On 31 March 1967, Tony Benn stated in a written reply in the Commons that each Phantom would cost £1.25 million, of which some 46 per cent related to items manufactured in the UK. This was the official 'flyaway' cost. The same day Merlyn Rees stated that each C-130 would cost just over £9 million: the previous estimate had been £7 million. Between March and June 1967, Government figures laid out the costs of buying 50 F-111Ks: the cost of the ten-year programme had escalated to £336 million, with a true average unit cost of £2.5 million, albeit the programme for 50 TSR-2s would have cost £610 million.

In the Commons on 16 January 1968, as part of a drastic, wide ranging package of economic measures designed to 'make devaluation work' – the Government having devalued in the previous November – Mr Wilson announced: 'We are discussing with the US Government future arrangements for offset orders for Phantom and Hercules aircraft.' Such measures were intended to reduce the dollar drain and help restore the nation's worsening balance of payments. At the same time, he announced the cancellation of F-111K, saving $700 million, he asserted.

In a written reply on 18 July 1968 Rees stated that while the US Government had originally agreed to grant credit of $700 million to cover the procurement of F-4M and C-130, the F-4K had subsequently been brought within the credit terms. In consequence, the US Government had agreed to increase the credit to $750 million for the estimated total credit requirement up to 30 June 1969, but the interest on the additional amount would be charged at 6 per cent not $4\frac{3}{4}$ per cent. The UK Government was discussing cancellation payments on the F-111K, and had undertaken to repay the $49 million drawn in credits before cancellation.

On 26 July 1968, a White Paper was published which set out details of an increase from £500 million to £528 million in the US Export-Import Bank credit to the UK, and announced an extension in the period in which credit could be drawn to 30 June 1969. (When the original agreement was concluded, the total of $1,200 million had represented £430 million, but this had increased to £500 million following devaluation.)

On 1 May 1968 John Stonehouse, Minister of State for Technology, stated in the Commons that the present estimated costs for the Phantom were about £1.4 million each for the F-4K and £1.5 million each for the F-4M. However, a report of the House of Commons' Public Accounts Committee, published on 8 August 1968, estimated that, after taking into account some £100 million of development costs, the total cost of each of the 170 F-4K and M which had eventually been ordered would be about £2 million, or twice that of the US models. The committee criticized the Government for having apparently accepted 'totally unreliable estimates' of the cost. In fact, the initial estimates made in February 1964 of the cost of developing the F-4K for the RN to accept the Spey and UK electronics was £25.3 million, of which £12.4 million related to engine development. By May 1965 the estimate, now for both F-4K and M modifications, was £45.5 million, of which engine development costs had more than doubled to £28.7 million. Even taking inflation into account, but balanced against the advantages of devaluation, development costs had rocketted. In consequence, the UK Phantom had the highest unit cost of any F-4 built.

While the operational excellence of the aircraft which resulted from this long, complex, expensive process cannot be disputed fundamentally, the F-4K and M cannot be seen as a financial success, and a basis for their procurement is thereby negated. Nor did the time that their development took hasten them into service earlier than the P.1154, invalidating the major expressed reason for their procurement.

British Phantom Procurement

SD-513-1RN, McDonnell JO 740, FY 1965

YF-4K-26-MC	2	XT595-XT596
F-4K-27-MC	2	XT597-XT598

SD-513-1-RAF, McDonnell JO 741, FY 1965

YF-4M-29-MC	2	XT852-XT853

SD-513-1-RAF-1, McDonnell JO 744, FY 1966

F-4M-31-MC	5	XT891-XT895
F-4M-32-MC	11	XT896-XT906
F-4M-33-MC	8	XT907-XT914

SD-513-1RN-1, McDonnell JO 748, FY 1966

F-4K-30-MC	2	XT857-XT858
F-4K-31-MC	4	XT859-XT862
F-4K-32-MC	8	XT863-XT870
F-4K-33-MC	6	XT871-XT876

SD-513-1-RAF-2, McDonnell JO 757, FY 1966

F-4M-33-MC	6	XV393-XV398
F-4M-34-MC	19	XV399-XV417
F-4M-35-MC	19	XV418-XV436
F-4M-36-MC	6	XV437-XV442
F-4M-36-MC	16	XV460-XV475
F-4M-37-MC	20	XV476-XV495
F-4M-38-MC	6	XV496-XV501

SD-513-1-1RN-2, McDonnell JO 758, FY 1967

F-4K-34-MC	7	XV565-XV571
F-4K-35-MC	7	XV572-XV578
F-4K-36-MC	7	XV579-XV585
F-4K-37-MC	7	XV586-XV592

Constructions by Calendar Year

Year	F-4K	F-4M	Total
1966	3	—	3
1967	2	2	4
1968	24	62	86
1969	23	54	77
Totals	52	118	170

British Sub-contracts

Company	Item	MAC Specification Control (S/C) No.	Approximate Value on 1966–67 Sterling Valuation Initial	Potential
BAC, Preston Div., Preston, Lancs.	Aft Fuselage Assy (upper)	32-331001-501		
	Aft Fuselage Assy (lower)	53-330501-501		
	Rudder Assy	32-24000-507		
	Stabilator	32-21103-309		
	Fixed Inboard l/e	32-11009-523/-524		
	Engine Access Doors			
	No. 1	32-321051-507/-508		
	No. 2	32-321052-511/-512		
	No. 2A	32-321057-501/-502		
	No. 3	32-321053-551/-552		
	No. 4	32-321054-521/-522		
	No. 5	32-321055-527/-528		
	Door Assy Air Starter	32-321059-33	3,110,000	11,100,000
Alan Bradley, Portsmouth	Caps and nipples	—	—	—
Cossor Electronics, Radar Div., Harlow	IFF Communications Set (GFE) SSR 1500 Transponder SSR 1503 Controller		63,000	318,000
Delaney Gallay, Biggleswade	Titanium Insulation Blankets	32-321083 32-321084 32-321085	128,000	410,000
Delaney Gallay, Cricklewood	Oil Radiator (× 2)	32-69018-11/-12	—	—
Dowty Electronics, Greenford, Mdx	Standby UHF Set D403P (GFE)		—	—
Dunlop Rubber, Aviation Div., Coventry	Flt Indicator Retract Cylinder Anti-Skid System Cylinder Assy Cylinder Assy Cylinder Assy	32-72252-3 53-41004 32-691111-1 32-691079-1 32-691138-1	1,370	7,450
EMI, Hayes/HSA	Reconnaissance Pod (GFE)		—	—
Electro-Hydraulics, Warrington	Nose Landing Gear Drag Brace Actuator Refuelling Probe Actuator Cylinder	32-451010-301 32-69737-5	21,800 8,330	120,700 32,000
Elliot-Automation, Rochester, Kent	Fuel Control and Gauging System Liquid Oxygen System Servo Amplifier Module Navigation Computer Auto-pilot System	32-58025 32-85003 893C520G4 AN/ASN-39A (Bendix) 32-87104	— 31,000 4,180 — 392,000	— 88,200 19,200 — 1,055,000
English Electric	Constant Speed Drives	Included in the engine costs		
Ferranti, Edinburgh	Inertial Navigation/Attack System Fire Control System	58-870551 AN/AWG-11/-12	3,445,000 —	6,270,000 —
H M Hobson, Integral Div., Wolverhampton	Hydraulic Pump 6gpm Hydraulic Pump 10gpm	32-69061-11 32-69062-11	68,750	340,000

Company	Item	MAC Specification Control (S/C) No.	Approximate Value on 1966–67 Sterling Valuation Initial	Potential
Hymatic Engineering, Worcester	Hydraulic Cylinder Assy	32-691050-1	—	—
Kollsman Instruments, Southampton	Pressure Altimeter (× 2)	L-81252-10-001 Mk 28	—	—
Louis Newmark, Reigate, Surrey	All-Altitude Bombing Computer	53-87011 (AN/AJB-7 Lear-Siegler)	366,000	1,645,000
	Attitude Indicator	32-13900-1	35,200	165,000
Marconi, Basildon	UHF Communications Set AD470 HF/SSB		—	—
Marston Excelsior, Wolverhampton	Fuel Cells			
	No. 1	32-58078-7		
	No. 2	32-58032-33		
	No. 3	32-58033-13		
	No. 4	32-58034-11		
	No. 5	32-58035-11		
	No. 6	32-58036-17		
	No. 7	32-581527-5	99,700	430,000
Martin-Baker, Uxbridge	Ejection Seat Mk 5 (× 2)	32-82022	221,000	937,500
ML Aviation, Maidenhead	Transformer Rectifier	MS17976-2 28VS100Y-10UK	—	—
Normalair, Yeovil	Flow Divider and Collector Valve (× 3)	32-409370-1	—	—
Plessey, Ilford	Spey Engine Gas Turbine Starter	—	—	—
	UHF/VHF Receiver/ Transmitter (PTR374)	32-87055-3		
	Transmitter Rectifier	53-790560-1 ??	175,000	750,000
Redifon Ltd, London SW	Amplifier	32-871077-3	3,090	15,800
Rolls-Royce, Derby	RB.168-25R Spey Turbofan (GFAE)		72,610,000 (530 engines at £137,000 each)	
Rosemount Engineering, Bognor Regis	Total Temperature Transmitter	(Contract No.66-0606-1) 32-87801-1/-3	6,600	34,200
Rotax, Willesden	Control Panel Regulator (× 2)	21B30-3A	—	—
Standard Telephones and Cable, London	Radar Altimeter STR 70	32-871076	152,000	750,000
Short Brothers and Harland, Belfast	Outer Wing Panels	32-15500-535/-536UK 32-19702-0305/-0306UK	925,000	2,830,000
Smith Industries (S Smith, Sons), Wembley/Cheltenham	Turbine Temperature Indicator (cockpit instruments)	RL-732 MV/CP/7	9,920	38,200
Teleflex Products, Basildon	Feel Trim System	32-62015		
	Feel Trim Actuator	32-63015		
	Feel Trim Actuator	32-64015	45,900	158,000
Ultra Electronics, Acton	UHF/VHF Standby Receiver/Rectifier	53-870550	Included in PTR374 costs (Plessey)	

Chapter 5
Development

The Royal Navy's Phantom, the McDonnell Model 98ET, or F-4K, was originally to be based upon the USN's F-4B, and was labelled only F-4RN or F-4B(RN). However, in 1963, the USN began drawing up specifications for a new version, based on the F-4B with an advanced fire control system and designated F-4J. The RN's F-4 was therefore based on the F-4J, and McDonnell termed the F-4K simply a 'Spey-powered F-4J'. In fact, the US Department of Defense initially applied the designation F-4J to the RN F-4 as well, when there was still doubt about whether the Spey would supercede the J79. The F-4K was ordered by amending the USN's F-4B/J Specification Detail SD-513 series. Following the F-4K programme go-ahead on 1 July 1964, the development and design phase was completed in mid-November 1965. Ground and wind tunnel tests began in late 1964 and ran through until June 1965, with further wind tunnel tests in the last three weeks of January 1966. The first F-4K flew on 27 June 1966, on schedule.

The Royal Navy required the Phantom primarily for the Fleet Air Defense role, to replace the Sea Vixen, and for attack roles, as a partial replacement for the Scimitar; the Buccaneer would take over other Scimitar roles. The USN's F-4A, B and J were Fleet Air Defense fighters, and for the USMC were Air Defense and Attack fighters. Development from the F-4B/J was thus straight-forward in this respect. However, the F-4K specification demanded several new features, although several were shared with the F-4J. The most radical was the introduction of the Spey. The second set of major changes was the incorporation of high lift devices and stronger landing gear to compensate for higher weights and operations from smaller British carriers; these were developed jointly for the F-4J and K. The third demand was

for an advanced radar weapon control system, satisfied by the integration of the AN/AWG-10 series pulse Doppler system, as selected for the F-4J.

New US and British avionics and equipment, and other changes and improvements being made to the F-4 series in general were also incorporated in the F-4K specification: development was a circular process. These included the addition of No 7 fuel cell in the rear fuselage to preserve balance as a result of the extra weight of the AWG-10, a feature shared with the F-4J. The improved AJB-7 all-altitude bombing system as fitted to the USAF's F-4C replaced the F-4B's AJB-3 in both F-4K and J. To cope with the increased avionics load, 30kVA generators mounted on each engine with constant speed drive units superceded the 20kVA units of the F-4A, B and C; they had been introduced on the F-4D, and were shared by the F-4J. The upper equipment bay, below the No 1 fuel cell – introduced on the USN's F-4G (modified B), and retained on the F-4C and J – housed the AWG-10's computer elements. A noticeable change was the deletion of the AAA-4 infra-red sensor, mounted in a fairing below the radome of the F-4A, B and C. More sensitive than an AAM's IR seeker, it detected IR radiation at greater ranges, slaved an AAM's seeker to its own, and launched the AAM earlier. Marginally effective in service, improved IR AAM and radar performance permitted its deletion without affecting AAM operation.

In essence, the F-4J was developed from the F-4B by replacing the Aero-1A weapon system with the AWG-10/Aero-27A system, introducing more advanced equipment, incorporating high lift devices, strengthening the airframe and undercarriage to permit 38,000 lb deck landing gross weight, and using F-4C and D improvements. In developing the F-4C from the F-4B, the USAF had adopted a policy of minimum engineering change, limiting changes to those strictly necessary for USAF requirements, importantly in the undercarriage and weapon system. Having carefully observed the changes introduced on the F-4C, the USN began to draw up specifications for the F-4J. However, in March 1964, the USAF was given the go-ahead to develop an F-4 more closely fitting its requirements; based on the F-4C, it was designated F-4D and had improved air-to-ground capability as a result of more advanced radar. The F-4J was, therefore, developed in parallel with the F-4D, but is a more advanced aircraft mainly as a result of the significant airframe changes needed to make a heavier aircraft compatible with carrier operations and the introduction of the sophisticated pulse doppler radar. Moreover, the F-4K's specification in turn influenced the F-4J.

The RAF required a multi-role fighter with mission capabilities similar to those of the USAF's F-4C and D: interdiction, close air support, counter air, and air superiority. In addition, reconnaissance and nuclear strike capabilities were required. Least emphasis was placed initially on air defence. To fulfill the air-to-ground role, an inertial navigation/attack system (INAS) was specified. The RAF's Phantom, designated F-4M,

was developed from the F-4K, which was already at an advanced stage of development. The F-4M was, in fact, developed virtually in parallel with the USAF's F-4E, which was intended to fulfil the same roles. Nevertheless, there was to be minimal engineering change from the F-4K: the F-4M was termed by McDonnell simply an F-4K with an improved INAS system.

In fact, the initial F-4M specification of 1965, a modification of the USN/RN SD-531, called for carrier capability. The Defence White Paper of 23 February 1965 suggested that the RAF Phantom's carrier capability would increase the Phantom force's flexibility and might mean less would be needed. However, with plans to phase out the RN's carrier fleet announced by the UK Government in 1966, the requirement for land-based reinforcement of the carrier-borne Phantom force was discarded and the carrier capability features were deleted from the specification in 1966. Apart from the INAS, the F-4M introduced HF radio, LCOSS, a radar altimeter, and other items for its air-to-ground roles.

UK Phantom project team, foreground left then clockwise round table: Alec Collins – R-R Resident Rep, Cyril Elliott – R-R Performance Department manager, John Dent – R-R Hucknall Flight Development manager, Don Crow – Fleet Air Arm rep, Eric Maddon, Ken McKenna, Bill Ross – VP Head of Flight Test (McDonnell), Jim Hanson – Flight Test Engineer F-4K&M Project (McDonnell)

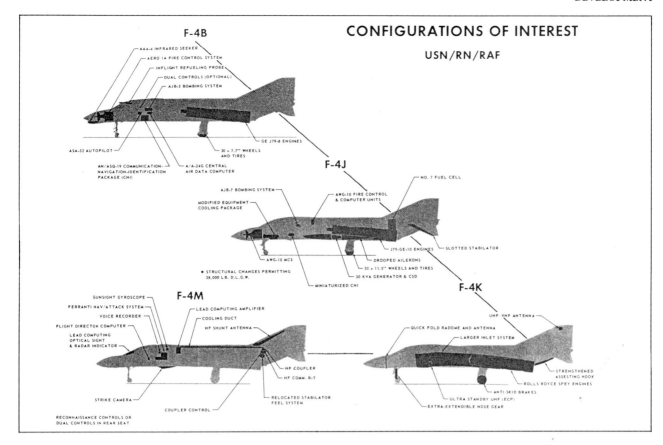

CONFIGURATIONS OF INTEREST

USN/RN/RAF

F-4B
- AAA-4 INFRARED SEEKER
- AERO 1A FIRE CONTROL SYSTEM
- INFLIGHT REFUELING PROBE
- DUAL CONTROLS (OPTIONAL)
- AJB-3 BOMBING SYSTEM
- ASA-32 AUTOPILOT
- AN/ASQ-19 COMMUNICATION-NAVIGATION-IDENTIFICATION PACKAGE (CNI)
- A/A-24G CENTRAL AIR DATA COMPUTER
- 30 x 7.7" WHEELS AND TIRES
- GE J79-8 ENGINES

F-4J
- NO. 7 FUEL CELL
- AJB-7 BOMBING SYSTEM
- MODIFIED EQUIPMENT COOLING PACKAGE
- AWG-10 FIRE CONTROL & COMPUTER UNITS
- AWG-10 MCS
- • STRUCTURAL CHANGES PERMITTING 38,000 LB. D.L.G.W.
- MINIATURIZED CNI
- DROOPED AILERONS
- 30 x 11.5" WHEELS AND TIRES
- 30 KVA GENERATOR & CSD
- J79-GE-10 ENGINES
- SLOTTED STABILATOR

F-4M
- GUNSIGHT GYROSCOPE
- FERRANTI NAV/ATTACK SYSTEM
- VOICE RECORDER
- FLIGHT DIRECTOR COMPUTER
- LEAD COMPUTING OPTICAL SIGHT & RADAR INDICATOR
- LEAD COMPUTING AMPLIFIER
- COOLING DUCT
- HF SHUNT ANTENNA
- HF COUPLER
- HF COMM. R-T
- STRIKE CAMERA
- COUPLER CONTROL
- RELOCATED STABILATOR FEEL SYSTEM
- RECONNAISSANCE CONTROLS OR DUAL CONTROLS IN REAR SEAT

F-4K
- UHF VHF ANTENNA
- QUICK FOLD RADOME AND ANTENNA
- LARGER INLET SYSTEM
- STRENGTHENED ASSISTING HOOK
- ROLLS ROYCE SPEY ENGINES
- ANTI-SKID BRAKES
- ULTRA STANDBY UHF (ECP)
- EXTRA-EXTENDIBLE NOSE GEAR

The F-4M programme go-ahead was given at the beginning of April 1965. The YF-4M engineering release was given in February 1966 and the manufacturing release in April 1966. The development and design phase continued until the end of September 1966 and was finalized in November 1966. However, by mid-1966, the F-4M programme was already behind schedule, through no fault of McDonnell's. Although the first YF-4M flew at St Louis on 17 February 1967, according to the revised mid-1966 schedule, the first delivery had originally been forecast in the Agreement of 9 February 1965 as occurring the previous month.

The F-4K's high lift devices, the same as the F-4J's, were demanded to improve its ability to operate from the RN's smaller carriers, particularly with regard to their shorter catapults, and to launch and recover at higher weights. They comprised drooped ailerons with BLC, larger leading edge flaps with BLC, stabilator slots and fractionally reduced stabilator anhedral, and an extra-extensible nose gear leg. A reduction of 8 per cent in approach speed was envisaged. The F-4M shared these devices except the slotted stabilator and had a standard F-4C-type non-extensible nose gear leg.

The fixed, inverted stabilator slot was developed by McDonnell for the F-4J and K to increase

From MCAIR Report B617, The Royal Air Force Phantom II, *1 August 1966. The British Phantoms were the only export F-4s to descend directly from USN variants*

rotational capability after a catapult launch. An aircraft's rotational capability is its ability to respond when, upon gaining a predetermined airspeed, the pilot increases the angle of attack in order to become airborne, by a positive rearward movement of the control column. The F-4K's stabilator then goes down, and thus the slot, by modifying the force on the aerofoil; gives greater downwards 'lift', to permit greater angles of attack. The slot extends the full span of the stabilator leading edge, and is a blunt, inverted aerofoil, the original stabilator had a blunt leading edge. The slot also increased control effectiveness at lower speeds on the approach. It was subsequently adopted on the USAF's F-4E.

The F-4A, B and C had inboard leading edge flaps. On the F-4J and K, these were fixed, and the outboard edges provided the flaps, of increased area. They are blown. Co-ordinated with the trailing edge flaps, they provide greater control effectiveness at lower speeds and higher angles of attack. Drooped aileron trials for the F-4K and J began in January 1964. They also are blown, and augment lift at low airspeeds. With landing gear

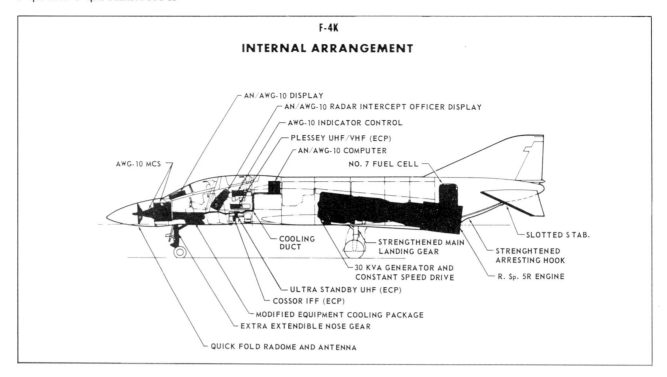

F-4K

INTERNAL ARRANGEMENT

- AN/AWG-10 DISPLAY
- AN/AWG-10 RADAR INTERCEPT OFFICER DISPLAY
- AWG-10 INDICATOR CONTROL
- PLESSEY UHF/VHF (ECP)
- AN/AWG-10 COMPUTER
- NO. 7 FUEL CELL
- AWG-10 MCS
- COOLING DUCT
- STRENGTHENED MAIN LANDING GEAR
- SLOTTED STAB.
- STRENGHTENED ARRESTING HOOK
- 30 KVA GENERATOR AND CONSTANT SPEED DRIVE
- R. Sp. 5R ENGINE
- ULTRA STANDBY UHF (ECP)
- COSSOR IFF (ECP)
- MODIFIED EQUIPMENT COOLING PACKAGE
- EXTRA EXTENDIBLE NOSE GEAR
- QUICK FOLD RADOME AND ANTENNA

down and flaps selected, the ailerons droop $16\frac{1}{2}°$, but continue to function differentially as ailerons with respect to the new zero position.

The Boundary Layer Control (BLC) system provides a laminar stream of high energy air which controls the development of the boundary layer over the wing, flaps and ailerons, thus affecting transition and separation; that is, the point of change from laminar or smooth flow, which provides lift, to turbulent flow. When the laminar flow separates from the wing boundary, as a result of low forward airspeed, turbulent flow produces drag and has negligible lift. BLC effectively compensates for low airspeeds by re-energising and speeding up the layer of air adjacent to the wing boundary. BLC thus provides a great range of useable lift co-efficients and, by delaying separation at greater angles of attack than without BLC, lowers the approach and touch-down speeds possible. The Spey gave more bleed air for BLC than the F-4J's J79, and thus an improved performance. BLC does not immediately cease with throttle retardation on landing.

Although the F-4K and M were developed in parallel with the F-4B-based F-4J, the substitution of the Spey turbofan for the J79 turbojet required substantial modifications to be made. The engine bays had to be redesigned and the fuselage widened; the large bellmouth afterburner nozzles required the lower aft fuselage to be modified and deepened. The air intakes had to be increased by 20 per cent in frontal area to cater for the Spey's greater mass flow. These changes required a different fuselage centre section, marred the area-

From MCAIR Report Phantom II for The Royal Navy

ruled aerodynamics and imposed several drag penalties – the most serious being the high base-drag underneath the engines. Air spill outlets had to be fitted to the fuselage, and a new inlet and nozzle control system installed. An additional 300 lbs of titanium, an expensive alloy, had to be incorporated in the aft fuselage to withstand the hotter exhaust gases.

The Phantom was the first reheat application for the Spey and the RB.168-25R, or Spey Mk 201, has since become the major military version. Closely based on the civil Spey-25, or Mk 512 (developed from the original Mk 505 via the Mk 506), the principal modifications were the addition of the reheat system with variable nozzles, and changes to the detail design of the compressors to meet the requirements of supersonic flight and air intake distortion. It was restressed for supersonic performance, incorporating new materials to meet the increased temperature and pressure conditions and flight loads imposed by a military rating. A major change from the Spey-25 was the introduction of a robust shaft and disc construction for the LP compressor. Static reheat boost of 70 per cent was achieved mainly by increasing the turbine entry temperature. The first Spey Mk 201 static bench test was made early in April 1965. By June 1965, it had delivered its planned thrust of 12,000 lb (5,000 kg) during bench tests and had exceeded its average reheat thrust. The engine gained flight clearance in late

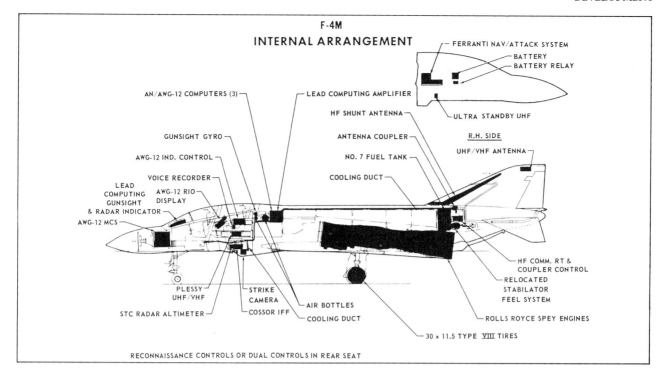

F-4M
INTERNAL ARRANGEMENT

FERRANTI NAV/ATTACK SYSTEM
BATTERY
BATTERY RELAY
ULTRA STANDBY UHF
R.H. SIDE

AN/AWG-12 COMPUTERS (3)
LEAD COMPUTING AMPLIFIER
HF SHUNT ANTENNA
ANTENNA COUPLER
UHF/VHF ANTENNA
GUNSIGHT GYRO
NO. 7 FUEL TANK
AWG-12 IND. CONTROL
COOLING DUCT
VOICE RECORDER
LEAD
COMPUTING
GUNSIGHT
& RADAR INDICATOR
AWG-12 RIO
DISPLAY
AWG-12 MCS
HF COMM. RT &
COUPLER CONTROL
RELOCATED
STABILATOR
FEEL SYSTEM
PLESSY
UHF/VHF
STRIKE
CAMERA
AIR BOTTLES
STC RADAR ALTIMETER
COSSOR IFF
COOLING DUCT
ROLLS ROYCE SPEY ENGINES
30 x 11.5 TYPE VIII TIRES

RECONNAISSANCE CONTROLS OR DUAL CONTROLS IN REAR SEAT

October 1965. Engine No 1 was delivered to McDonnell at St Louis in early February 1966, followed shortly by the second, and by the third later in the month. The fourth arrived in late April. Six pairs were delivered each at monthly intervals until December 1966 when the delivery rate was increased.

Being a turbofan, the Spey offered greater fuel and afterburner efficiency over the turbojet J79. Estimates were for 30 per cent shorter take-off, higher top speed, much longer range or higher loads, faster acceleration, 30 per cent lower SFC, 20 per cent quicker climb to high altitude and faster response to throttle movements. However, performance estimates deteriorated as a result of problems in matching the inlets and nozzles with the airframe.

The Spey is quite a bit bigger in diameter than the J79, partly because it is a bypass engine. It is also shorter. Therefore the installation bay had to be re-engineered to accept the Spey. To facilitate this McDonnell proposed and Rolls-Royce agreed that each define an envelope. One was the envelope that surrounded the engine and the other was a slightly larger envelope, essentially the engine bay, within which the installation should not encroach. In theory about 0.5 inch separated the two envelopes. Any excursion outside either envelope was negotiated between the two parties, and a new envelope ensued. While this is now standard practice in certain circumstances, at the time it was innovative as far as Rolls-Royce and McDonnell were concerned.

McDonnell's project engineer insisted on

From MCAIR Report The Royal Air Force Phantom II

constructing a large scale mock-up of the installation. Initially, he did this by building up large plywood patterns which resembled the negotiated installation in advance of Rolls-Royce getting an actual engine bay. There was also a wooden mock-up of the engine which was installed so that various access points, such as for tightening bolts, could be checked. The whole exercise was thoroughly conducted.

The RN laid down strict timings for re-installation of the engine, and forcefully stressed the difficulty of doing this on a pitching deck. They made absolutely certain that serviceability and installation features were given the highest priority, and many features were re-engineered to satisfy the RN.

The mock-up finally became the installation bay proper, and a full-sized fully dressed engine was sent out to St Louis. This was used to demonstrate the ability to carry out the installation, which was brought down to about half an hour to take one engine out and a further hour to re-install. This was considered to be no mean feat. At the same time as the F-4K programme, McDonnell had developed and built the Gemini space-capsule, the launch of which took place while the Spey installation was demonstrated. For the benefit of the television networks, a Gemini capsule was in the bay next to the installation rig. Rolls-Royce's team met many of the broadcasters and felt privileged to sit in the capsule.

Intimately connected with the development of
the engine installation is the engineering of
the intakes to provide good aerodynamic
characteristics over the widest possible speed and
altitude range, while keeping drag to a minimum.
To allow for the greater mass flow of the Spey
compared with the J79, 240 against 169 lb/sec, the
air inlet ducts and the engine tunnel sections were
enlarged by increasing the fuselage width by some
6 in. This involves a small loss of wing area, but
does not increase span. As a result of the known
critical characteristics of turbofan engines with
regard to intake flow distortion, Rolls-Royce
undertook an intensive intake investigation and
proving programme. A full-size F-4K fibre-glass
mock-up intake system was sent over from St
Louis, in which a Spey was tested in worse
conditions than the aircraft would expect to
encounter. As a result of this work no significant
engine matching problems were anticipated.

It is also necessary to maintain the correct air
mass flow to the engines under all flight
conditions. This is achieved by rotary valves in the
engine tunnel arranged to dump surplus air. The
movement of the valves is a function of duct Mach
number and is operated by actuators on command
from the air data computer (ADC). However, to
cope with the demand for airflow at low speeds,
the F-4K and M have auxiliary air intake doors,
one above and one in the belly below the rear
chamber of each engine, which are open for take-
off and landing. These air spill devices are

*F-4K slatted stabilators on final assembly jigs at BAC
Strand Road. Built as single structural assemblies, they are
based on torque boxes. The darker panels are titanium, the
lighter ones steel and ('fragile') aluminium*

*USN F-4J aboard HMS Ark Royal during cross-decking
operations. The F-4J formed the basis for the F-4K and
M, sharing high lift devices, but the intakes and centre and
aft fuselage section differ greatly*

controlled by the ADC. All intake management is automatic and needs no attention from the crew.

The fixed and moveable engine intake ramps were redesigned. The function of the ramp system is to vary the position of the two shock waves which form at the apex of the 'V', in order to provide the greatest pressure recovery over the whole performance range. Each intake is a double-external, single-internal shock system. The functions of the fixed, forward ramp are to bleed off the de-energized boundary layer air before it enters the engine intake, and to fix the position of the first oblique shock wave so that it is clear of the intake at all speeds. Attached by vertical hinges to the rear of this ramp is the moveable ramp, which has two sections and is shaped like a very shallow, vertical 'V'. The two sections close and open to change the angle of the 'V', thus changing the area of the intake throats. Their movement is programmed as a function of the free stream total temperature, and is controlled by an hydraulic actuator moving in response to demands from the ADC.

Lt Michael S Seider, USN, who flew both the F-4J and F-4K, made this comparison:

The only major difference in the Royal Navy version of the Phantom is the twin-spool Spey bypass engine. The almost 25 per cent increase in thrust in maximum reheat over the American F-4J gives the F-4K better initial acceleration. But its increased drag does not give the K model a great advantage throughout the flight envelope. At high level its performance deteriorates faster than the American models. While the airframe limits are the same for top speed, the low level acceleration of a clean K is very impressive even to an experienced F-4J man.

The F-4K arrestor hook was strengthened for operations on smaller RN carriers and is stressed to 4.8G. The F-4M has the same hook for use on runway wires. Hook operation is energized hydraulically, controlled by a handle in the forward cockpit, and falls to the fully down position under its own weight, and the action of an hydraulic dashpot. The 4.7 m flat diameter ring slot brake parachute, housed in a compartment in the tail cone, is similar to the F-4J's, and can be used for spin recovery. It is deployed by pulling a handle in the forward cockpit. The F-4K's built for the RN had catapult spools recessed under the fuselage centre body; the F-4M did not.

The F-4K and M were built equipped with the Martin-Baker Mark H5 ejector seat. In 1957 the Secretary of the US Navy took the decision to instal Mark H5 series seats into nine USN front-line aircraft, including the F4H-1 (F-4A), although the first six F4H-1 prototypes were equipped with Stanley ejection seats. The Mk H5 was a cartridge-operated runway level/130 kt seat developed by Martin-Baker under contract to McDonnell, and equipped all production F-4A, B, C and D aircraft.

In 1965 decisions were taken by the Bureau of Naval Weapons (now NAVAIRSYSCON) to modify the Mark H5 seat to include an under-seat rocket motor, designed and developed by Martin-Baker, to achieve zero-zero performance, and to fit a McDonnell designed and developed sequence firing system. The seat was re-designated Mk H7. Following engineering and test effort, the total system was subjected to system tests on the SNORT sled track at China Lake, California, during 1967, at speeds between zero and 600 kt. The USAF jointly funded the engineering and test effort of the improved system which entered Fleet and USAF squadron service in 1968.

The RN and RAF observed the effort to introduce the modified system, but elected not to participate in funding the Engineering Change Proposal (ECP) and preferred to retain the Mk H5 seats, pending subsequent modification to a Type 7 standard in the UK, which reduced initial costs on the F-4K and M development and procurement. The H5 was produced by Martin-Baker entirely in the UK. Martin-Baker has produced over 11,000 Mk 5/7 seats for the F-4, all ordered by McDonnell. Standard US harnesses were initially used on the UK Phantoms, until discarded as unsatisfactory. The ejection seat parachute for the F-4K and Marks H5 and H7 was the Irvin (GB) Ltd I24.

The USN's F-4s had a 20 inch (51 cm) extensible nose oleo leg to improve attitude for catapult launching, but an extra-extensible nose leg was designed for the F-4K to give a larger angle of attack for launching at higher weights from the shorter catapults of British carriers. McDonnell had proposed such a device from their initial studies. Extra-extensible nose gear for future use on the 'F-4RN' had been tested aboard USS Forrestal (CV-59) on 11 April 1963 and found satisfactory, following trials carried out at NATC, Patuxent River, by Lcdr (now Rear-Admiral) William Ramsett, USN, of NATC Carrier Suitability section. Two trials proposed to take place aboard Ark Royal were not conducted. The F-4K's 40 inch (102 cm) leg extension allowed wind over deck requirements to be reduced by 11 knots (20 km/hr) ie the extended leg gives 11 knots WOD effect. The F-4K's extra extensible leg is, essentially, a function of the length of the catapult and WOD. When the UK was considering the F-4K for operations in the tropics, with high temperatures and no wind, meaning 'no lift in the air', the extra extensible nose gear was essential; in such conditions, the Sea Vixen struggled for lift and climb. The F-4K's leg has two sets of torque links between the wheels for extension/normal, in contrast to the single set of the F-4M's standard leg. The leg is pneumatically extended and returns to its normal length upon selection of landing gear 'UP'. It retracts

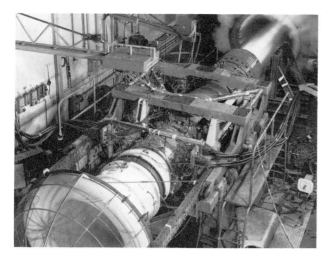

A Spey in the static running engine test facility at Rolls-Royce Derby

RIGHT
At BAC Strand Road, a completed F-4M rear fuselage section showing the double-walled underside with titanium shingles, the rudder and stabilator actuation and feel-trim system, and (left) the fuel vent pipe

Spliced YF-4K centre fuselage section and mainplanes. The fixed inboard leading edge was fitted during final assembly, and part of the leading edge BLC duct is visible. F-4K and Ms were built alongside other F-4s

backwards hydraulically. The nose wheels are hydraulically steerable and self centring, the steering unit being located on the front of the upper oleo casing.

The main landing gear legs of the F-4K and M are of ultra-high tensile 140-ton steel, and were strengthened to allow a maximum landing weight of 36,000 lbs (17,252 kg) force and 24 ft per second (7.3 m/second) sink rate for landing-on at higher weights, and steeper approach angles. Similar changes were applied to the F-4J.

Goodyear took over the substantial wheel and brake contract from General Tires from the F-4C onwards. Auto Specialties of St Joseph and J & M designed and supplied the brakes and wheels respectively, all of conventional design, to both. The F-4J, K and M have the same wheels and brakes, which facilitates support arrangements with the USN. An anti-skid system, introduced on the F-4C for operations from runways, was specified for the British F-4s. Designed by Hydro-Wire, it was licence-built in the UK by Dunlop. Tyres skid if wheel deceleration is greater than the traction co-efficient as a result of a wet runway surface, or an uneven runway surface producing poor tyre-to-runway compliance which continually alters the braking coefficient, causing skipping. Simplistically, the anti-skid system consists of an exciter ring, a cogged plate attached to the rotating part of the wheel; a fixed sensor which 'counts the cogs' (rpm); a control box comprising a velocity converter which interprets rpm in terms of velocity, and thus acceleration and deceleration, and a skid rate and locked wheel detector; and an hydraulic valve control which controls the proportion of pilot-applied brake force which is transmitted to the brakes.

The best deceleration that can be obtained during the landing roll is programmed into the control box as a base or aim point. By comparing the actual with the desired deceleration, the box gauges if more or less is required to keep the wheel at the desired deceleration rate. If the wheel is indicating no skid tendencies, the box allows full pilot applied pressure to the brakes; if deceleration is too fast, and the wheel is thus progressing too deeply into skid, the box relieves the brake

The first Spey installation in YF-4K1 on 19 March 1966. The keel, upper heat shields, fuselage side panel, and belly doors form the engine bay. Note the left Spey's thrust trunnion and side link attachment

pressure to the wheel to bring it back to the correct speed. The desired deceleration rate of the wheel is termed the skid threshold; it determines the point at which the system starts to relieve brake pressure. The amount relieved is virtually proportional to how deeply the deceleration has penetrated the skid threshold. The system takes all pressure off the brake at the lock-up threshold. This is not necessarily when the wheel has locked, but represents a deceleration condition where full relief of brake pressure is necessary to accelerate the wheel back towards free-rolling velocity. The system works symetrically: deceleration on both wheels is dictated by the wheel with the lowest coefficient, so that the aircraft continues in a straight line.

Pulse Bias Modulation (PBM) dictates the length of time required to put full pilot applied pressure back on the brake after the wheel has come up to speed following a skid. Each time the wheel skids, the PBM circuit is charged, the amount determining how much of the pilot-applied pressure is initially put back into the brakes after recovery, increasing the proportion with time. In a sequence of skids, the amounts remaining from previous charges are added to subsequent charges. Within a few cycles, therefore, the system has 'sampled' the runway and has adjusted brake pressure to runway conditions. As the aircraft starts decelerating, the amount of brake pressure it can tolerate increases, and the cumulative PBM charge dissipates, and thus the brake pressure allowed through is increased.

Upon activation, the system checks itself; if the system fails, it automatically shuts itself off, and a light comes on in the cockpit. Upon touchdown, the pilot puts the power to idle, deploys the brake 'chute, and holds the stick full aft (BLC does not cease immediately upon throttle retardation, so power can be taken off just before touch-down for short landings). The pilot does not brake until the nosewheel is on the ground, partly because of nose gear loads, and to ensure that the wheels are up to speed, which is required for anti-skid operation. Full aft stabilator and the brake 'chute rapidly reduce speed to 100 knots, below which brakes can be used; above this speed rudder steering can be used; below, nose steering can be used in addition. Anti-skid protection ceases at around 10–20 knots, as the pilot requires full control of brakes for taxying.

The F-4K and M shared UHF/VHF equipment. The Plessey PTR373 Receiver/Transmitter and Transmitter Rectifier was the main communication equipment. It was specified by MoD. The equipment is located under the rear cockpit, and the antenna in the top of the fin. Dowty Electronics (Ultra, part of Plessey) produced the UHF Standby Receiver Amplifier in conjunction with the PTR374, the

small D403P UHF Airborne Emergency Transmitter/Receiver, used when the main set fails. Military aircraft are dependent on UHF to maintain the controller to aircraft and aircraft to aircraft communication links which are essential to the conduct of effective, co-ordinated operations. This has led to increasingly sophisticated and reliable UHF sets, but failures do occur. In the event of failure, the D403 enables the Phantom to continue to operate safely, in most cases without premature return to base.

The Dowty D403P, a military specification version of the D403M, was developed under contract from McDonnell and was fitted to all British Phantoms. Introduced in 1968, D403 became the standard UHF standby radio with the RAF, RN and others. Developed as a fully transistorized successor to D303, and half its weight and volume with generally improved specification, D403 is 4.75 in height, 3.5 in wide and 10 in deep, and weighs 5 lbs. It comprises a main assembly chassis in which are mounted the three modules, the transmitter and the receiver, mounted side by side on top of the third element, the modulator/transient suppressor. Modular construction, easy access to components and easy interchange are features. Full transistorisation eliminates warm-up period. The unit has been designed for remote mounting so that the only addition required in the cockpit, where space is at a premium, is a combined power on/channel switch. It operates on two channels, and has a frequency range of 238–248 MHz. In its emergency role, once the initial international distress frequency (243 MHz) has been made, a second channel for approach and landing instructions is opened, thus occupying the distress channel for the shortest necessary time.

In common with other F-4 models, the F-4K and M have TACAN (Tactical Air Navigation) equipment. A military air navigation aid, the TACAN system comprises a fixed or mobile ground or seaborne transmitting unit and an airborne unit which reduces the ground transmitters signal to a visual presentation of azimuth (bearing) and distance information. TACAN is a pulse system operating in the UHF band (300–3000 mc, around 1,000 MHz), not through the conventional VOR (VHF omnidirectional range) air navigation aid equipment, which operates in the VHF band (108 to 117.95 MHz). *Ark Royal* was equipped with a TACAN transmitter. TACAN can be used to fix CAPs. TACAN can also generate inputs for the navigation and weapons control systems.

The F-4M introduced HF equipment, the AD470 HF/SSB (single side band) communications equipment produced by Marconi. It is a high power set for long range communications, especially useful for aircraft to base contact for reconnaissance tasks. The HF radio provides instant contact with ground bases out to the limit of range over the horizon, when UHF would be limited by line-of-sight, dependent on altitude. The first supersonic aircraft equipped with HF was the RF-4C, and it was proposed for the RF-4M. The HF shunt aerial is in the fin leading edge, and the RT and antenna coupler and coupler control are located in the rear fuselage, behind the No 7 fuel cell, which was of reduced size compared to the F-4K's to accommodate this equipment, while the stabilator feel system was also relocated below the HF equipment as a result. The F-4K did not have HF equipment.

In peace and war it is essential to distinguish friendly from enemy aircraft quickly, accurately and reliably, a requirement underlined by the increasing accuracy of air defence systems. It is vital in an environment where interceptors are capable of shooting down a target well beyond visual range by radar contact alone. Identification Friend or Foe equipment (IFF) has been in use since World War II. However, the valve-technology from that period became increasingly limited during the 1950s. In 1963, taking advantage of the benefits of solid-state design techniques, Cossor commenced development of a transistorized IFF transponder, featuring reduced weight and high reliability. Designated SSR 1500, initial design was undertaken for TSR-2. As another example of spin-off from TSR-2, UK MoD specified the SSR 1500 IFF Mk 10A transponder for the F-4K and M.

A two-stage transmitter section was designed, based on two ceramic planar triodes, to achieve the required high power. Forming an oscillator/buffer amplifier circuit, this method reduces the effect of antenna mismatch. The design concept incorporated full mode and code facilities to ensure compatability with existing and future military and civil ground systems. Designed to operate without serious restrictions on altitude, temperature and shock, the SSR 1500 has a maximum altitude of 100,000 ft, a temperature range of −55 to +125°C, and requires no shock damping or special cooling. These are important factors in high performance aircraft which valve-technology could not meet. The SSR 1500 uses silicon transistors and fibreglass circuit boards.

The SSR 1500 packaging was selected to approximate to ARINC $\frac{1}{2}$ ATR long concept (4.7 × 18.4 × 7.6 inches) to simplify installation design problems. It weighs 30.5 lbs. The SSR 1500's Control Unit, designated SSR 1053, weighs 2 lbs and measures 5.8 × 3.3 × 3.8 inches, and has antenna Type 100B or High Speed Type 4169.

Subsequently, the SSR 1520, an SSR 1500 repackaged in a one ATR short case size (10.1 × 9.7 × 7.6 inches) to simplify retrofitting of the APX25 and ARI 5848 rear-warning radar systems,

became the RAF's standard IFF Mk 10A transponder, fitted to all front line aircraft and some Naval helicopters. Over 2,400 IFF 1500/1520s were purchased by HM Government before production ended in about 1976.

A ground station or another aircraft interrogates an unidentified aircraft's IFF transponder. If the correct, friendly, modes are being employed an identifying signal is returned. The Cossor IFF 3500 airborne interrogator, designed for use in any type of aircraft, is specified by UK MoD for the RAF's Phantom, Tornado F.2 and Nimrod AEW.3 from 1983. It has a narrow beamwidth, previously held to be unattainable, and is claimed to yield extremely high resolution. Automatic code changing eliminates incorrect code selection by reducing pilot workload and improves security.

Westinghouse was the main contractor for the Phantom II's radar and fire control systems from the beginning of the programme. A succession of improved models was produced based upon the F-4A's APQ-72 search and track pulse radar and APA-157 continuous wave illuminating radar for passive homing AIM-7 missiles, the Aero-1A system. The versions which followed the APQ-72 were the results of advancing performance and adding air-to-ground modes to the original air interception modes, and progressive introduction of solid-state electronics. However, Westinghouse had begun serious development of pulse Doppler radar in the mid-1950s. The first production type equipped the Boeing Bomarc IM-99 missile. The second, the APQ-59, was integrated with the ASW-25 weapon control computer to produce the AN/AWG-10 airborne multi-mode missile control system. The AWG-10 was adopted by the USN for the F-4J because it offered considerable advances for air defense fighters over previous systems. It was also proposed for the USAF's F-4E, but the new APQ-120, the culmination of Westinghouse's first F-4 series, was selected. Selection for the F-4J, and the advanced in performance offered, made the selection of the AWG-10 for the F-4K and M logical and attractive in terms of cost, development time and mission suitability. To meet British requirements, modified versions of the AWG-10 were developed by Ferranti for the F-4K and M, designated AWG-11 and -12, respectively. In 1965, McDonnell stated that this multi-mode, search and track pulse Doppler system would 'significantly increase the British Phantom's air-intercept capability.'

The system is of modular construction, with 29 line replaceable units (LRU). The APG-59 nose package comprises the transmitter, receiver, RF oscillator, scan pattern generator, trackers and power supplies, and the 32-inch diameter radar dish and antenna. The nose radome hinges to starboard and the installation runs forwards on

telescopic rails for all-round inspection and
maintenance purposes. On the F-4K, to reduce the
aircraft's length to the standard limit of 54 ft RN
carrier lifts and hangars, the radar dish and
antenna fold 180° to starboard with the radome for
stowage.

The ASW-25 computer comprises the system's
three remaining units, the computer elements and
the one-way data-link, housed in the upper
equipment bay. The nose package and the
computer elements are cooled by air ducted from
the aircraft's conditioning system; the nose
package also has liquid air cooling. The AWG-10
system required a modified equipment cooling
package. The F-4M's AWG-12 differs from the F-
4K's AWG-11 in another important respect, in
that the ASW-25 is interfaced with the Ferranti
INAS.

The radar operator's controls include an
indicator, indicator control, radar set control,
antenna control, and built-in test equipment
(BITE) circuit which enables the operation of the
29 LRUs to be checked in flight, thus expediting
ground maintenance. The pilot has an indicator
and display. It is the RIO's task to control all
phases of radar operation.

The AWG-11/-12 provides pulse Doppler (look-
down) and pulse air-to-air search and tracking
modes, detection and ranging modes, high and low
level mapping, navigation, and terrain clearance
modes, beacon homing, air-to-ground interdiction
and bombing ranging modes, and a variety of
ECCM. It also provides missile launch
computations and semi-active illumination for the
AIM-7 radar homing missiles through a weapon-
aiming computer which provides range and closing
speed information. It is interfaced with other
aircraft systems.

When introduced on the F-4, the AWG-10 was
the most advanced air intercept radar in the world.
Pulse Doppler radar is essential in order to meet
the range of modern combat requirements, and to
take advantage of developments in missiles. Pulse
Doppler radar alone can either detect or reject
targets moving on or close to the ground, thus
enabling an aircraft at altitude to detect an aircraft
at ground level, but to reject an object moving on
the ground; modern missiles can acquire such an
aircraft target and home onto it – this is termed
'look-down, shoot-down' capability. Moreover, in
air combat, only pulse Doppler can avoid blind
velocities, the angular directions where aircraft
cannot be seen, and reject clutter.

Pulse repetition frequency (PRF) is the
frequency of emission of pulse from a radar.
Range is determined by measuring the time to
return, but there are range ambiguities at distances
corresponding to the pulse spacing, least at low
and most at high PRF. Doppler shift is a
phenomenon which results in a shortening or

lengthening of a basic frequency due to the
relative motion of the radar and target: it therefore
reveals the target's relative motion. A frequency
sensitive radar receiver with filters to analyse the
frequency content of returning energy can
determine if the radiation emitted has returned at
exactly the transmitted frequency, or if it has
shifted. Such a radar is a Doppler system. Radars
which analyse both pulse data and Doppler shift
are pulse Doppler radars. Doppler radars tend to
be of the medium and high PRF types
(10,000–30,000, and 100,000–300,000 pulse per
second). While the medium PRF has less range
ambiguities, the high-PRF offers better target
velocity discrimination over a wider range.

The basic receiver in a PD radar derives target
range, bearing and range rate. An extra computer
stage conducts tracking functions in order to
convert this receiver information into target data
for the crew and weapon system. This computer
stage sifts the information from the receiver and
converts the relative position data into tracks.
These are presented relative to a stable ground
reference, such as latitude and longitude. PD
radars can distinguish, therefore, between returns
from the ground and from moving targets, and
thus have a reliable 'look-down' capability, able to
detect low-flying aircraft at long ranges, an
essential development in conjunction with 'snap-
down' AAMs, and especially in Europe where the
threat is mainly low level. A high speed digital
computer is required to perform the receiver
computing, and only since these became available
in the early 1970s has PD radar become standard.
The speed of the computer determines how many
targets can be tracked simultaneously.

For attack roles, the F-4M required an INAS.
Developed by Ferranti, the INAS was based upon
work undertaken for the TSR-2. Problems were
encountered in interfacing the INAS with the
AWG-12 which delayed trials and service
introduction programmes. Coupled with the
AWG-12, the INAS gave the F-4M exceptional
capability in the air-to-ground roles. Replacing the
Litton equipments in the USAF's F-4s, the INAS
was interfaced with other weapon-aiming and
navigation facilities, including TACAN, horizontal
situation indicator, radar altimeter, the air data
computer, and LCOSS. INAS equipment requires
to be aligned before missions and was not until
recently suitable for carrier operation. The
computer elements require to be maintained at a
constant temperature, and are therefore connected
to an external power supply on the ground. The
system comprises an HUD, and control unit, and
the main LRUs: the computer, inertial platform,
power supply, electronics and interface modules. It
is housed in the lower part of the upper equipment
bay. The INAS controls are located on the aft
cockpit's starboard console.

The INAS was designed to provide exceptionally accurate navigation to targets by a series of en route checks, and a series of complex attack and withdrawal manoeuvres at low altitudes. The INAS provided high and low level navigation, air-to-ground interdiction and bombing and terrain clearance modes. The combined AWG-12, INAS and AJB-7 could control any combination of weapons the F-4M can carry and gives the F-4M the capability of attacking both air and ground targets by day or night, in all weathers and in severe ECM environments.

The F-4M also required lead computing optical sight (LCOS) equipment; the F-4K did not. The original equipment was semi-automatic ('wind-up') but automatic (ALCOS) equipment was later fitted. The F-4M's LCOS equipment comprises a display located with the radar indicator in the pilot's line of sight under the windscreen, and a two-axis computing gyroscope, gyro mount and a lead computing amplifier mounted behind the AWG-12 computer in the upper equipment bay (the standard F-4 position). Aircraft manoeuvres generate rate and acceleration signals in the gyro lead computer, the radar measures range to the target, and the air data computer supplies the aircraft's angle of attack, and air density and airspeed data. The pilot's aiming reference is displayed in the correct direction to introduce lead angle and gravity corrections. Analogues of the aircraft's roll angle and range information are also projected onto the combining glass. In ground attack modes, other aircraft systems are used to generate corrections for drift, and offset bombing is possible. The HUD projects the aiming reference by means of a collimated reticle display in the pilot's line of sight. In the air-to-air mode, the equipment displays missile fire control information by means of a servoed aiming reference. In the ground attack mode, the pilot adjusts the aiming reference manually to control gunnery, rocket firing and bombing displays.

From the start of the programme, the Phantom II's main armament was the Raytheon Sparrow III, carried semi-recessed in four positions – stations 3, 4, 5, and 6 – under the fuselage and ejection launched. The AI radar systems developed for the Phantom II were primarily tasked with controlling these missiles. The purchase of the F-4K and M Phantom for the British Services included the procurement of stocks of AIM-7E-2 Sparrow IIIs for self-defence when operating in the ground attack or reconnaissance roles and for interception in the maritime air defence role. A quantity were ordered in 1965 directly from Raytheon, although test equipment was produced in the UK by Cossor Electronics, a Raytheon subsidiary. The more advanced AIM-7F, then under development, was to be considered as the subject for a further order.

The AIM-7 was designed for the US Navy as an all-weather, medium range air-to-air missile (MRAAM), able to operate at high altitudes. It is one of the most versatile and widely used of US missiles. The Sparrow III family are all similar with a length of 12 ft (3.66 m), a diameter of 8 in (0.20 m) and a span of 3 ft 4 in (1.02 m). The total weight of the AIM-7E-2 is some 400 lbs (228 kg). It has a cruise speed of Mach 3.5 plus, and a range of 28 miles (44 km), dependent on weather conditions. It has a semi-active radar homing guidance and control system, and has a 'jump' capability of several miles. The interceptor's radar detects a target out to about 40 miles range, and feeds range and speed information to the AIM-7, which acquires the target at about 15 miles. It is locked-on at about 12 miles range, and launches between 12 and 8 miles. The 60 lb HE warhead is a continuous rod type.

In addition to AIM-7, the F-4 can carry four AIM-9 Sidewinder short range air-to-air missiles (SRAAM) on the inboard pylons. The essence of Sidewinder is a low cost, mass produced, relatively simple missile. AIM-9 has an infrared homing and guidance system which detects and homes on to the hot exhaust gases of a target, basically for rear-on attacks. It requires no special equipment on the launching aircraft, and can be fitted to many operational types for short range offensive and defensive purposes. It has few moving parts and offers easy maintenance. Development began as a US Naval Ordnance Test Station project in 1949. It is named after the lethal snake which corkscrews across the desert, because gyros in the rear fin tips give a twist in flight, leaving a spiral smoke trail.

The British Phantoms were initially armed with the AIM-9D Sidewinder IC. Externally similar to the AIM-9B, the AIM-9D has a higher thrust Rocketdyne solid-propellant motor which increased the range and speed. It has a 10 lb HE warhead, a proximity fuse and a Raytheon/Philco-Ford Mk 18 Mod 1 infra-red guidance system. Its speed is in excess of Mach 2 and its ceiling exceeds 15,000 m. In fine weather, the AIM-9D was the most effective weapon of its type. Under certain circumstances, for instance where the target was moving against a land or cluttered background or in attack from nearly astern, it was more effective than the passive radar homing AIM-7. The AIM-9 accounts for the highest proportion of F-4 combat kills, but it could be distracted by any source of heat stronger than that from the target aircraft, notably by the sun itself, and a pursued pilot could evade an AIM-9 by 'going vertical' into the sun, then reversing. The AIM-9D is 284 cm long, 12.7 cm in diameter, and spans 60.9 cm. It entered US service in 1965. The AIM-9D was progressively superceded on UK Phantoms by the much more advanced AIM-9L from the late 1970s.

When the Phantom was designed fighter philosophies concentrated upon all-missile armament, and consequently the Phantom had no internal guns. It was believed that AAMs combined with radar control would be more relevant to meet the foreseen threats, but lessons had to be relearnt, particularly from US experience over Vietnam. A gun is more effective than a missile in many air combat situations. The ultimate answer was an integral gun armament, applied to the F-4E, which has an M-61 rotary cannon. The interim solution was the installation of gun pods on external stores points, which have the advantage of being interchangeable with other stores, permitting mission flexibility, albeit with a drag penalty. A gun is also a very effective close support weapon against soft targets, such as troop concentrations and vehicles, and fast patrol boats.

McDonnell had studied fitting gun pods to the Phantom before aircrews started calling for them. The first system was the SUU-16/A with an M61A1 20 mm Vulcan rotary cannon, mechanically driven by a ram air turbine which is lowered into the slipstream, a drive which restricts the rate of fire at air speeds below 350 kt (650 km/hr), and creates drag, but it can be electrically or hydraulically driven. One of these pods could be carried on each of the outboard and the centreline pylons, endowing the F-4 with a tremendous punch. The next model, the SUU-

23/A (XM-25) uses a GAU-4/A 20 mm Vulcan rotary cannon which is driven by gases generated by the ammunition; it is therefore completely self-driven. The appearance, performance and hitting power of the SUU-16/A and -23/A are otherwise identical, but the latter is 12 lb heavier. They are interchangeable and both were designed specifically for high performance aircraft in close support and air defence missions. The F-4M was designed to carry the SUU-16/A and the SUU-23/A; the latter became the standard RAF Phantom gun pod. The F-4K was not adapted to carry the pod, but ex-RN F-4Ks in RAF service were eventually modified to carry the SUU-23/A. The pod does not affect either performance or load, and stores can be carried on the other pylons.

Excellent for air defence and ground attack roles – 'gives a fair old hose' – the SUU-23/A is a devastating weapon. It is capable of destroying a convoy of vehicles with HE ammunition in one pass, particularly relevant to the RAF Phantom's interdiction role in Europe, while it has the accuracy and fire power to destroy targets that bombs and rockets have difficulty in hitting. A quick burst can dig a trench six feet deep. The

SUU-23/A, lifted by its 30-inch centre suspension. The aerodynamic pod houses the GAU-4/A 20 mm six-barrelled rotary cannon, the linkless feed and the ammunition drum

SUU-23/A is particularly well-suited to engaging ground targets from ranges of 700 m or more.

The pod is aerodynamic in shape and is designed to attach to standard 30-in centre double-lug suspension racks (MIL-A-8591), but is compatible with other racks and thus a wide range of tactical aircraft. The RAF Phantoms carry it on station 5, the centreline, only. The pod provides ammunition storage and feed and electronic control support for the operation of the GAU-4/A 20 mm rotary cannon. Power input from the parent aircraft are 208 VAC, 400 Hz cycle, 3-phase, 10 amp, and 28 VDC, 3 amp. The electrical output of the control panel is 28 VDC for control voltage and 320 VDC for firing voltage.

The gun system itself comprises the GAU-4/A Gatling-type cannon, the linkless feed ammunition chutes which contain the ammunition canister, and the drive coupling between the gun and the ammunition drum, in the rear of the pod.

The GAU-4/A has an exceptionally high normal rate of fire of 6,000 rounds per min (6,600 maximum), a high muzzle velocity of 1,036 m/second and exceptional accuracy and reliability. Multi-barrel design increases heat dissipation and reduces barrel erosion. All six barrels are rigidly clamped together in a cluster and attached to the forward end of the breech rotor which rotates anti-clockwise, in the direction of firing, in a stationary housing. Barrel rotation and the operation of the action are driven by the gases generated by the ammunition. Four barrels have small ports drilled in them to allow propellant gas to pass into a piston and cam mechanism, within the barrel cluster, from whose action the barrel receives its rotary motion. The piston is mounted on a cam shaft, which only moves fore and aft. A cam follower mounted on one pair of barrels is forced round the cam path by the fore and aft movement of the piston. The breech bolts are mounted on trackways on the gun rotor and a cam path on the gun housing causes the breech bolts to travel backwards and forwards as the rotor revolves, providing the normal gun functions of feed, chamber, lock and fire, extraction and ejection. An electric governor holds the gun's firing rate at a constant 6,000 rounds per min. The gun can fire continuously until all ammunition is expended.

A 3-phase electric inertia starter provides initial barrel rotation. The gun is run-up by a flywheel behind the breech. The starter accelerates the weapon to an approximate rate of 3,750 rounds per min in about 0.2 sec, then disengages automatically. The gun gas pressure drives it up to 6,000. The time to maximum firing rate is 0.3 seconds, and the stopping time is 0.5.

Interchangeable barrel muzzle clamps provide different shot dispersion, the minimum giving an accuracy of 80 per cent of the rounds inside an 8 mil cone. Standard M50 electrically-primed 20 mm ammunition is used in a variety of types, including HE, incendiary, and AP with or without tracer.

Poor feed reliability and the problem of link disposal associated with belt feed at the Vulcan's high rates of fire led to the adoption of a linkless feed system, a conveyor belt in flexible chuting about 4.6 m long. The system provides positive control of ammunition throughout all storage and feed operations. The ammunition drum contains 1,234 rounds stored between radial partitions; 40–70 remain to keep the conveyor system full. A central rotor moves the rounds into the conveyor in a multi-stage operation. The drum feed system is driven by a shaft coupling to the gun, which develops about 40 hp, sufficient to operate feed system and gun rotation. Cartridge cases are ejected during firing, and once the firing button has been released, the gun is cleared automatically, ejecting a few live rounds, eliminating 'cook-off'.

The SUU-23/A is aimed using a gunsight or radar fire control system. It is tied into the radar for radar lock and ranging but can be operated with degraded radar. Specifications: Length 197 in (5.05 m); diameter 22 in (560 mm); weight 1,720 lb (785 kg) with 1,200 rounds, 1,045 lb (489 kg) empty; CG shift when ammunition is expended, 17 in forward. GAU-4: Weight 264.55 lb (120 kg); length 6 ft 1¾ in (1,875 mm); recoil travel, +6 mm; average recoil force 3,990 lb (1,810 kg); round weight 0.55 lb (0.25 kg); projectile weight 22 lb (0.1 kg).

The UK Phantoms required stronger stores racks than the US F-4s for three main reasons. First, UK Phantoms were required to carry heavier bombs than US F-4s, 1,000 lb against 500 lb. US F-4s have not carried the number or individual size or weight of bombs that UK Phantoms were required to carry. Better stores separation characteristics were also required. Secondly, RN Phantoms were required to land back on carriers with bombs up, because the RN could not afford to jettision bombs if unused – unlike USN F-4 operations where F-4s did not land back with bombs up, but jettisioned. Moreover, the RN's Phantoms were landing back with heavier individual bombs and a greater number. Thirdly, the UK Phantoms were required to carry the new generation of ground attack weapons, retarded tail system bombs and BL755, which required predictable release points. Originally, the UK Phantom's were equipped with Carrier Bomb Triple Ejector (CBTE) racks manufactured by MB Metals to a similar design as the US Triple Ejector Rack 9A (TER 9A), fitted to US F-4s; the CBTE had three, single-piston Ejector Release Units (ERU), the ML Aviation ERU No 121, similar to the US type. However, the UK CBTE had three 1,000 lb bomb capability. The main loads of the CBTE were three 1,000 lb HE Medium Capacity (HEMC) bombs or three 600 lb Cluster Bomb BL755 Mk 1 No 2, or three MATRA 155M 68 mm rocket launchers. The UK MoD specified the CBTE under ECP 9016, along with specialized stores as shown in the following table.

Store	Weight, lb	I.	2.	5.	8.	9.
Original Specification						
Mk 81 General Purpose Bomb	270	3	3	3	3	3
Mk 82 General Purpose Bomb	525	3	3	3	3	3
Mk 83 General Purpose Bomb	1,000	2	2	3	2	2
Mk 57 Special Bomb	500	–	–	1	–	–
AIM-9D Sidewinder IC	190	–	2	–	2	–
LAU-10/A Rocket Launcher	533	3	3	3	3	3
Lau-3/A Rocket Launcher (Aero 7A)	427/480	3	3	3	3	3
Aero 8A Practice Bomb	610	–	–	1	–	–
SUU-16/A M-61 20 mm cannon	1,702	1	–	1	–	1
Reconnaissance Pod	2,300	–	–	1	–	–
Wing Fuel Tank, 370 US Gal	234	1	–	–	–	1
Centreline Fuel Tank, 600 US Gal	235	–	–	1	–	–
Suspension Equipment						
Conventional Weapons Pylon	92	1	–	–	–	1
Wing Missile Pylon	150	–	1	–	1	–
Aero-27A Ejector Rack (Internal)	51	–	–	1	–	–
Weapons Adapter (Centreline)	55	–	–	1	–	–
Weapons Adapter (Inboard)	24	–	1	–	1	–
Weapons Adapter (Outboard)	24	1	–	–	–	1
LAU-7/A AIM-7 Launcher	87	–	2	–	2	–

Store	Weight, lb	I.	2.	5.	8.	9.
Engineering Change Proposal 9012 (MARTEL)						
AS37 MARTEL, Anti-Radiation	1,135	–	1	–	1	–
AJ.168 MARTEL, Television	1,167	–	1	–	1	–
Pylon	148	–	1	–	1	–
Launcher, AS.37/AJ.168	130/163	–	1	–	1	–
Equipment Pod	500	–	–	1	–	–
Equipment Pod Adapter Pylon	139	–	–	1	–	–
Bomb rack (Aero-27A)	51	–	–	1	–	–
Engineering Change Proposal 9016						
MC Mk 10 General Purpose Bomb	1,040	2	2	3	2	2
SNEB Rocket Launcher	394	–	3	3	3	–
Retarded Practice Bomb	29	4	4	4	4	4
Practice Bomb	26	4	4	4	4	4
8-inch Lepus Flare	176	2	2	2	2	2
UKMoD CBTE	95	1	1	1	1	1
Engineering Change Proposal 9021						
Wing Fuel/Strobe Light Tank	489	1	–	–	–	1

Station 3, 4, 5 and 6

Weapons

One AIM-7E-2 is positioned on each of stations 3, 4, 5 and 6, and a Strike Camera, weighing 50 lb, could be carried on station 4.

Chapter 6
Technical

The construction of the F-4K and M airframe was essentially similar to that of all other Phantoms. The airframe consists of seven major assemblies: forward, centre, and aft fuselage; wing centre section and port and starboard outer wing panels; and the stabilator. The sub-assemblies from which the major assemblies were constructed were designed to be as large as possible in order to minimize the weight penalties and load concentrations which result from the use of bolted joints. The sections were constructed independently and passed along the production line before being brought together in the final

assembly area. Each assembly operation was organised to minimize the time required at later stages, because the F-4 is very dense. There are 54,197 ft of electrical wiring, 8,856 wires and 400 wire bundles or assemblies (it was the first aircraft with braided, compact, wire bundles), 4,000 ft of tubing, and 643,000 rivets, bolts, nuts, washers, etc. Although the F-4's design preceeded the

The production block in which YF-4K1 was built (26) also included the first five production F-4Js, simplifying rejigging

The mainplane, centre fuselage and tail of YF-4K2 ready for splicing, showing the torque box, upper wing bulge for the larger wheels, and the emergency ram air turbine's compartment on the left of the fuselage

large-scale use of digital software, whose advantages for the aircraft designer lie principally in their light weight, compact, easily accessible modular construction, the F-4's equipment was arranged in a very logical, accessible and economical fashion. From the start of major assembly, it took eight months until delivery.

The F-4's wings have an average chord of 5.1 per cent, a sweep of 45°, and an incidence of 1 per cent. The NACA sections are 0006.4-64 (mod.), 0074-64 (mod.), and 0003-64 at the root, fold-line and tip respectively. The centre wing section is flat. The outer wing panels have extended chord – dogtooth – to correct a tendency to pitch-up in high 'g' manoeuvres, and 12° anhedral to correct lateral instability.

The wing centre section is the major airframe structural assembly. It forms a one-piece structure from wing fold to wing fold, spanning 27 ft 6.6 in. It is based upon a torque box, which carries the major loads and forms the structural backbone of the aircraft. The torque box assembly passes through the fuselage and is assembled in two halves joined at the centre-line. It extends between the forward and the main spars at 15 and 40 per cent chord respectively. The torque box is sealed to provide two integral fuel tanks, with a total capacity of 630 US gal.

Of 'C' section, the wing's foward and main spars were machined from forgings 14 ft long. The centre wing rear spars, the centre-line rib between the left and right halves of the torque box, the wing fold ribs and two strong intermediate ribs aft of the main spar in the area of the main undercarriage trunnions were also machined from forgings. The upper and lower torque box skins were machined from flat 2.5 in (6.35 cm) thick aluminium billets; in the machining process integral stiffening 'spars' almost parallel to the main spar, and integral lands for rib and spar attachments were produced. The skins were tapered in both directions from the maximum stress areas at the wing/fuselage intersection; after machining, they were pressed to aerofoil curvature.

The centre wing trailing edge assemblies are of one-piece honeycomb construction. The fixed inboard leading edge and the leading edge and trailing edge flaps, ailerons, outboard and inboard spoiler assemblies and spoiler actuator doors, and speed brakes are of conventional all-metal construction, although the aft 50 per cent of the ailerons and trailing edge flaps are of honeycomb construction.

The outer wing panels were constructed from roll-tapered sheets of between .1 and .3 in thick, employing chemical milling to form the lands for the sub-structure attachments. The trailing edges are single aluminium honeycomb structures aft of 70 per cent chord. The panels have a stressed skin. The leading edge flaps are of conventional aluminium structure.

The all-moving stabilator, or horizontal tail, was built as a single structural assembly. It is of all-metal, cantilever construction with stainless steel ribs and stringers with an Hastelloy/stainless steel leading edge and a stainless steel honeycomb trailing edge. The inner section, situated above the jet efflux and, therefore, subjected to high and variable temperatures, is skinned with titanium, whereas the outer sections are skinned with aluminium. The stabilator pivots at about 50 per cent chord and has an an anhedral of 23° 15'. The F-4K, like the aerodynamically similar F-4J, has fixed, inverted, leading edge slats; the M does not.

The forward fuselage section was constructed in left and right halves to allow most of the complex internal wiring and piping to be fitted before the halves were spliced together, thus minimizing the time required. The major structural components of each half were a keel web, upper and lower quarter panels, and forward engine air intake duct and duct lip, each of which was constructed separately. Alclad aluminium and machined extrusions formed the majority of the structures, but forgings were

BOTTOM
F-4K right hand forward nose assembly spliced on the jig, comprising the duct, and upper and lower quarter panels, each built separately. Note the fuselage equipment spade, unskinned laminar ramp, and retractable fuel probe housing

TOP LEFT
F-4M fin, at BAC, and template at left. Note the three fuselage attachment points, HF antenna coupler below front spar, HF shunt aerial, and leading-edge anti-collision light and stabilator feel pressure pick-up/static heater apertures, and the latter's tube

TOP RIGHT
An F-4M rear fuselage section, complete except for the fin tip, at BAC Strand Road, showing the extensive heat shielding and double-walled lower section, through which air is blown for cooling

RIGHT
With YF-4K1's right Spey installed, the first installation of the left Spey followed, the same day, 19 March 1966. The tail cone and arrestor gear were removed. Work continued on the remainder of the airframe

Spey Mk 202 afterburner

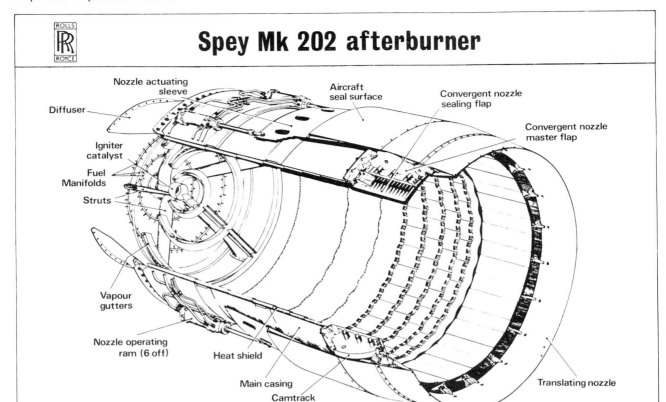

Nozzle actuating sleeve

Diffuser

Igniter catalyst

Fuel Manifolds

Struts

Vapour gutters

Nozzle operating ram (6 off)

Heat shield

Main casing

Camtrack

Aircraft seal surface

Convergent nozzle sealing flap

Convergent nozzle master flap

Translating nozzle

DTG

8519A

used in areas of load concentrations, including the nose undercarriage support fittings, the engine inlet ramp actuation system, support points and the inlet leading edge. The inlet ducts were designed with machined leading edges, closely-spaced ribs, and heavy inner and outer skins to ensure that they were smooth and did not flutter or distort.

The centre fuselage section, 22 ft 6 in long, was based upon seven main bulkhead frames, a keel assembly and two left and two right upper longerons, which together formed the centre fuselage structural assembly to which was added the left and right side panels.

The keel is of titanium and steel to withstand the high temperatures to which it is subjected and to give strength to bear the engine and torsion loads. Titanium was also used for the inner linings between the engine compartments, and between the engine compartments and fuel cell bays, the main engine mounting pickups, and critical frames and ribs. The lower section provides the tail hook trunnion pick-up point. Two left and two right main longerons extend from the first to the seventh frames.

Fuel cells Nos 2 to 6 are located in the compartments between the first to sixth frames, above the engine compartments. They have concave, curved floors and flat, unstressed alloy sheet upper panels. The fuel cell floors/engine

compartment linings incorporate titanium heat blankets and are of double wall construction through which air bled from the engine is blown and exhausted through louvres in the fuselage side to provide cooling for the cells. No 7 cell is located between the sixth and seventh frames. It has no floor, as fairing assemblies enclose the lower areas on either side of these two frames, which are positioned between the two jet nozzles and are therefore of titanium. The fuselage 'spine' is formed by the fuel cell doors.

Access doors stretch the full length of the engine bay, four smaller doors between the second and third frames on either side, and one large door between each of the third and fourth, and fourth and fifth frames, while a clam door behind the fifth frame is hinged horizontally mid-way up either side panel. The six main engine access doors comprise alloy skins and formers with titanium inner skins.

The aft fuselage section was built in two halves, upper and lower structural assemblies, spliced horizontally to facilitate assembly. Situated above the jet efflux, the aft fuselage section is in a critical heat area, with the lower part continuously exposed to very high temperatures. Therefore, the lower section has a skin of double wall construction with ram air cooling, blast fairings, and insulating blankets and an outer layer of ceramic-coated titanium shingles. To minimize buckling resulting from the large temperature changes in this area, the latter are installed with prominent mounting screws through over-size holes. The vertical fin assembly was permanently fixed to the aft fuselage section after the upper and lower assemblies had been joined. The stabilator was then installed, followed by the tail cone assembly, below and behind the stabilator, and housing the drag chute, and then the drag chute/tail cap. The rudder and the fin tip assemblies were then added.

The Spey

The Spey is a two-shaft turbofan with an engine inlet air mass flow of 92.53 kg/sec (204 lb/sec) and a by-pass ratio of .62:1 at take-off conditions. The by-pass ratio means that for every 1.62 kg mass of air which passes through the gas generator section only 1 kg is ducted through the engine and combusted, while 0.62 kg is ducted over the inner casings of the engine through the by-pass duct.

The cold, slow-moving by-pass air is mixed with the hot gas stream aft of the turbines, which produces an exhaust jet of relatively low velocity, and, consequently, high propulsive efficiency. Moreover, because the combusted gas stream also has much of its energy removed by the engine's turbines in the process of compressing both the by-pass and gas-generator air flows, the Spey is able to run at high temperatures without reducing its propulsive efficiency.

The by-pass principle has two important results for the Phantom. First, a significant proportion of the total airflow through the engine has not been through the combustion section. Therefore, there is a large amount of oxygen still available in the combined exhaust jet, and thus the temperature rise possible in a turbofan's reheat pipe is greater than that of a turbojet. Consequently, the thrust boost potential is greater. Secondly, there is a considerable supply of bleed air available to meet the Phantom's heavy BLC requirements, exceeding that available from turbojets.

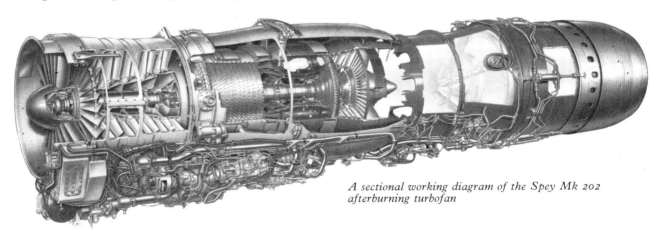

A sectional working diagram of the Spey Mk 202 afterburning turbofan

The right hand side of a Spey Mk 202

Compared to a turbojet, the turbofan cycle's high thermal and propulsive efficiencies results in significant improvements in the cruise specific fuel consumption (measured in pounds of fuel per hour per pound of thrust), and the addition of the reheat system provides a higher level of boost. All these benefits may be translated into terms of long aircraft range, large weapon load, excess energy and high rates of acceleration.

The Spey's compressor section is divided into two separate units mounted on concentric shafts and each powered by its own turbine. This two shaft concept enables a higher overall pressure ratio to be obtained in the compressors for the same, relatively few, stages of compression, because each compressor can operate at its optimum speed. Seventeen compression stages achieve an overall pressure ratio of 20:1.

The five-stage low pressure (LP) compressor is driven by a two-stage LP turbine. The drive shaft passes through the centre of the high pressure (HP) drive shaft and is supported by four bearings. The first and fifth stage compressor rotor blades have mid-span spacers, or 'clappers', for increased rigidity and tolerance of the pressure fluctuations associated with supersonic aircraft intakes and the operation of the reheat system.

The twelve-stage HP compressor is driven by a two-stage HP turbine through the HP shaft which is supported by three bearings. Clappers are fitted to the first stage rotor blades. Variable HP compressor inlet guide vanes are coupled with a handling bleed from the seventh stage to ensure satisfactory operation at 'off-design' speeds. A maximum of 20 per cent of the airflow through the HP system is available for aircraft services and BLC flap-blowing, bled either from the seventh or twelfth HP compressor stage. The turbine discs, HP nozzle guide vanes and the first stage HP turbine blades are all air-cooled.

Combustion takes place in ten inter-connected straight flow combustion liners which are housed in a tubo-annular casing. A duplex fuel spray nozzle, with main and primary flows, is located at the entry to each liner. Two igniter plugs light all ten burners.

The by-pass duct is an annular chamber which surrounds the engine from the delivery end of the LP compressor and ends in a fixed area, chuted mixer downstream of the turbines, where the by-pass and combusted gas flows are mixed.

The reheat boost of the Spey Mk 202 is fully variable from an initial boost of about 10 per cent to 65 per cent at sea level, static conditions. Modulation of reheat boost is provided by metering the flow of fuel. The afterburner jet pipe has an internal diameter of 940 mm and consists of a diffuser section, a burning section incorporating a heat shield, and a nozzle section.

The burner section consists of three concentric vapour vee-gutters mounted, downstream of four multi-bar fuel injection manifolds, on five radial struts. The self-contained catalytic igniter is located in the hub of the vapour gutters. Primary fuel is fed to the igniter and gutters, and the main fuel flow is distributed to the manifolds. The flame stabilises on the vapour gutters.

The nozzle section has a variable area primary nozzle and a fixed area, translating, secondary nozzle. The primary, convergent nozzle consists of alternate master and slave flaps, operated by the longitudinal movements of the secondary nozzle. A cam is attached to each master flap to provide a track for a roller mounted on the secondary ejector nozzle. When the secondary nozzle is moved forwards or rearwards, by six rams using engine oil as the hydraulic medium, the rollers move over the cam profiles and reduce or increase the area of the primary nozzle by opening or closing the flaps. When full reheat is selected, the secondary nozzle is in its rearmost position and the primary nozzle is therefore at its maximum. The afterburner sections are infinitely variable between fully closed and fully open, and are activated by movements of the pilot's throttles past the 100 per cent 'cold' power gate. Movement of the nozzle is a function of throttle position and exhaust gas temperature and is automatic.

The function of the engine fuel system is to provide the engine with fuel in a form suitable for combustion, and to control the flow for easy starting, acceleration, and stable running at all operating conditions and altitudes, without exceeding the maximum limitations of the engine.

The pilot's engine throttle lever controls the separate engine and reheat systems and opens and closes the HP shut-off cock. The fuel flow to the engine is controlled by varying the output of the HP fuel pump in response to signals from the fuel flow regulator which takes account of the selected rpm, indicated by the pilot's control lever. To ensure that maximum engine operating limits are not exceeded, and to maintain selected rpm, and, during rapid control lever movement, optimum fuel flow to the burners, the system is controlled by signals of gas turbine temperature, HP compressor delivery pressure and temperature, and LP and HP shaft rotational speeds.

The Spey standard (Mks 201 and 202) and fast (Mks 203 and 204) reheat control systems were developed by Dowty Fuel Systems Cheltenham, and comprise five separately mounted units. Following pilot control throttle movement, the system's controls and vapour core pump meter the fuel injected into the reheat burner system, and thus the gas stream, to ensure reliable ignition and efficient burning over a range of pilot-selected fuel flows. This is achieved by ensuring that fuel flow and nozzle area are matched. The pressure in the jet pipe is monitored by a ratio control unit in the pipe, so that the functioning of the engine compressor is unaffected by combustion in the reheat system. Ignition and cancellation, following throttle movement, are automatic. There is a small continuous circulation of fuel round the system's units for cooling when reheat is not in use.

Reheat is selected by moving the pilot's engine throttle lever into the reheat band. An isochronous valve within the throttle selection and shut-off unit prevents fuel entering the vapour core pump at less than 80 per cent of shaft speed. The flow is metered downstream of the pump. The throttle control varies the flow by positioning the total flow metering valve. The vapour gutter flow pressure drop regulator ensures that a fixed proportion of available fuel flow for all conditions of reheat is fed to the vapour gutter metering valves. This prevents either rich or weak extinction during rapid changes of reheat boost, while the reheat acceleration control (spill valve) prevents overfuelling during the early stages of slam reheat control. Following engine air signals, the engine ratio rams pneumatically position the vapour gutter metering valve, and therefore adjust the total flow metering valve to match the engine parameters for the prevailing conditions. Metered

fuel is delivered to the main and vapour gutter manifolds via a manifold distribution valve. Ignition is by catalyst supplied by main engine fuel pressure from a catalyst flow control.

The Spey is located in the Phantom through three mountings: a thrust trunnion and a side link attachment on the compressor intermediate casing, and a link attachment on the by-pass mixer flange. The thrust trunnion takes vertical, longitudinal and side loads. The side link attachment caters for vertical loads only. The side link and trunnions are interchangeable so that the trunnion is always mounted on the inboard side of the engine; thus the Spey can be installed on either side of the Phantom. The rear link attachment takes vertical and side loads, and is positioned so that the loads are transmitted tangentially to the engine casing. The aircraft linkage at the rear and side link attachments provide for engine expansion.

The Spey is a completely self-contained propulsion unit. The accessory units are mounted

A right hand view of a Spey, on an installation dolly, at St Louis. A Spey can be installed in either the right or left engine bay

on a gearbox attached to the underside of the intermediate compressor casing/by-pass duct. The gearbox is driven through bevel gearing and a radial shaft from the front of the HP compressor shaft. The aircraft accessories are mounted on an additional gearbox located under the front bearing housing, the drive for which is via a shaft from the main engine. Mounting all engine accessories in this cool environment is a basic part of the Spey's concept.

The Spey also possesses a basic self-sufficiency, requiring only electrical power for energising the gas turbine starter and igniter boxes, and fuel to initiate and maintain operations. Engine starting is via a small turbine which is spun up electrically from the aircraft's battery on the F-4M; however, like J79 Phantoms, the F-4K requires external assistance. The pilot's throttle lever initiates engine starting, modulates dry heat, initiates reheat lighting and modulates and cancels reheat. The oil system is completely self-contained.

There are four variants of the augmented Spey:

Mark 201 (RB.168-25R): the original unit, equipped with an air starter. These engines were converted to use a gas turbine starter with a resultant change in mark number, to Mark 202.

Mark 202 (RB.168-76R): equipped with a gas turbine starter.

Mark 203: equipped with a rapid reheat lighting system for service with the RN, enabling a substantial thrust increment to be obtained within 1.5 seconds from pilot selection, with maximum boost achievable within 3 seconds, up to an altitude of 5,000 ft, for use in carrier recovery overshoots. It was in service by May 1971.

Mark 204: equipped with a fast reheat lighting system for service with the RAF, enabling 30 per cent thrust boost to be achieved in 1.5 sec from selection, with maximum boost attainable within 3 seconds, up to maximum altitude of 45,000 ft, for use in air combat and interception. Development of this mark began in 1970.

The performance of the Phantom's Spey is consistent with AIA intake pressure recovery; no air or power off-takes; fuel calorific value of 10,370 kCal/kg; reheat jet pipe and ejector nozzle with no airflow to ejector nozzle; LP speed restoration at high aircraft speeds; and a minimum standard engine. The Spey Mk 202 dressed power unit weighs 4,060 lb (1,842 kg), including the engine, accessories, installation features and the afterburner with its associated fuel, control and operating system, but excluding the constant speed drive unit, alternator, gas turbine starter, hydraulic pumps and fuel flowmeter, which are not supplied by Rolls-Royce.

Flying Controls

The flying controls of the F-4K and M comprise the stabilator, rudder, ailerons, spoilers, airbrakes and leading and trailing edge flaps, and the boundary layer control (BLC) system.

The stabilator is mounted high to compensate for the tendency of the wing's upswept outer panels to create roll when the aircraft yaws, and to avoid the jet efflux. In order to minimize structural and weight problems associated with a high horizontal tail configuration, the stabilator has an anhedral of 23° 15'. The anhedral positions the outboard section to ensure good longitudinal stability through a wide range of angles of attack on the wing, and good directional stability throughout the useable Mach range. This total solution was reached as a result of extensive wind-tunnel testing and analysis on the XF4H-1. The F-4K's stabilator slats ensure adequate control effectiveness at the lower landing speeds of which it is capable. The stabilator pivots at about 55 per cent chord. Neutral is horizontal, negative is depressed and positive is raised. For landing, the stabilator is neutral, and is fully depressed on touch down to kill speed.

To operate the stabilator, pitch control demands from the pilot are fed via push-pull rods, cables and bellcranks to dual servo-valves which meter hydraulic fluid to the working section of a tandem, irreversible actuator. Independent hydraulic systems feed each of the actuator's two sections to ensure adequate control response if one fails. An hydraulic autopilot servo is mounted on the actuator and provides a parallel input into it. There is no manual reversion in the event of failure. A bob-weight is included in the control circuit to give the required stick force per 'g'.

Artificial feel is imparted by a ram-air pressure bellows acting through bellcranks on the stabilator trim actuator. (The ram-air intake is below the static-pitot on the fin.) A change in airspeed causes a corresponding change of ram pressure which causes the bellows springs to become imbalanced. The resulting force is transmitted to the control column and operation of the control column trim switch causes the trim actuator to balance the force between the bellows and spring assembly. Operation of the autopilot moves the control column.

Rudder pedal demands are transmitted via push-pull rods, cables and bellcranks to the servo-valve

of a power actuator which supplies hydraulic fluid to one side or the other of the unit, thus moving the rudder. In the event of hydraulic failure, manual reversion is possible; the movement available depends upon the air loads on the rudder. An hydraulic servo for yaw-damping and autopilot operation is incorporated in the servo-valve. Operation of the autopilot does not move the rudder pedals.

An hydraulic cylinder with pressure on both sides of a differential-area piston supplies artificial feel to the rudder pedals at the rate of about 4 lb per degree of rudder deflection below about 250 kts. Above this speed, a pressure switch in a pitot-static system cuts off hydraulic pressure to the low area side of the piston, producing a pedal force of 18 lb per degree of deflection. When the rudder has been moved to the desired position, an electric trim actuator, controlled by a console-mounted switch, trims out the forces. The rudder is

Taking-off from Rolls-Royce Hucknall, XT858's air spill outlets in the fuselage sides and belly are open for low speed flight, and the engine-fed BLC system is operating on the flaps

interconnected with the ailerons at low airspeed.

An aileron and spoiler system provides lateral control. The system is fully-powered by two independent hydraulic systems. The inset ailerons deflect 1° up and 30° down, and are mounted on the outer half of the inner wing panels, inboard of the flaps. The spoilers, normally flush with the wing upper surface are elevated through 45°. The ailerons and spoilers operate in conjunction, the ailerons limited to downwards movement, and the up function supplied by the spoilers. As the aileron on the ascending wing is depressed, the spoilers on the descending wing rise.

Lateral control demands are transmitted to the servo-valves of the aileron and spoiler hydraulic jacks via bellcranks and push-pull rods. Each aileron has dual-system irreversible jacks powered by both hydraulic systems. Each of the two spoiler sections on one wing is operated by a single system irreversible jack, energized by its own hydraulic supply so that only one section of spoilers on each wing moves in the event of one system failing.

A trim switch on the control column operates the lateral trim system which repositions the ailerons by means of a reversible motor and actuator system. The control column follows the trim movements. Artificial feel is supplied by double-action spring cartridges, which provide a force proportional to control column movement.

When flaps are selected, both ailerons depress 10 per cent to augment the lift at low speeds but continue to function differentially as ailerons, moving with respect to their new zero position. Below a certain airspeed, an aileron-rudder interconnection system (ARI) operates, causing a rudder displacement proportional to aileron displacement, and enabling co-ordinated turns to be made at low airspeeds.

An airbrake is located on the underside of each inboard wing panel aft of the wheel well. Hydraulically-operated and hinged at their forward edges, they move downwards and forwards upon selection, controlled by a three-position switch on the pilot's control grip. The switch positions are 'IN', 'OUT' and 'STOP', respectively for airbrakes retracted, fully extended, and stopped at an intermediate position in the travel.

The trailing-edge flaps are located inboard of the ailerons and the leading-edge flaps are located on the outboard half of each centre wing and on the outer wing panels. The inboard leading edge, providing the leading edge flaps on earlier models, is fixed on the F-4J, K and M. The flaps are blown. They are hydraulically-operated. Leading and trailing edge flaps are co-ordinated. A single lever, aerofoil-shaped for easy identification, in the pilot's wing flap control panel controls the flaps. The lever has three positions, 'UP', 'HALF' and 'DN' (down). In the 'UP' position all the flaps are

retracted. When retracted the leading edge flaps are locked by overcentre linkages and the trailing edge flaps by internal locks in the actuators. Selection of 'HALF' moves the leading-edge flaps to the full position, 60°, and the trailing edge flaps to 30° depression, and operates the leading edge but not trailing edge flap BLC. This position is used for take-off. Selecting down keeps the leading edge flaps at full with BLC and moves the trailing edge flaps to full, 60°, and operates the trailing edge BLC. This is used for landing.

The flight control systems designed and manufactured by the General Electric Corporation, USA, for the F-105 and F-4 implemented the control concept of mechanical primary plus stability augmentation (pseudo-fly-by-wire). An electro-magnetic autopilot, the F-4's system contains speed/height/Mach lock facilities, and is a three-axis stability augmentation mechanization with no gain change ie the ratio of power delivered by the pilot's force transducer to the load placed on the system is unity. It is non-redundant and operates with limited authority. The pilot relief modes are provided with parallel actuation by the same actuator as used for series actuation when only stability augmentation is engaged. In an emergency, the paddle switch, a lever shaped like a spoon in front of the control column and easily in reach, cuts out all autopilot control and transfers to pilot control.

The system's sensors consist of Type KR-7 rate gyros, as on F-105, with magnetic damping, and 3-phase motors with single-phase pick-off (a sensing device that responds to angular movement to effect a control response). Linear accelerometers, which are fluid damped, spring restrained and temperature compensated, are used for lateral control and 'g' cut-off normal acceleration limiting. A force transducer in the pitch (stabilator) channel gives a signal proportional to force for use in autopilot steering modes.

The system was one of the first extensive uses of transistors. The functions (adder, network, servo-amplifier, etc.) are packaged in individual modules with point to point wiring. The system has BITE to isolate Line Replaceable Units (LRU). Autopilot synchronizing is accomplished using electro-mechanical devices, as on F-105.

Fuel

The total internal tankage of the F-4M is 1,991 US gal of Avtur/50, which weighs a total of 13,240 lb (Avtur/50 weighs 6.65 lb per US gal). In common with other F-4 models, the F-4K and M have an integral wet cell of 315 US gal (1,192 lit) capacity in each half of the wing torque box. The F-4K and M have seven flexible fuel cells in bays in the upper fuselage, No 1 below the upper equipment bay in the forward fuselage assembly, and Nos 2 to 7 in the centre fuselage. The F-4J, K and M introduced the No 7 cell in the extreme rear of the centre section. It is of smaller capacity in the M because it was built with HF equipment in the same bay, unlike the K. Cells Nos 2 to 6 have fuel filler access caps above them. Each tank has an internal contents units, and transfer pumps are located in each, feeding into a fuel transfer line running between them.

Three external fuel tanks may be carried. The centreline (station 5) tank has a capacity of 600 US gal (2,271 lit) weighing 3,990 lb, and an empty weight of 235 lb. It is some 22 ft long. One wing fuel tank – Sergeant Fletcher – may be carried on each outboard wing pylon (stations 1 and 9). Each has a capacity of 370 US gal (1,400 lit) and an empty weight of 234 lb. The total weigh of their fuel is 4,921 lb. The total external fuel capacity is 1,340 US gal of Avtur/50, weighing 8,911 lb. The rail and equipment carriage weighs 277 lb. (For reconnaissance, a tank/strobe light was available, with fuel in the forward 80 per cent, and a light in the after section. It resembled the wing tank, and had an empty weight of 389 lb.) The external wing tank fuel vent system shut-off valves, low-level shut-off valves, and tank shut-off valves and tank pressure regulator are located above the rear of stations 1 and 9 outboard of the main landing gear bay, and between the internal wing tank and the rear spar. All external tanks may be jettisoned.

Each fuselage and wing tank has a low pressure cock, and feeds into a common pipe which is divided into two to supply one engine each. The fuel lines run above the fuselage tanks to an interconnector, which, with the nose down, gravity feeds fuel to a collector tank below cell No 2. The internal wing cells and the external tanks feed directly. Each external wing tank feeds into a pipe running through the internal wing tank, at the rear, to the main fuel system in the fuselage. Delivery to the engine is made via independent pipes to each engine; each pipe has a delivery boost pump. Each engine's delivery pipe enters the engine bays adjacent to the keel and curves around the front of the engine to connect with the engine fuel pump below the forward engine casing.

Fuelling and de-fuelling are carried out at a single point under the fuselage, at a rate of some 250 US gal per min. There is a single refuelling line running above the fuselage tanks. The F-4K and M have as standard a flight refuelling probe – although it has not been used in RAFG – which is located adjacent to the rear cockpit on the starboard. It extends forwards on an hydraulic support arm. All internal and external tanks can be refuelled in flight.

There are three fuel vents. The internal and centreline tanks are vented to atmosphere through a common pipe and manifold running above the fuselage tanks, which, passing through the rear fuselage, under the stabilator control jack and over the drag chute, terminates in a prominent pipe under the rudder. The external wing tanks are vented through pipes in the rear of the inner panels outermost ribs.

Systems

There are two air-conditioning systems, one for the cockpits and a cooling system for the electronic equipment. Both systems use air bled at high temperature and pressure from the engine HP compressor by blowers. The bleed air passes through piping in the lower forward fuselage to the equipment cooling units located below the front cockpit. The air conditioning ram-air intakes on either side of the nose supply air for the units' bleed air heat exchangers, located one behind each air intake, and for the nose-mounted AWG-11/-12 radar package's liquid-air heat exchangers above and behind the intakes.

The equipment cooling air is passed from the cooling units through ducts to the electronic equipment bays. The radar package in the nose is also cooled by air. The main duct extends below the cockpit floors, with a branch to the UHF and IFF below the rear cockpit, up to the AWG-11/-12 computer located at the top rear of the forward fuselage section, in the upper equipment bay. In the F-4M this bay also houses the lead computing amplifier.

The F-4M also differs from the F-4K in having HF communications. The HF communications RT and coupler control and antenna coupler are located behind fuel cell No 7 in the after fuselage section equipment bay. A cooling duct extension runs above the fuselage fuel cells to this bay.

Air conditioning for both cockpits is by a combined freon/temperature control system, drawing air from the electronic equipment air-conditioning system. The cockpit conditioning air is also used for windscreen demisting, blown from a duct under the panel at the front of the windscreen, and for rain removal, blown from an external duct in front of the windscreen, and for suit pressurisation, pressure suits being worn at all times. (For crew breathing purposes, a liquid oxygen converter of 10 lit capacity, whose lox container is located below the front seat with the evaporator behind it, supplies oxygen to the crews' oxygen masks via pressure regulators. The seats are equipped with personal oxygen supplies for use during ejection.)

The pneumatic system draws air from the engine bleed air supply via the electronic equipment cooling system. The air is compressed to about 3,000 psi by an hydraulic motor-driven air compressor. The pneumatic system provides high pressure air for canopy operation, nose wheel oleo strut extension, ram-air turbine extension and retraction, and the emergency operation of leading and trailing edge flaps and undercarriage emergency blowdown, and for wheel brakes, which are also served by hydraulic power.

Air for the leading and trailing edge BLC system is bled from the seventh and twelfth stages of the HP compressor of both engines. Air for the leading edge flap BLC is bled at about seven atmospheres from each engine through ducts exiting above the keel into a common duct. The leading edge flap duct is attached to the front of the wing torque box and runs inside the fixed inboard leading edge and leading edge flaps. The duct continues through an interconnection at the wing fold line to the outboard flaps. The air is released through BLC slots along the flap hinge line over the top surface of the wing. BLC air for the trailing edge plain flaps is fed through a duct running between the trailing edge flaps and the flap closure beam, and directed over the flaps.

There are three hydraulic systems, each operating with Skydrol 500 at a pressure of 300 lbs in^2 (210 kg/cm^2). Hydraulic power is supplied to the dual control aileron, spoiler and stabilator actuators by two pumps, one on each engine. Another pair of engine-driven pumps supplies a utility system for energising the leading and trailing edge flaps, the airbrakes, rudder, main and nosewheel retraction, mainwheel brakes, nosewheel extension and steering, wing folding mechanism, and the arrestor-hook. Each system has an associated hydraulic accumulator, one of which is located in the front of the port main undercarriage bay, along with an hydraulic reservoir. There is no emergency hydraulic power for the ram-air turbine.

The primary electrical source is the AC generator. Early F-4's had 20 kVA generators, but, to provide the greater electrical power required by more powerful systems, the F-4K and M are fitted with two engine-mounted 3-phase 200V generators of 30 kVA. They are driven through constant-speed drive units to ensure that the output frequency is a constant 400 c/s. In the event of one generator failing, each generator can independently supply the entire AC load, including the two fully-loaded transformer rectifier units (TRU), without load-shedding. The generators are controlled by switches on the generator control panel in the cockpit. A generator drive by the ram-air turbine can supply emergency power down to 130 kt IAS. Two 100 ampere TRUs, energised from the 200V AC supplies from the generators, supply power at 28VDC. Each unit is capable of supplying the DC bus system without load-shedding if one fails.

For engine starting on the F-4K a ground power unit, to energize the aircraft AC bus system once the electrically driven starter turbine has been energized by the TRUs, is coupled to an external power connection point under the fuselage. However, the F-4M has an internal 24V battery solely for engine starting, and requires no external power although it has the same external power connection for emergency or ground testing purposes. No other F-4 model, the F-4K included, has an internal battery. On the F-4M, it is extremely useful on deployments and for quick reaction alert (QRA).

Chapter 7
Trials and Tribulations

The money allocated to the F-4K/M programme covered the development and trials flying at McDonnell and elsewhere in the USA as well as in the UK by Hawker Siddeley, the sister design firm, and at the Aeroplane and Armament Experimental Establishment (A&AEE), Boscombe Down, Wiltshire and by others. Flight testing before full production was carried out by McDonnell Engineering and Experimental Test Pilots at St Louis, Edwards AFB, Naval Air Test Facility (NATF), Lakehurst, NJ, and Naval Air Test Centre (NATC), Patuxent River ('Pax'), Maryland. The F-4K and M passed through the St Louis production line in the same way as other F-4 models, and test flying consisted of normal post-production flights by production test pilots, except for those specific to the Spey and new equipment. The flying acceptance trials before the aircraft was accepted into UK service were conducted by A&AEE. The considerable effort expended to make the F-4K and M as problem free in operational service as the US F-4 models, which had had no groundings, was largely rewarded.

The Ministry of Technology had an office in St Louis throughout the F-4K/M programme, closing on 20 October 1970. It provided liaison and support during development, trials and production phases. UK manufacturers, as described earlier, also had teams in St Louis to provide support during these phases. After production test flying, F-4K and M aircraft were delivered to Ministry of Technology charge in St Louis, before being ferried to the UK by US crews to be taken on charge by the RAF or RN, or, if for trials in the UK, to remain on Ministry charge and allocation. (The Ministry has been superceded by MoD [Procurement Executive].) For instance, the fourteenth production F-4K, F-

4K14, MCAIR ship number 2602, serial XT868, first flew on 1 May 1968, and, following trials, was delivered to Ministry of Technology charge in St Louis on 8 August 1968. It arrived in the UK at Yeovilton on 27 August 1968 and was taken on Naval charge the following day. The Naval Air Service Unit (NASU), Yeovilton prepared it to issue standard. It was issued to No 767 Sqn on 9 January 1969.

The formers and jigs for the F-4K were completed in June 1965 and manufacture of major assemblies was well advanced by December 1965. The first Spey flight engine was delivered on schedule to St Louis in early February 1966, with the second, almost on time, soon after. There were a number of unexpected problems when they were bench tested at St Louis, not least with fuel leaks. These were subsequently understood and cured. A key reason appeared to have been the very low temperatures to which they had been exposed when they were airfreighted out from the UK.

On the afternoon of 19 March 1966, with 98 days to go to the scheduled date of the first F-4K flight, the first Spey was installed in the YF-4K1 (the first pre-production F-4K, XT595, MCAIR number 1449). A series of intensive ground tests was run on YF-4K1. A further problem arose with the installed Spey, and it took considerable careful analysis by the resident Rolls-Royce team to finally trace it to a very obscure electrical design feature. It was corrected in time to keep the schedule.

YF-4K1 first flew on 27 June 1966 (on schedule) and was publicly demonstrated next day. It was something of a hybrid. Although powered by two Spey Mk 201 engines, it had a high proportion of US equipment and components. As it was initially intended for engine trials only, there was no requirement that it contained British manufactured items or equipment. For calibration purposes, it was equipped with a long pitot-static probe in the radome tip and instruments in the nose. The YF-4K2, XT596, MCAIR number 1527, first flew on 30 August 1966.

As the first British Phantoms to fly, XT595 and XT596 were to undertake the engine development and performance programme. The first two production F-4Ks, XT597 and XT598, and the two YF-4Ms, XT852 and XT583, were for systems and weapons trials, and completed the batch of six development and trials aircraft. Other aircraft were also used for specific tasks. F-4K1, XT597, a fully instrumented trials aircraft, began the systems and weapons trials shortly after it flew on 1 November 1966. It was joined by the first YF-4M, XT852, after it flew on 17 February 1967, although it was not fully equipped, the major omission being the INAS. F-4K2, XT598, also an instrumented aircraft, flew on 21 March 1967 and joined the trials programme ahead of the second YF-4M, XT853.

A Phantom FG.1 under trials with A&AEE Boscombe Down is catapulted from HMS Eagle during the successful British carrier compatability trials in June 1969, in which three FG.1s were flown by A&AEE pilots

YF-4K2 XT596 seen on 31 August 1966. Bud Murray was MCAIR's F-4K project test pilot, while Joe Dobronski was MCAIR's chief test pilot. H Cliff Rogers was chief test pilot for Rolls-Royce

YF-4K1 XT595 on its first flight on 16 July 1966, with an instrumentation pitot probe. The profile illustrates the further aft positioned Spey burners, greater thrust angle and deeper belly compared to J79-powered F-4s

At first, the engine development and performance trials were promising, confirming only aspects of performance and those problems which had been anticipated. Tests showed that the estimated performance, base upon the specification for the minimum performance of the Spey Mk 201 engine, was conservative in cruise by about 2 per cent at sea level and 3 per cent at high altitude. It was confidently expected that the introduction of the Mk 202 would result in 2 to 3 per cent improvement in overall mission performance. The Spey turbofan's 30 per cent lower SFC over the J79 resulted in some 10 per cent increase in radius of action, and a 15 per cent greater ferry range, an important effect in view of the decreasing number of en route staging facilities the RAF and RN could use for ferry operations during the late 1960s and 1970s. The Spey also gave a better take-off and climb performance and more rapid low-level acceleration. The latter results from the fact that the Spey has greater power and thrust than the J79, but the weights of the J79 and Spey-powered Phantoms are not considerably different; thus, the power-to-weight ratio is loaded in favour of the UK Phantoms. Indeed, even in the early 1980s, few aircraft can accelerate more rapidly than the F-4K or M at low level. However, the UK Phantoms have a lower operational ceiling than the US F-4J and performance deteriorates more rapidly at altitude, but, in the European air combat theatre, this is not a serious failing. The main anticipated problem was that the greater overall fuselage width, increased depth below the jet efflux and destruction of the area-ruled

XT857, the third production F-4K, seen over St Louis on 7 December 1967. It has EROS collision avoidance equipment

XT852, proclaiming itself the first YF-4M, seen on 23 February 1967, carrying EROS pods. Externally the F-4K and M were identical, apart from the former's catapult spool and hold-back points, slotted stabilator and nose gear door approach lights

aerodynamics resulting from the Spey installation increased drag, off-setting some of the Spey's advantages.

It is to be expected that problems will be found in installing a new engine into an airframe, and a development programme is structured for the purpose of identifying, understanding and correcting problems. The civil Spey was a first generation turbofan, and the RB.168-25R was the first reheat application. The design of the afterburner and systems therefore ventured into new areas. Monitoring of engine temperatures and

pressures and co-ordination with afterburner fuel flow was particularly vital.

It is thus hardly surprising that reheat problems developed during the trials. The engine responded slowly to rapid throttle movements and the afterburner suffered what was officially described as 'combustion instability at altitude'.

The magnitude of the problem was not appreciated in the UK until Air Vice Marshal Derek Hogkinson, Assistant Chief of the Air Staff for Operational Requirements, and Air Commodore (later Air Vice Marshal) Colin Coulthard, Director of Operational Requirements (RAF) flew the aircraft at St Louis. Returning immediately to the UK, they informed Ronald Harker of Rolls-Royce that the Spey Phantom was non-operational until the engine and reheat handling had been considerably improved.

This was a serious situation for Rolls-Royce. David Huddie, the managing director, urgently organized for an early F-4K to be sent to Rolls-Royce's Hucknall, Derby test facilities for investigation rather than in the USA. Hucknall was a flight test airfield, with test facilities, an experimental manufacturing organization, and an engineering installation organization comprising design, stress, aerodynamics, fuel systems and noise specialists. The Spey problems were solved in the Mk 202. The clearance of the F-4K and M for service was delayed and considerable post-delivery modification was necessary to bring them up to standard, while early delivered aircraft were subject to some operational limitations. An upper speed limit of Mach 1.9 to keep within compressor outlet temperature tolerances remains the only restriction on the F-4K and M, but it is somewhat academic as the maximum speed is in that region.

On 11 July 1967 F-4K4 XT858 was delivered to the Ministry of Technology for Rolls-Royce's Spey investigations. The first F-4K in the UK, it was flown into Hucknall by Rolls-Royce test pilot Jimmy Jackson, who had flown on the engine development programme at Edwards AFB, with crew member Johnny Butcher. It was delivered to the Ministry for service acceptance in April 1968, and was one of the first three F-4Ks delivered to Yeovilton on 29 April 1968. Serving briefly with No 700P Sqn, it returned to the Ministry to continue Hucknall's Spey trials in 1968–70.

Rolls-Royce continued development of the Spey in the UK after Phantom service deliveries had begun in connection with the development of improved versions and fast reheat. The RN required a different mark, the 203, with a slightly different reheat control system to give a more rapid lightup after an overshoot during carrier recovery. The RAF also had a requirement for a quick reheat to improve acceleration and climb for future use in air combat.

As with the Spey-engined Buccaneer, the Phantom's original deployment in the low level strike/ground attack roles in RAF service placed an extremely heavy demand on engine life through the use of high power at low altitudes. Use was

XT858 outside Rolls-Royce's Hucknall test facility hangar. The code VL, in white, is Yeovilton's, and 724 is XT858's code from No 700P Sqn

LEFT
Phantom FG.1 XT858, on loan to the Ministry of Technology from the RN for Rolls-Royce's Spey continuation trials, seen in the engine test rig at Rolls-Royce's Hucknall test facility

intensive and by May 1971 the Marks 201, 202 and 203 had accumulated over 80,000 hours in RAF and RN service. Experience of reheat Speys during trials and in RAF and RN service, the first such use, resulted in a number of changes being introduced to improve cooling and reliability of turbine components. This was largely a result of a series of turbine blade failures between 1969–72 due to the engines, despite the modifications, being run at temperatures for which they were not designed. Reliability had been improved to a satisfactory level by mid-1972 and the changes allowed the life of the engine to be developed by 1978 to a point where Marks 202 and 203 had declared times between overhauls of 1,000 hours.

From the pilot's point of view, in overall terms, the Spey gave the F-4 a large increase in thrust, but it also increased the drag and altered the area-ruling. In consequence, the British aircrews did not end up with a better Phantom. Compared to the F-4J, it is less good at high altitude, but marginally better at low altitude, and has rather better fuel consumption and acceleration. On the F-4J, Mach 2.1 is the upper limit, compared to Mach 1.9 on the F-4K and M. The F-4J, K and M are very much the same in terms of handling. In combat, acceleration, specific excess energy, and the ability to unload gravity fast are the determinants: the F-4K and M have these in abundance. However, like all F-4s, the British Phantoms are 'not a fighter pilot's dream to fly in terms of the Hunter or Spitfire – much more of a rock of an aeroplane.'

The F-4K carrier suitability trials commenced with catapult launches from field facilities at NATF, the first taking place on 6 January 1968. The first F-4K launches witnessed by UK personnel, including a representative from the Royal Aircraft Establishment (RAE) Bedford and Rolls-Royce personnel, were carried out at NATF on 29 and 30 January 1968, when 28 launches were made. The same UK representatives watched the first arrested landings, which were contractor's demonstration trials, at NATC between 15 and 26 January 1968.

The first carrier suitability trials at sea with the F-4K were undertaken on USS *Coral Sea* (CVA-43) off the coast of California. The programme lasted between 15 and 22 July 1968. One British and two NATC pilots flew the trials, which were

The F-4K's initial carrier compatability trials were successfully conducted aboard USS Coral Sea *(CVA-43) by two trials F-4Ks, XT597 and XT857, flown by an NATC and two British pilots, in July 1967*

again observed by an RAE representative in connection with the development of new British catapult and arrestor gear, and by Rolls-Royce personnel. The aircraft used were F-4K1, XT597, a fully instrumented trials aircraft, and F-4K3, XT857, an instrumented back-up aircraft. Respectively, they made eighteen and four launches and arrested landings on 18 July 1968. Compared to the F-4B, the F-4K had a 10 mph reduction in approach speed as a result of the high lift devices, shared by the F-4J, but it was also lower than that of the F-4J partly as a result of the increased BLC bleed air from the Spey turbofan against that from the J79 turbojet. The F-4K's catapult performance was also better than that of the F-4J as a result of the large power advantage and the greater lift made available by the extra-extensible nose leg.

The systems and weapons trials in the USA were generally satisfactory, and the performance of the AWG-11/12 was a revelation. But, although it was a design development problem rather than a trials problem, delay in overcoming the F-4M's Ferranti INAS's incompatibility with the AN/AWG-12 MCS disrupted the trials programme. The INAS prototype and been scheduled for delivery in December 1966, in time to begin trials with the YF-4Ms. Following delivery of the first, incomplete system in August 1967, limited trials commenced, but full trials awaited a complete prototype. The first production INAS arrived at St Louis in October 1968, but the first service deliveries of F-4Ms without INAS had nevertheless gone ahead from July 1968. Early production aircraft were retrofitted with the INAS after it had been cleared for service. One

anticipated problem, unstable stores separation, began to manifest itself during trials in the USA, but was not rectified until after the aircraft was in service.

The Defence White Paper of 16 February 1967 anticipated that the first F-4K deliveries to the UK for the RN would be made during 1967, with the first operational RN unit commissioning at Yeovilton in March 1968, while the first RAF F-4M squadron would be formed in 1968–69. During a defence debate in the Commons on 27 November 1967, Healey attributed the delays in deliveries of the Phantom which had now been announced solely to difficulties in the development of the INAS and the Spey. However, he did not appear to be duly concerned that the target dates bought at the expense of the British aviation industry in 1965–66 would not be met. He said that the delays would assist in saving several million pounds on the 1968–69 defence budget!

The first three of the Royal Navy's Phantom FG.1s, XT858, XT859 and XT860, arrived at RNAS Yeovilton from the USA on 29 April 1968. Under the codename Project TRANSPLANT, the Phantoms, with three drop tanks, were flown from the USA by American civilian crews via the Azores route. The Phantoms were appropriately escorted the last leg of the flight by Sea Vixens of No 892 Sqn, RN, and the crews were met with a champagne welcome.

The following day, 30 April, No 700P Sqn was commissioned under Cdr A M G Pearson, RN at RNAS Yeovilton, as the RN's Phantom Intensive Flying Trials Units (IFTU). The squadron worked closely with data supplied by A&AEE, but was distinct from A&AEE's Naval Test Squadron,

'C' Sqn of A&AEE's Flying Division. No 700P's aircrews had converted to the Phantom in the USA, and the unit was to follow a six month trials and 'work-up' programme. It would then form the nucleus for the training squadron, No 767, and the operational squadron, No 892. It completed its task in early 1969.

Of the first three RN FG.1s, XT858 and XT860 were taken directly onto No. 700P's charge on 30 April 1968, and XT859 on 21 May 1968. Between 1 and 20 May 1968, XT858 undertook trials of the Jet Blast Deflectors (JBD) developed for *Ark Royal* at RAE Bedford, although still on No 700P charge. Returning to Yeovilton for two months, it was transferred to the Ministry of Technology for Spey trials on 26 July 1968. XT861 and XT862, delivered to the RN on 24 June 1968, were taken on No 700P charge on 11 and 3 July 1968 respectively, while XT864, delivered on 22 July 1968, was taken on No 700P's charge on 3 September 1968. However, No 700P did not have its full complement of seven aircraft until XT863, delivered on 2 August 1968, and XT869, taken on RN charge on 7 August 1968, were issued to No 700P on 3 and 30 October 1968 respectively.

The squadron also introduced the Phantom FG.1 to the British public when XT859/725 was the solo demonstrator at the 1968 Farnborough, creating impressive sonic bangs on the first public day. No 700P's FG.1s were resident for the display days courtesy of Rolls-Royce.

No 700P completed its task in early 1969. Three

XT862/722 of No 700P Sqn (IFTU): the unit carried no distinctive emblem, and its aircraft were coded in the 700 range, in white on the nose

of its aircraft, XT863, XT864, and XT869, were transferred to No 767 Sqn on 7 January 1969, and the remainder to No 892 Sqn on 31 March 1969, when these squadrons formed.

Before any new equipment can be accepted for British service, trials are conducted over a set period. A&AEE, Boscombe Down carries out the acceptance trials of all new military aircraft and associated equipment and weapons, and modifications to aircraft in service for the British services. The tasks are formulated by MoD (Procurement Executive), formerly by the Ministry of Technology, upon whose charge the trials aircraft are taken. The trials are planned, controlled and co-ordinated by the Performance Trials Management Division, and Groups in this and other Divisions carry out the work on the trial. The Flying Division administers, plans and analyses the actual trials, and its squadrons, dividing the work according to aircraft type, fly the trials of aircraft and equipment. 'A' Sqn flew the FGR.2 and 'C' Sqn the FG.1 trials.

The Naval Test Squadron, which received its first Phantom FG.1s in 1968, was an integral part of A&AEE. Formed on 1 June 1945 solely to test Naval aircraft, it was officially 'C' Sqn of Flying Division. Although its personnel were exclusively Naval, it was entirely under the direction of A&AEE and RAF discipline in exactly the same way as the other test squadrons.

XT597, the first F-4K and a fully instrumented aircraft used in the USA trials, went directly to A&AEE for trials in 1969 following delivery from the USA on Ministry of Technology charge in early August 1969. It was not taken on Naval charge. It undertook further trials at A&AEE in 1970, and later became the resident Phantom laboratory aircraft, operated by 'A' Sqn of Flying Division. XT865 and XT857, also instrumented aircraft, remained on Ministry charge following delivery to the UK in September and November 1968 respectively, and were used for trials by A&AEE from November 1968. They were taken on RN charge in October 1970. Their instruments were removed by NASU and they were modified to issue standard and subsequently issued to No 767 Sqn. XT872 was taken on Naval charge on 27 September 1968, but was used by A&AEE for trials between 22 and 27 November 1968, then going to RAE Bedford until 31 January 1969. Another FG.1, XV567, delivered in June 1968, was also used by A&AEE.

Groups within A&AEE are responsible for trials of specific areas. For instance, FGR.2 XV410 was used for radio trials in 1969–70 and FGR.2 XT898 for navigation trials in 1971–72 by the navigation and radio group which carries out trials of all radio and radar equipment for navigation and operational use. The performance group is responsible for assessing the handling and

performance of aircraft under trial and powerplant and control and handling systems. It works closely with manufacturers, monitoring their trials. The Engineering Division assesses aircraft systems and operates environmental rigs and installations. The photographic group carries out the trials of all photographic equipment and provides photographic support for the other Divisions. FGR.2 XV406 made the first flight with the EMI reconnaissance pod at HSA's test base, Holme-on-Spalding Moor, in 1969, and undertook the trials of the pod at A&AEE in 1970 and 1971. The pod was accepted for service in 1970. The Armament Division is responsible for the clearance trials on all aircraft armament, assessing carriage release and jettison of weapons and stores.

Store separation problems were experienced with the UK Phantom's original stores carriers, the MB Metals CBTE with single-piston ML Aviation ERU No 121s. These were similar to the US F-4's TER 9A, which were known to suffer problems. The problem was compounded by the requirement for the UK Phantoms to carry 1,000 lb bombs, against 500 lb on US F-4s, and new ground attack weapons which demanded predictable, stable release. Therefore, the UK MoD decided to regun the CBTE with the ML twin-piston ERU No 119 Mk1, which has a pitch control capability. This modification was carried out by MB Metals about 1970, and considerably improved bombing capability. It was also adopted on West German F-4s.

The twin-piston ERU, such as the ML ERU No 119, is the most successful solution to the problems of unstable stores release, ballistic dispersion, and unpredictable trajectory which were encountered, especially as speeds increased and stores become more sophisticated, with 'free-fall' (ie 1 g) and single ejector piston release. The two pistons' thrust can be varied to suit a store's characteristics, compensating for air disturbance around the aircraft and controlling pitch to give level, stable release. The two pistons eject the store rapidly from the area of disturbance. Ballistic performance of stores is consistent, bombing patterns are repeatable, and accuracy greater.

Since 1974, XT597 has been an A&AEE laboratory aircraft, under three headings. First, it is used as a 'pacer' with a special nose for a long pitot-static boom. Its airspeed and altitude recording system has been very closely calibrated and it is used to calibrate the systems of other aircraft. For example, it was used to establish the airspeed and altitude errors in the Concorde pitot-static system. Secondly, it is a high-speed test

No 700P Sqn Phantom FG.1 at Yeovilton. In the intakes are the total temperature transmitters (Rosemount SD model 102AR2U-UK) which provide accurate all-weather air temperature measurement to permit automatic engine control by the ADC

vehicle for navigation equipment, with another nose housing the equipment under test and instruments. Thirdly, it is a photographic trials vehicle for tests of new cameras and optical systems at high altitudes. Until 1983, when it appeared in MoD(PE) 'raspberry ripple' fleet colours, it remained in basically RN colours, with red wing tips and fin and 'A&AEE' in white on the spine aft of the cockpits.

Although RAE Bedford had no direct involvement with the development of the F-4K and M aircraft, its connection with the RN version was considerable because new catapult and arresting gear was being introduced. Proposals to replace Mark 13 arrestor gear with direct acting (DA) gear in carriers were made in 1963–64. Trials with DAX1 gear in an arrested landing deck (ALD) at Bedford airfield were undertaken between November 1965 and July 1967, including tests with Scimitars, Sea Vixens and Gannets in March 1966. In July and August 1968, trials of centre-span ropes on DAX2 gear were undertaken on ALD at Bedford.

The first F-4K delivery was scheduled for April 1967 but was delayed. In September 1967, therefore, a full-scale mock-up of the F-4K, nicknamed *Omega*, was 'offered-up' to a BXS4 steam catapult on the raised Catapult Assisted Launch Equipment installation (CALE) at Bedford airfield to check the compatibility of the holdback mechanism, shuttle spreader, etc. The mock-up was used for trials into 1970. RAE Bedford also undertook the development and trials of *Ark Royal*'s catapult JBD system.

Between 27 November 1968 and 30 January 1969, FG.1 XT872 was allocated to Bedford from No 700P Sqn, RN for catapulting and arresting trials. XT872 carried out sixteen catapult launches and 22 'taxi-in' arrests using Mark 13 arrestor gear installed on ALD. XT857, a fully instrumented F-4K, was also used for catapult trials in 1969. RAE Bedford later carried out further arrestor gear trials: FG.1s XT870 and XT865 were lent by the RN to MoD(PE) for trials between 1 and 21 October 1974 and 20 March and 12 April 1975 respectively.

Phantom FG.1 engaging an emergency barrier during RAE Bedford trials on 19 August 1970. The nylon net absorbed the Phantom's kinetic energy, greater than in previous RN aircraft because of higher weight and approach speed

This full-scale mock-up F-4K was used on the raised catapult installation (CALE: catapult assisted launch equipment) at Bedford airfield to check the compatability of the F-4K and the BXS4 steam catapult

LEFT
Phantom FG.1 XT858 on the CALE base at RAE Bedford on 31 December 1969 during trials of the jet blast deflectors for Ark Royal's catapult areas. It has no RN insignia or codes

XT857, a fully-instrumented trials F-4K on loan from the RN to the Ministry of Technology from November 1968 to October 1970, leaving RAE Bedford's raised catapult during trials on 31 December 1969

BELOW
Phantom FG.1 XT857 on the assisted landing deck (ALD) at RAE Bedford during trials of the new rotary hydraulic arrestor gear for Ark Royal on 10 December 1969. Note the kink in the wire

In April 1966, RAE Bedford's Naval Air Department had received confirmation that an emergency barrier was required for carrier Phantom operations. Further trials with a nylon net barrier were conducted with an FG.1 in August 1970. Composed of nylon to absorb kinetic energy, and stowed in pallets, it resembled the USN's system.

In June 1969, discussion took place with RAE Bedford on performance limits for airfield arrestor gear for the Phantom. Runway hydraulic arrestor gear (RHAG) became standard for Phantom airfields, to limit the landing run and minimize wear on brakes.

In March 1969, FG.1s carried out 121 'approach touch and goes' on HMS *Eagle*. These were followed by initial deck-landing and catapult trials aboard *Eagle* in June 1969, when three Phantom FG.1s from A&AEE, XT857, XT865,

Phantom FG.1 725 of No 700P Sqn flies low over HMS Hermes, *then a commando carrier. In 1964, consideration had been given to operating the Phantom from the* 'Hermes'-class carriers

A&AEE Phantom FG.1 HMS Eagle's *port catapult during trials flown by A&AEE pilots, carrying four 1,000 lb (454 kg) bombs on CBTEs, one of several configurations tested. A CBTE weighs 131 lb (59.4 kg) unladen*

Phantom FG.1 XV569/'013' of No 892 Sqn on Saratoga's *port catapult during the operational trials in October 1969. The double torque links of the 40-in extensible nose oleo, unique to the FG.1, are extended*

and XV567, flown by Boscombe Down pilots, carried out 61 arrested landings. RAE Bedford participated in both these trials. During *Eagle's* refit between September 1966 and April 1967, more powerful arrestor gear was fitted, and her deck was locally strengthened. Although these modifications were for the Phantom, she was not reconstructed for their operational use, only for detachments during trials and emergencies, because her deck would have required to have been strengthened, like *Ark Royal's*.

Operational trials of the RN Phantoms were undertaken in October 1968 on USS *Saratoga* (CV-60) which was suitable for operational trials of the FG.1 because she was of comparable size to *Ark Royal*, and also incorporated a fully-angled deck. The smaller *Coral Sea* (CVA-43), of the immediate postwar 'Midway' class, commissioned in 1947, had been suitable for the shorter compatibility trials in 1968. The trials aboard CV-60 were flown by members of No 892 Sqn because they were for aircrew operational qualification, but Roll-Royce engineering personnel were involved and A&AEE had a trials officer present.

During catapult launches from CV-60, it was found that the Spey's heat and thrust, greater than the J79's, and exacerbated by the downwards angle produced by the 40-in extensible nose gear, turned CV-60's deck plates viscous, causing severe buckling and even holing. This problem had been anticipated in the reconstruction of the *Ark Royal* whose catapult points had water-cooled deck panels and jet blast deflector screens installed.

The intensive flying trials to test *Ark Royal's* new catapults and arrestor gear began when the first aircraft embarked on 10 March 1970. The main Phantom trials took place during May 1970. Four Phantom FG.1s were borrowed from No 892 Sqn by A&AEE for the calibration trials and were flown by Boscombe Down pilots under the technical direction of A&AEE trials officers. The trials were observed by Rolls-Royce personnel. After the squadron's Operational Readiness Inspection (ORI) in April 1970, three No 892 Sqn crewed Phantoms joined the carrier trials. Many different levels of aircraft take-off weights were combined with different ship speeds. Some launches were made with reheat and others without, with various stores loads and combinations. A group of scientists and engineers from A&AEE and RAE Bedford recorded each launch to gather data from which to produce statistics and graphs to be used as a ready reckoner for all launch operations. All recoveries were recorded in a similar manner to establish the maximum permissible landing weights and compare them with the design limitations. After the trials were completed at the end of May 1970 the Royal Navy's Phantom FG.1 could be declared fully operational.

Chapter 8
Training

RAF Coningsby in Lincolnshire was selected as the main strike/ground attack and reconnaissance Phantom FGR.2 base in the UK. In February 1968, in accordance with the policy of centralizing support facilities, No 228 Operational Conversion Unit was formed there under Air Cmdr Derek Bryant in preparation for the Phantom's entry into service. The first OC Flying was Wg Cdr Howe. As it was designated as the RAF's Phantom FGR.2 conversion and refresher training unit for both aircrew and groundcrew, No 228 OCU was divided into three squadrons. The first squadron was responsible for flying conversion and air defence training, the second for strike/ground attack and reconnaissance training, and the third for groundcrew training. Its earliest task was to train its instructors and maintenance personnel on the Phantom FRG.2, although all of No 228 OCU's first instructors had completed F-4 instructors' courses in the USA.

The RAF's first FGR.2 (XT891) was delivered to No 23 MU, RAF Aldergrove, Northern Ireland on 20 July 1968. After acceptance trials, it was flown to No 228 OCU on 23 August 1968, followed the same day by others. By early 1969, there were over twenty FGR.2s at Coningsby, including XT891, XT893, XT899, XT901, XV395 and XV396. The first Phantoms at No 228 OCU were equipped with dual controls but could be converted to an operational configuration. Only a proportion of UK Phantoms are capable of dual control, and none are permanently dual-equipped because that would restrict the radar operator. A detachable control column can be plugged into the rear cockpit, and appropriate instruments can be fitted in some Phantoms if required. In fact, the view from the rear seat is poor, limiting the usefulness of dual control.

As the first Phantom FGR.2 unit to be established, No 228 OCU initially performed a 'trials flying' function. The Phantom's capabilities brought surprises. A few months after the Phantom's arrival at No 228 OCU, Wg Cdr Howe flew a typical Hi-Lo-Lo-Hi mission on a medium fuel load. Climbing hard from Coningsby, he flew high out over Anglesea and let down over the Irish Sea and returned over North Wales at low level for a 'reconnaissance' sortie, then cruised at altitude to Coningsby, from where he still had enough fuel for a 600-mile diversion!

The aircrews for the first course at No 228 OCU assembled in late 1968. The course began in January 1969 and was completed on 2 May 1969. The crews from the course provided the nucleus for No 6 Sqn which had formed at Coningsby on 16 January 1969, and became operational on 6 May 1969, taking over FGR.2s from No 228 OCU, such as XV466. The course was effectively No 6 Sqn's work-up. The crews from the No 2 Course became the nucleus of the RAF's second FGR.2 unit, No 54 Sqn, which began forming at Coningsby on 1 September 1969. Initially, the majority of aircrews for No 228 OCU were selected from officers who had completed flying tours on fighter/ground attack or reconnaissance squadrons. This meant that more training time could be devoted to familiarising aircrews with the new aircraft itself, and that they could become operational rapidly.

The support and administration problems created by the Spey's inadequate turbine blades and the shortage of replacement engines, restricted No 228 OCU's schedules. Training was suspended for a while following the No 9 Course, although the requirement for aircrew had slackened by then. Priority in the supply of engines was given to operational squadrons. Although the problem was never serious enough to affect front-line strength

RN technicians work on RAF Phantom FGR.2s XT898
and XT891, 'zapped' with 'Fly Navy' at Yeovilton. RAF
Phantoms were delivered in standard RAF tactical Dark
Green, Dark Sea Grey and Light Aircraft Grey
camouflage

XT891, the first Phantom FGR.2 delivered to the RAF,
during post-production flight trials at St Louis. Between
first flight and Ministry of Technology acceptance there
was a period of between one and three months

appreciably and had largely been resolved by mid-1972, it did retard the Phantom re-equipment programme, particularly the supply of aircrews. No 228 OCU staff instructors made temporarily redundant after the No 9 Course were posted to squadrons to make up some of the deficit.

In July 1970, as the number of Phantoms at Coningsby increased, the OCU was allocated the 'shadow' designation of No 64 Sqn, and its aircraft then bore No 64 Sqn's markings on the fin. In an emergency, No 64 Sqn could be called upon as a second-line operational squadron, and has participated in exercises on this basis, with the aircraft flown by OCU staff instructors. In September 1972, No 45 Sqn reformed at RAF Wittering on Hunter FGA.9s, tasked with maintaining a reserve of pilots at operational pitch for Phantom FBSA squadrons, in case of war.

Until 1974–75, the emphasis at No 228 OCU was upon strike/ground attack and reconnaissance, the roles in which the FGR.2 was initially deployed. Aircrews for No 892 Sqn, RN and No 43 Sqn, RAF were trained in the air defence role on Phantom FG.1s by No 767 Sqn until 1972, then by the Phantom Training Flight until 1968. However, from 1974, when the Phantom FGR.2 was re-assigned to the air defence role in the UK and Germany, No 228 OCU's training programme changed its emphasis to air defence. No 228 OCU then came under No 11 Group Strike Command rather than Support Command.

The majority of Phantom FGR.2 aircrews have come directly from Flying Training Schools. From commencing *ab initio* training, it takes three years

Phantom FGR.2 XV429 of No 228 OCU at Coningsby, 18 September 1969. It was transferred to No 54 Sqn when it formed from the OCU's No 2 Course. Initially, all FGR.2s passed to the OCU, as the only FGR.2 operator

TOP RIGHT
Phantom FGR.2 XT909 of No 228 OCU. This aircraft later went to RAFG. The OCU's aircraft carry no unit insignia. Serials were carried on the fin, initially in white then black, but were later removed

OPPOSITE
Phantom FGR.2 XV409 of No 228 OCU takes-off in 1982. An ex-No 111 Sqn machine, it wears the air superiority grey scheme, and small muted 'pink and lilac' roundels

to train a Phantom pilot to operational readiness. Following the Officer Training Unit, he begins with the flying training course on the Jet Provost. Selected for fast jets, he proceeds to Valley to fly the more demanding Hawk, formerly the Gnat, followed by the Brawdy tactical weapons course, where he will first fire weapons. Creamed off to fly Phantoms – Phantom pilots must be the best pilots – he will then go to No 228 OCU, where he meets 'his' navigator. The navigator, after passing from OTU to the Navigation School at RAF Finningley for theoretical training, will gain air experience on Bulldogs, then move to Dominie navigation trainers and Jet Provosts for low-level nevigation. If his accuracy and timing are of the high standards required of a fast jet navigator, he will pass on to Brawdy to learn the skills and procedures necessary for high speed and tactical flying, and air combat. Selected for Phantoms, he is then posted to No 228 OCU.

However, before going to No 228 OCU the trainee Phantom aircrews will go through the Aero Medical Centre, RAF North Luffenham. There they are taught the aircrew survival features and procedures specific to the Phantom, and are introduced to aviation medicine theory. They undergo fitting out in flying clothing, harness fitting in a mock-up Phantom cockpit, ejection seat adjustments, parachute harness tests, pressure chamber and physiological monitoring tests in full flying kit, and a cold weather survival course. During training, the aircrews will have undergone dinghy drill, and at any point may be whisked off on an 'impromptu' survival exercise in the wilds at any time of year, but such exercises are routine. From North Luffenham, aircrews pass to Mountbatten for specific survival training which includes being trailed behind a Land Rover and a power boat in full kit by the parachute harness to simulate a landing! Survival training is a specific aspect of flight safety, and is continued on operational squadrons, aircrew having to do two wet dinghy drills, one at sea, per year.

The navigators' course at No 228 OCU begins with a six-week period covering theoretical and practical training in the missile control system procedures and the theory of the inertial navigation system. The pilots then join the navigators, forming aircrews, and attend a further two weeks ground school to learn the aircraft systems and operating methods.

The pilot flies five or six dual-control sorties with a staff pilot instructor before going solo with an OCU staff navigator for two sorties, while the navigator will do two or three sorties with an OCU staff pilot. Then, comparatively early in the course, they begin to fly together as a crew. The course normally tries to keep a navigator and a pilot together throughout, as on a squadron, although on a squadron other factors such as leave will prevent this from time to time. However, during the course there is a need for further dual instruction for both the navigator and the pilot. During the flying training course, the aircrews fly some 100 hours before becoming operational. The course covers conversion to the Phantom FGR.2 – some of which is flown in dual control aircraft with staff instructors – followed by training in air defence and, formerly, reconnaissance and strike/ground attack, with weapon practice sorties on the ranges. After posting to a squadron, new Phantom crews undergo further training before being declared fully operational.

A Phantom first conversion course lasts six months, and a refresher course three. Today, aircrews on ground tours do no flying, and so must do a short refresher course of a few hours on Jet Provosts or Hawks before going to No 228 OCU for a first conversion or refresher course on Phantoms. Aircrews on ground tours are not

qualified on type because it is not 'cost-effective' in terms of the support required, rather than the fuel expended, to keep them flying. They would normally return to their last squadron for refresher or qualification flying, but squadrons have little flying time to spare, and any extra strain on them must be carefully monitored to give their crews maximum flying time, which is dependent upon available engineering and administrative support. Currently, the RAF is running a small scale trial of two-week refresher course for aircrews on ground tours, who return to their last squadron as normal practice. The RAF is almost unique among air forces in not having staff on ground tours flying in a 'dual' capacity.

Training on the FG.1 in the air defence and maritime roles was conducted concurrently with No 228 OCU's operations by specialized units. By an order dated 12 December 1968, the Flag Officer Naval Flying Training, Rear-Admiral C K Roberts DSO, commissioned the RN's Air Warfare Fighter Training (Phantom) Unit, No 767 Sqn, at RNAS Yeovilton on 14 January 1969. Commanded by Lt Cdr Peter C Marshall, RN, it was responsible for the conversion training of pilots and observers for the Phantom FG.1 for both No 892 Sqn, RN, and No 43 Sqn, RAF. The former was the RN's only operational Phantom unit, and the latter had formed instead of the second RN unit, operating in the maritime air defence and tactical air support roles. To assist in its task, the RAF lent No 767 Sqn some of its first FG.1s. They retained their RAF camouflage but had RN markings, and were operated alongside No 767 Sqn's FG.1s which were in Naval camouflage. No 767 Sqn had an initial official

Phantom FG.1 leaving St Louis for the 4,900-mile delivery flight to Yeovilton. Flight refuelling was required. Full external and internal tanks give 2,085 nm unrefuelled ferry range, or 2,305 by dropping the tanks

BELOW
No 767 Sqn's nine Phantom FG.1s, including those on loan from the RAF, at Yeovilton. This unit trained all British FG.1 crews for No 43 Sqn RAF and No 892 Sqn RN until July 1972

establishment of nine aircraft, but this became eight from 22 September 1970.

A number of the Phantom FG.1s delivered directly from St Louis to No 23 MU at RAF Aldergrove for RAF custody were allotted from the MU on loan to RNAS Yeovilton for attachment to No 767 Sqn. The RN collected the aircraft from No 23 MU. The period of the loan could be modified. Forming part of the original strength of No 767 Sqn, the RAF lent XT873, XT875 and XT876 on 10, 27 and 17 January 1969 respectively. XT873 and XT875 were flown to No 23 MU for return to RAF charge on 17 March and 30 July 1969 respectively. XT876 was retained longer, but crashed into the sea on 10 January 1972. The RAF also lent XV572 on 6 May 1969, which was returned on 24 March 1970, and lent XV579 on 19 June 1969. XV579 was returned to RAF charge on 31 July 1972, at the same time as the FG.1s on Naval charge serving with No 767 Sqn were transferred to RAF charge before the unit disbanded the next day.

No 767 Sqn's instructor staff totalled only ten aviators, small in comparison with most training units, but they were highly experienced. The first instructors had been trained in the USA. Each

Phantom FG.1 XT158 of No 767 Sqn during deck landing practice (DLP) at Yeovilton. The squadron's FG.1s bore Yeovilton's code, VL, and a three-figure digit in the 150 range from Yeovilton's batch, both white

TOP
One of the FG.1s the RAF lent the RN solely for training purposes with No 767 Sqn. They retained RAF tactical camouflage. No 767 Sqn's insignia was a yellow diving gull with black legs and outline

course lasted approximately four months and consisted of 70 hour's flying, 25 hours in the simulator, 25 hours air intercept training and a sustained instructional programme. Training included deck landing practice at Yeovilton, 'touch and goes' on *Ark Royal*, and simulated and live catapult launches.

The course began with two weeks ground school, where the aircrew were taught the complexities of the aircraft systems, and the alien US terminology, such as landing gear, stabilator, and horizontal situation indicator (compass), but they soon became bilingual! The training syllabus was designed to systematically develop the skills required to operate the Phantom FG.1 to its limits, to do which the aircrews had to learn in detail the capabilities of the FG.1 and its weapon

Phantom FG.1 XT867 at Yeovilton, 7 July 1967. When No 767 Sqn disbanded on 1 August 1972, its FG.1s passed to the RAF, PTF and No 892 Sqn. XT867 went to No 23 MU for a modification programme, before going to No 892 Sqn

system. They learnt the contrasting skills required for intercepting Mach 1 plus bombers at 50,000 ft, seeking out an intruder flying fast at ground level, attacking ground and amphibious targets, managing maritime combat air patrols, and surviving air and ground or ship-based defences.

From more or less 'text book' interceptions, the course progressed to air combat manouevring (ACM) to master the fine skills required for the 'sport of kings' – fighter against fighter combat. The basic principles of air combat may not have changed since Oswald Boelcke enshrined them in his *Dicta Boelcke* in 1915, but the Phantom's acceleration and rate of climb and the resultant closing speeds of combat and the fleetingness of openings for attack have meant that decisions must be instantaneous and correct. Moreover, the Phantom's advanced radar and weapons system intensified the complexity of skills and procedures required to manage interceptions and combats, and to fully exploit the considerable increase in capability and potency over previous fighters with which the system endowed the Phantom.

The final phase of the No 767 Sqn course was an intensive period of air-to-ground weaponry practice, for No 892 Sqn's secondary role was attack and army ground support. Crews had to be able to deliver their weapons accurately in all weather conditions by day or night. The course culminated in a strike mission which was planned, briefed and executed by the officers on the course, while the squadron staff took the role of an enemy air force. No 767 Sqn also provided Phantom experience for maintenance crews after Short Aircraft Maintenance Courses on the Phantom at Yeovilton's Technical Training Department. The trainee controllers at Yeovilton's Aircraft Direction School's facilities also honed their skills controlling the squadron's Phantoms.

On 3 December 1969, flying FG.1 XT868, No 767 Sqn's CO, Lt Cdr Marshall was engaged in air interception exercises off Lands End when a 'heavy blow' struck the aircraft, followed by severe vibration. Hydraulic fluid coated the windscreen, obscuring vision. Both engines flamed out. Thinking he had collided, Marshall prepared to eject, but his experience – he was 39 – bade him stay. XT868 was still controllable, despite severe buffeting. Another FG.1 formated on him and reported that XT868's radome and scanner assembly had ripped off, and the starboard engine, intake, wing leading edge and fuselage were badly damaged. In spite of these problems, Marshall decided to fly the 130 miles to Yeovilton. With virtually no forward vision, pronounced yaw and continued severe buffeting threatening to wrest control from him, the final approach to Yeovilton was extremely hazardous, but his skill enabled him to land. On 17 February 1970, the award of the Air Force Cross to Marshall was gazetted, the first time it had been awarded to a Naval officer for gallantry. He was commended for 'cool thinking and personal courage' and placing his life at risk 'in the full realization of the great value to be gained from bringing the aircraft back for technical investigation.' On 29 May 1970, he was also awarded the Boyd Trophy for 1969.

During its commission, No 767 Sqn converted over 100 aircrew, including most of the RAF officers of No 43 Sqn, and all RN, RAF and exchange officers who flew with No 892 Sqn. The last course, seven aircrew, finished training shortly before No 767 Sqn disbanded on 1 August 1972.

The Post Operational Conversion Unit Phantom Training Flight, later shortened to Phantom Training Flight (PTF), formed at RAF Leuchars on 1 September 1972. Superceding No 767 Sqn, the PTF was tasked with converting aircrews for the RN until the requirement ceased. No 767 Sqn had disbanded as a result of the MoD decision that the RAF would be responsible for all RN fixed-wing support and training from 1972. Consequently, the PTF was an RAF unit, under RAF control and discipline, and was jointly used by the RN and RAF as a refresher and conversion flying unit for the FG.1.

All the PTF's instructors were Naval aviators, except the squadron commander, a former Naval officer who transferred to the RAF. By 1974, there were only seventeen RN Phantom qualified pilots, many on their third operational Phantom tour. The deficit was made up from RAF officers. The PTF conducted RN pilot and observer refresher and RAF conversion training on the FG.1, providing replacement pilots for *Ark Royal*. The training was highly flexible and, because of the small numbers of aircrew involved, each officer received a personal programme depending upon his background and experience. RAF conversion aircrews normally had Phantom experience, initially ground attack, and most of the RN refresher aircrews had *Ark Royal* experience. The course included ACM, interception, low-level navigation, ground attack, bombing and interdiction, and deck landing practice on *Ark Royal* when she was in Home waters.

The PTF's aircraft included those transferred to RAF charge from No 767 Sqn. They retained the RN finish of gloss Dark Sea Grey and White with roundels in six positions and no fin flash. However, they lost the 'ROYAL NAVY' fuselage markings, but did carry a badge on the fin based on No 892 Sqn's, an *Omega* with a dagger vertically through it. Of No 767 Sqn's FG.1s, XT857, XT861, XT866 and XV569 were among those allotted to RAF charge on 1 August 1972, the date the unit disbanded. They were formally transferred to RAF charge by Form 179 and struck off RN records on 10 August 1972. They were dual control aircraft. All served with the PTF at Leuchars until 1978 They were coded 'U', 'V', 'W' and 'X' of the

Dual-control PTF FG.1 XV569 at Leuchars, with Leuchar's RN code 'LU' in white. Later, coded 'X', its rudder carried the PTF's black Omega *and silver, black and yellow dagger on a black-edged diamond*

PTF respectively. Following the PTF's disbandment on 31 May 1978, its aircraft were repainted in standard RAF camouflage and issued to the front-line RAF squadrons at Leuchars, or stored. The PTF's aircraft were unique among RAF F-4s in being carrier operable.

Lt Michael S Seider, a US Navy exchange pilot with No 892 Sqn, RN in 1974, recorded his impressions of conversion to the RN's Phantom FG.1 from the F-4J:

My actual training began at Royal Air Force Station North Luffenham in Northamptonshire at the RAF Aero Medical Centre. I received my flight clothing and survival equipment which was fitted by RAF flight surgeons. A very comprehensive fitting procedure followed, including the testing and refitting in cockpit mockups. I received the F-4 high-altitude course which included a 60,000-ft-pressure-breathing, low-pressure chamber ascent, all in my new kit. I was given all the aviation medicine lectures and a cold weather survival course was included.

The flying equipment has some very good items that the US Navy might look into. The dry immersion suit could be an improvement over some of our wet suit designs. It is a double layer of fabric that becomes waterproof after it has been soaked. The cloth breathes while it is dry, making long hours in it bearable if not exactly comfortable. Rubber seals at the feet, neck and hands give good protection once you're in the life raft. For all sceptics, as I was myself before my April dunking in the cold North Sea, it really works as advertised.

After departing North Luffenham, British Rail deposits you at HMS *Vernon*, a naval installation in Portsmouth where the thrill of the dunker awaits you. Very similar to Dilbert, the Royal Navy version is less terrifying because it doesn't roll over; it just submerges. Orientation in a British helicopter version is also required because helicopters are used for COD and even fixed-wing aviators can expect to be flown around in one. You receive four rides in this machine, one at each sitting position. The cockpit enters the water and rotates 180° in either direction. For a fixed-wing aviator who has done a loop, it is not very disorientating and the escapes are actually fun, assuming you know how to swim.

After Portsmouth it's off to Scotland for ground school and assorted survival drills. Ground school lasted two days and a third was used for wet-dinghy and wet-winching drills in the North Sea with the SAR squadron.

Having completed all the preparations for flight, one last item remained, a test of my knowledge in the British version of the 2F-88 or Phantom flight simulator. The biggest advantage of this trainer is its visual display. Various airfields can be projected and it has a plate for *Ark Royal* as well. Night landings on the simulated *Ark* are quite realistic. After this phase I was certified competent to fly in the Fleet Air Arm.

Before reaching *Ark Royal* and 892 NAS, I was sent to the PTF in Scotland for my conversion training in the Rolls-Royce Spey-powered Phantom. I managed to complete the conversion course in about five weeks and even found time for some golf at St Andrews. As I was

the only student for a portion of the time, I normally flew twice a day and, on one occasion, three times.

Normally, the first sortie is established as a performance demonstration. I was given a one-on-one air combat maneuvring flight instead. That happened to be the program of the week when I started flying. Having been a RAG instructor, it was falsely assumed I knew everything I needed to know and I was launched right into the ACM phase.

Most of the RAF aviators going through the PTF are Strike Command experienced, so air-to-air training is emphasized. The course does include low-level navigation exercises throughout the numerous lochs and valleys of the Scottish Highlands.

I had radar flights and also flew bomber profiles, normally against ECM Canberras. The Phantom can simulate the other two threats nicely, and typical evasion includes high-G maneuvers to break pulse-Doppler locks. Loops and drastic altitude changes are also favorite tricks. These realistic evasion techniques make for exceptionally well trained air defense crews.

The normal brief for air intercept flights also includes a countering turn into the fighter upon visual sighting by the bogey. The AWG-11 radar with the 1971-update modifications is exceptionally reliable. The squadron does not fly an airplane with unserviceable radar. Availability on board 'Ark' is not seriously reduced by this policy.

Air-to-air tactics are very similar to US Navy-developed techniques. The same tactical manuals and publications that we use are employed by the Fleet Air Arm. Tactics are practised on every sortie in Scotland.

With minimal air space restrictions, a section of aircraft launched as a pair and, at the field boundary, split into battle (loose deuce) formation. Even on air intercept sorties, transit to and from the operating area is in battle formation with turns, attacks and counters being practised. This amounts to approximately 20 minutes of fundamental ACM practice per sortie.

Redifon produced five Phantom digital flight simulators, four for the RAF and one for the RN. They were the most sophisticated training simulators built until then. Their main advantage lies in their display systems. The first FGR.2 simulator entered RAF service at Coningsby in mid-April 1970, and one course began simulator training shortly afterwards. About the same time, the RN's FG.1 simulator was installed at RNAS Yeovilton, and an FGR.2 simulator at Bruggen.

The system has five components; the fuselage unit on a three-axis motion system; the Visual Flight Attachment (VFA); the Land Mass Attachmen (LMA) for radar use; the Pilot and Navigator Instructors' operating consoles; and the Redifon R.2000 digital computer. The VFA and LMA have separate camera systems. The main innovation was that the VFA and MFA produce a radar picture of the area over which the simulator is flying, and this is used in conjunction with its radar set. In visual and radar or visual/radar modes, the three-facet VFA model mechanism and separately coupled LMA system permits quick and automatic changes of external scene.

For training in the bombing role with either conventional or special practice weapons, such as the 4 lbs retarded or 28 lbs ballistic bomb, UK Phantoms can be equipped with the ML Aviation Carrier Bomb Light Stores (CBLS) No 100 Mk 1. A light, aerodynamically faired carrier, the CBLS has four ML Aviation ejector rack units for stores up to 103 mm diameter and 750 mm length, and weights up to 35 kg. The No 200 superceded the No 100 in production.

A BL755 practice cluster bomb was developed which is completely representative of the live weapon, including bomblet release and dispersion, except that the bomblets are inert. For air-to-ground rocketry practice, the Type 250 smoke and Type 252 inert SNEB 168 mm rocket rounds, carried in the MATRA RL F2 training or 155M standard launcher, realistically simulate live firing. Both the BL755 and SNEB practice weapons are carried and fired in the same manner as the live rounds.

For live air-to-air missile training, the Jindivik drone target can be used, but in simulated interceptions against other aircraft, AIM-9 airframes, minus wings and warhead but retaining a live seeker for lock-on, are fitted with datalink

Simulator airfield model (4 × 14 nm), above. Carrier and ground attack models were also used. The models are mounted on a three-facet mechanism, below. A separate 24,000:1 (33 × 120 nm) land mass model and camera system caters for high visual/radar flight/navigation

equipment to relay the Phantom's position, attitude and status during all phases of the attack and 'firing' to ground-based computers. The computer data permits post-flight analysis of every aspect of the attack to a greater degree than with a live firing. Drill and inert AAM rounds are painted blue, in contrast to the white of live

The simulator permits simultaneous or separate pilot and navigator training in ground attack, air-to-air combat, and routine or emergency procedures. Crews must do at least one check ride per month

rounds. Camera guns can also be carried for missile and gun training.

Flight Refuelling's Rushton towed target system

is used for air-to-air SUU-23/A gunnery.
However, the company later developed a high
speed air-to-air gunnery target for use at speeds in
excess of 350 kt primarily by UK Phantoms and
Yugoslavian MiG-21s. It comprises either a radar
reflective, fabric, three-winged dart, measuring 8.2
by 1.2 m, or a banner target, and a container,
carried on the Phantom's outboard pylons, which
houses and deploys the 500 m tow rope and target.

*Pilot's view from the simulator over the airfield approach
path, showing the absolute fidelity in instrumentation,
systems and controls – only the stress levels of real flight
are absent, but procedures can be thoroughly rehearsed*

This system's higher speeds and radar reflective
target provides a greater degree of realism. A
Phantom FGR.2 of No 23 Sqn carried out trials of
this sytem in late 1980.

Chapter 9
No 38 Group: Tactical

The British Phantom is essentially a multi-role aircraft, and the RN used it as such. The RAF assessed multi-role use of the Phantom, but considered it impractical. Although the RAF has used it in all of its roles, the RAF's Phantoms are used in only one role at a time. A case in point is No 41 Sqn which was considered for tactical reconnaissance and ground attack dual roles with the Phantom. However, it was declared as a tactical reconnaissance unit, because the role demands specialization and it is not possible to attain the desired standards of excellence in dual roles. This single role philosophy pervades all RAF aircraft use, and is not peculiar to the Phantom. Far from being a waste of potential, this is a practical, long proven policy. It is a compliment to the Phantom that it can perform several roles separately and excel in them all. The RAF first deployed the Phantom as a tactical aircraft for offensive support operations.

The British Government assured NATO that the RAF's Phantom and Buccaneer forces would be deployed primarily in Europe, but to prove the Phantom in British service the first squadrons were based in the UK. The Phantom FGR.2 began to replace the Hunter FGA.9 in No 38 Group, Air Support Command in 1969, followed shortly by Harriers. RAF Coningsby, for the purposes of centralizing support, had been selected as the base of the RAF's entire UK Phantom FGR.2 Fighter-Bomber/Strike/Attack (FBSA) force, and No 228 OCU had been established there in preparation. Three squadrons were to form there, first Nos 6 and 54 operating in ground attack roles, and then No 41 Sqn in the tactical reconnaissance role. The Phantom FGR.2's primary role was ground attack and close support for the Army, with a secondary tactical reconnaissance role, and air defence a third.

Complemented by the Harriers of No 1(F) Sqn at Wittering, they provided the short range, offensive support element of No 38 Group for Army Strategic Command. Although assigned to SACEUR's strategic reserve, the Phantoms would not necessarily have been committed to the Central European NATO region during an emergency. Also in 1969, No 43 Sqn became operational at RAF Leuchars with Phantom FG.1s in the air defence role and assigned to No 11 Group in Strike Command.

On 10 January 1969, No 6 Sqn disbanded as a Canberra bomber unit at RAF Akrotiri after 54 years of continuous service overseas. On the same day, No 6 Sqn (Designate) Sqn (FBSA-Phantom) formed at Coningsby under Wg Cdr Harcourt-Smith DFC, whilst the crews were still converting on the No 1 Course at No 228 OCU, so that the squadron did not have to disband entirely. This was very unusual. In fact, the first No 6 Sqn FGR.2s were at Coningsby on 1 January 1969. From January until April 1969 there were 24 aircrew. All the aircrew on the course had previously completed ground attack and air defence tours. The course finished on 2 May 1969 and on Tuesday, 6 May 1969 the squadron started operationally with ten Phantoms under Sqn Ldr A J Bendell AFC, (a pilot) and Sqn Ldr L W A Rowe (a navigator) as Flight Commanders, and Sqn Ldr W E Hobby as Navigator Leader. The squadron had worked-up on OCU Phantom FGR.2s, and took some over to form its initial complement, including XV466. On 1 August 1969 all crews were operational. More aircrew arrived so that in February 1970 there were eighteen pilots and sixteen navigators. On Tuesday, 1 July 1969 the squadron's twelve Phantoms had taken part in the fly past for the Prince of Wales' Investiture at Caernarvon Castle. No 6 Sqn was assigned to the strike fighter role under the control of No 38 Group; its secondary reconnaissance role was dropped shortly before the squadron converted to Jaguars. Being the RAF's first FGR.2 unit, it was used to prove the type in squadron service and to undertake the first overseas detachments.

The existing No 54 Sqn was renumbered No 4 Sqn (UK Echelon) on 1 September 1969 and on the same day the new No 54 (Designate) Sqn (FBSA-Phantom) formed at Coningsby on Phantom FGR.2s. The first aircrews were from the second No 228 OCU course and the squadron worked up on OCU aircraft, taking over some on formation. No 54 Sqn, as the RAF's second Phantom FGR.2 unit, flew many of the early squadron operational type proving detachments, and on 8 December 1969 two No 54 Sqn Phantoms left the UK to deploy out to Singapore Armed Forces Base Tengah, the first such visit.

Nos 6 and 54 Sqns ran out to Tengah each year. Normally Phantoms deploying out to Tengah from Coningsby would land to refuel at Dhubai or Sharsah in the Persian Gulf. However, on 19 May 1970, Phantoms of Nos 6 and 54 Sqns left the UK to deploy in one hop to Tengah, refuelling in flight several times. Arriving next day, they established a record for the flight of 14 hours, 8 min and 19 sec.

Nos 6 and 54 Sqns were part of the UK Mobile Force in the ground-attack role in No 38 Group. Their role was to deploy at short notice to support NATO or UK out of theatre. In this capacity, the squadrons went out to Cyprus during the Turkish invasion in August–September 1974. The siren sounded at Coningsby at 6 pm one evening, calling a full alert, although the crews did not know the reason. By 8 am next morning No 6 Sqn had twelve fully-armed Phantoms on the pan at RAF Akrotiri, having flown by the most direct route to Cyprus, even though the trip involved some sensitive overflights. No 54 Sqn quickly followed. Three experienced No 43 Sqn aircrews, flying Phantom FG.1s in the air defence role from Leuchars, flew in to fly with and brief the 'mud-movers' – ground attack crews – in Phantom air defence. For overseas deployments, No 38 Group crews were trained in in-flight refuelling, unlike RAF Germany Phantom crews.

During its last year of Phantom operations No 6 Sqn was unique in being trained for the night ground attack role using flares, against such targets as bridges, ships, and fast patrol boats. Two Phantoms carrying Lepus flares, navigating by terrain-mapping radar, would lead three or four 'bombed-up' Phantoms at low level to the target, then pull up and over it, loosing the flares. The 'bombed-up' Phantoms, spaced out at two miles,

RIGHT
No 6 Sqn ham it up for the Press shortly after the unit had re-formed (see below)

No 6 Sqn's initial complement of Phantom FGR.2s at Coningsby on 14 February 1969, from No 228 OCU's No 1 Course, before application of squadron markings. RAF Phantom FGR.2s were originally to be deployed to the Middle and Far East

would follow the flare ships in from different directions as circumstances permitted, and dive on the target. Three or four Phantoms could attack under one lot of flares. SNEB and bombs were the main weapons used, but the squadron also practised night straffing with the SUU-23/A.

Flares and night could be very disorientating and pilots who set up too steep a dive had to be warned by other crews. The navigators proved invaluable in these operations. A strange and frightening phenomena encountered was 'Phantom shadow' when the Phantom's own shadow, bounced by the flares from cloud, would encounter the Phantom and 'simulate' a mid-air collision.

A series of training exercises was carried out by No 6 Sqn in the night attack role over the waters of the Skagerrak against fast patrol boats, and at night on the ranges at Decimomannu. In 1973-74, No 6 Sqn also undertook DAWN PATROL exercises off Sardinia, deploying to Gruzzamise near Naples and using the flare range at Cape Talada for night flare attack training.

No 6 Sqn undertook regular squadron exchanges to France, Italy and Germany, while armament practice camps (APC) were held mainly in Cyprus. No 6 Sqn's detachments included the following: Bruggen, Germany, 13 June 1969; Akrotiri, Cyprus, 22 September 1969 for the first APC; Andoya, Norway, 25 February 1970; Akrotiri, 4 May 1970; Cervia, Italy, 4 June 1970; Gütersloh, Germany, 20 September 1970; Decimomannu, Sardinia, 30 September 1970; Laarbuch, Germany, 24 May 1971; Decimomannu, 19 May 1971; Baden Soellingen, Germany, 12 July 1971; Akrotiri, 2 July 1971; Decimomannu, 18 January 1972; Tengah, 1 April 1972; Decimomannu, 13 July 1972; Hopsten, 3 October 1972; Decimomannu, 8 January 1973; Tengah, 28 March 1973; Gruzzamise, 4 June 1973; Karup, Denmark, 21 June 1973;

Television crew interviews the American civilian ferry pilot of the last FGR.2, the 118th, delivered to the RAF at Aldergrove on 29 August 1969. The last FG.1, the 52nd, arrived at Yeovilton on 29 July 1969

No 6 Sqn FGR.2s take-off from Akrotiri on 30 October 1969 during their first APC. Its flying-can-opener emblem was applied to the fin in 1969 on a red-outlined white disc, and moved to the nose a year later, displaced by the dark blue 'Gunner's Stripe', edged light blue, with red chevrons

Decimomannu, 26 July 1973; Akrotiri, 18 September 1973; Karup, 29 April 1974; Akrotiri, 1 July 1974; Akrotiri, 25 July 1974.

No 41 Sqn, disbanded on 18 September 1970 as a Bloodhound 2 SAM unit, reformed as a Phantom FGR.2 unit under Wg Cdr B J Lemon at Coningsby on 1 April 1972. The third and final member of the Coningsby Wing, it had waited to form until the RAF Germany Phantom re-equipment programme was advanced. Only 15 weeks later, on 12 July 1972, it was declared operational by AOC No 38 Group – which had become part of Strike Command on 1 July 1972 – although the squadron did not reach full operational strength for some months. It was the second British Phantom squadron to specialize in tactical fighter reconnaissance in support of land forces. No 2 Sqn (the first) had formed in January 1971 at Laarbuch assigned to RAFG, and pioneered the use of the specially-developed EMI reconnaissance pod which also equipped No 41 Sqn's FGR.2s. The addition of the pod to such a high performance aircraft, while still retaining the full weapons capability of the ground attack variant, was a great advance over the Canberra and Hunter dedicated PR aircraft.

Ground attack was a secondary part of No 41 Sqn's duties. Such a combination of roles is unique in the RAF. The unit's aircraft would undertake ground attack in the context of armed

FGR.2 XV405 of No 64 Sqn (No 228 OCU) at Coningsby on 29 March 1974. No 64 Sqn's insignia, carried on the fin only, is a yellow Scarabee on a black-ringed white disc, flanked by a white-edged red and blue 'trellis'

fighter reconnaissance sorties. As proof of its dual role capabilities, No 41 Sqn took second place in the reconnaissance competition BIG CLICK held out of GAF Eggebeck in September 1974, while in May 1975 it won the coveted Buchanan Trophy tactical bombing competition, scoring 996 points out of a possible 1100. Like Nos 6 and 54 Sqns, No 41 Sqn undertook regular overseas detachments, including to Tengah. In August 1973, No 41 Sqn deployed to Tengah to take part in Exercise PALE JADE 4. Working with HMS *Tiger* and Royal Australian Air Force units, the Phantoms carried out invaluable reconnaissance training over the South China Sea and the Mallacca Straits.

As part of No 38 Group, the Coningsby wing worked closely with the Army. In one limited war scenario, securing a landing strip and seizing an enemy position in enemy territory, a No 41 Sqn Phantom would fly a reconnaissance sortie over the target. Final planning would be based on analysis of the evidence gathered. Before the assault, Phantoms would soften up the target area's defences with SNEB, bombs and strafing, taking out radar and gun posts, anti-aircraft systems, armoured and soft skin vehicles, artillery, hard installations and troops in the immediate vicinity. Then, Pumas would disembark troops to secure a landing strip. Harrier GR.1s would reduce the enemy and provide close-support for the final assault, and Hercules C.1s and Andover C.1s would ferry in the heavier equipment.

The Phantom is a 'magnificent ground attack aircraft', stated one FBSA pilot, with good ground-mapping radar, and the capability of carrying free-fall or retarded or cluster bombs on five pylons, SNEB rockets and the devastating SUU-23/A while retaining four AIM-7 for self defence. Carrying the SUU-23/A and the AIM-7 did not compromise its ground attack capability. It was possible in one 20-minute slot during APC to combine three weapon training elements: four passes retarded bombs, four passes SNEB, four passes SUU-23/A, and the odd dive-bombing attack. This was hard work for the crews, but the results were consistently excellent.

The SUU-23/A is a devastating ground attack weapon. During a BBC television documentary No 6 Sqn's CO strafed a convoy of fully fuelled vehicles with the SUU-23/A using HE ammunition. One quick pass ripped them all up and set them on fire. In 1973, No 6 Sqn went to Cyprus to participate in a fire-power demonstration for CENTO nations. The representatives watched from the cliffs above Akrotiri as various aircraft types attacked barges with bombs and rockets, but it was the Phantoms which demolished the barges with their SUU-23/A cannons, the others hardly getting a look in!

The typical battlefield and tactical targets against which the RN and RAF Phantoms would have been committed were dispersed or massed main battle tanks, light armoured tracked or wheeled vehicles, light, medium or heavy-wheeled or self-propelled artillery, mortars, electronic warfare installations, bridges, pontoons, soft vehicles, convoys, and dispersed logistics vehicles, infantry, airborne dropping zones parked or dispersed aircraft, minehunters and minesweepers, coastal vessels, fast patrol boats, surfaced submarines, amphibious assault craft, and beach-heads, barges, supply depots, and missile sites.

Modern tactical and ground attack aircraft rely upon high speed/low-level capability to penetrate enemy battlefield air defence systems. The Phantom's high speed/low-level capabilities, a product of airframe, engine and radar performance, were a considerable advance over the Hunter's, particularly in terms of survivability and effectiveness. The necessity for tactical operations to be carried out at very low level and high speeds has been proven in successive limited conflicts, and is largely a response to the increased effectiveness of surface-to-air missile systems (SAMs). It also has the advantage of surprise.

Vulcans, Victors and No 6 Sqn Phantoms at RAF Tengah during BERSATU PADU, *a five-power exercise in Malyasia from April to July 1970, involving 25,000 men and a large airlift from the UK*

High speed/low-level attack also permits a variety of evasive and withdrawal patterns to be flown which enhance the aircraft's ability to survive. It was precisely for such patterns that the Phantom FGR.2's INAS was designed.

To overcome problems inherent in such attacks, Hunting Engineering developed the British bomb retarding tail system which, in conjunction with a new delayed fuse, ensures aircraft safety and accurate delivery of HE bombs from very low level. Four spines deploy from the tail upon release, with fabric stretched between them like an umbrella. This decelerates, or retards the bomb, allowing a safe distance between the aircraft and the 'debris envelope' before the bomb explodes. The system has been in British service since 1968 and was employed by both the RN and RAF Phantoms. The Type 117 retarder tail is designed for Mks 6, and 9 to 19 series 1,000 lb (454 kg) HE medium capacity tactical and battlefield bombs, in two versions, each 1.35 mm long: the Mk 3 (584 mm span) for external carriage, and the Mk 4 (419 mm span) for either external or internal carriage. The Type 118, 970 mm long and 463 mm in span, was developed for British Mk 1/2 540 lb HE medium capacity battlefield bombs. Both types can be adapted to other bombs, including the US Marks 64, 65, 82, 83, and 117.

The Coningsby wing was comparatively short-lived, the Phantom FGR.2 being superceded in the FBSA roles by the SEPECAT Jaguar, releasing the Phantoms to replace the increasingly inappropriate Lightning in the air defence role.

The Jaguar officially entered RAF service with Nos 6 and 54 Sqns in June 1974. No 54 Sqn disbanded as a Phantom unit at Coningsby on 23 April 1974, handing over the squadron number plate to No 54 (Designate) Sqn (FBSA-Jaguar) which formed at Lossiemouth on 5 June 1974. However, part of the disbanded Phantom unit retrained in the air defence role to form the nucleus of No 111 (Designate) Sqn (Air Defence-Phantom) at Coningsby on 1 July 1974. On 1 June 1974, No 6 (Designate) Sqn (FBSA-Jaguar) formed at Lossiemouth under Wg Cdr R J Quarterman, to whom Wg Cdr B W Lavender AFC, a first-tour Phantom pilot who had commanded No 6 Sqn since 29 December 1972, formally handed over command. The aircrews of the Phantom unit began to retrain in the air defence role at No 228 OCU or converted, and on 30 September 1974 No 6 Sqn (FBSA-Phantom) was formally disbanded, the Jaguar unit taking over the squadron number plate. However, on 1 October No 29 (Designate) Sqn (AD-Phantom) formed at Coningsby with Wg Cdr Lavender as CO and No 6 Sqn aircrew among its complement.

No 41 Sqn's re-equipment with Jaguar in the tactical reconnaissance role was delayed until RAFG's Jaguar squadrons had been brought up to full strength. No 41 (Designate) Sqn (AC-Jaguar) formed on 1 October 1974 at RAF Coltishall under Wg Cdr C J Thompson. For the next six months it worked up while the Phantom squadron remained operational at Coningsby. No 41 Sqn (AC-Phantom) disbanded on 31 March 1977 and on 1 April 1977 the squadron standard and number plate were handed over to the Jaguar squadron at a parade reviewed by AOC No 38 Group, AVM P G K Williamson CBE, DFC.

FGR.2 XV496 at Cottesmore on 15 September 1973, bearing No 41 Sqn's red Cross of St Omar, black XLI and yellow crown on a white disc with red bars edged white. The fin's Cross is edged white, its crown, black

Chapter 10
Royal Air Force Germany: Tactical

NATO forces in Europe are deployed in a defensive arc from Northern Norway to Southern Turkey. The Central Region stretches from Denmark's southern border to Austria's northern border. The air power in the Central Region's northern sector is provided by the Second Allied Tactical Air Force (TWOATAF), comprising RAF Germany, USAFE elements, and West German, Netherlands, and Belgian air force elements operating from their own countries. In the southern sector, air power is provided by the Fourth Allied Tactical Air Force.

TWOATAF's area of responsibility covers about 60,000 square miles. It stretches from the East/West German border north to the Danish border and west over the North Sea to meet UKADR; it then runs south along the French border to Luxembourg's northern tip, then north of a straight north-east line to Kassel and Gottingen, below which is the FOURATAF sector. TWOATAF's war headquarters are in Holland. The commander is usually the RAF officer who is also C-in-C RAFG.

In peacetime TWOATAF's defensive forces, the interceptor and SAM units, are assigned to the control of the Supreme Allied Commander Europe (SACEUR). The offensive forces remain under national control and command, essentially a political requirement. Therefore, in peacetime HQRAFG is responsible for the operational training and readiness of units assigned and of the logistics and administrative elements. Thus, RAFG's Phantoms were under national control when serving in the tactical roles, but have been assigned to SACEUR since being redeployed to air defence from 1977. In the event of war, Commander TWOATAF would assume

Canberra PR.7 WH779 and Phantom FGR.2 XV426 of No 31 Sqn at the squadron's reformation ceremony, the last RAFG FBSA-Phantom squadron to form

operational control of all assigned defensive and offensive forces at a prescribed stage in the NATO alert system. Then, all RAFG units would be assigned to SACEUR.

RAFG's major commitment is providing nuclear strike, conventional attack, interdiction, ground support, reconnaissance, and air defence forces for NATO air power and for the immediate support of NATO land exercises and wartime operations in the Central Region. In peacetime RAFG also discharges a national commitment, like all NATO-assigned RAF formations, by defending the integrity of West Germany's airspace and keeping open the Berlin air corridors in accordance with the Bonn Convention.

RAFG's FBSA-Phantom squadrons began to form once the Coningsby-based Nos 6 and 54

FGR.2s, 1972, carrying No 17 Sqn's black and white chevrons as an arrowhead and (on the port only) a red and white segmented shield bearing the unit's gauntlet, red and black outlined black or white in contrast

TOP
XV464, 1972, wearing No 14 Sqn's red St George Cross on a black-outlined white disc under a knight's helmet and flanked by wings, both yellow with black outlines and details. The black-edged white bars carried medium blue diamonds

Sqns were established, priority having been given to re-forming UK-based units for operational trials reasons. RAF Bruggen was selected as the base of Nos 14, 17 and 31 Sqns in the strike/attack roles, while No 2 Sqn, tasked with tactical reconnaissance, was based at Laarbruch. Bruggen, Laarbruch and Wildenrath, the 'clutch' airfields, lie

95

No 2 Sqn's FGR.2s wore its knot device on a white disc flanked by white triangles over a black panel. White triangles on the fins bore aircraft codes. For low-visibility requirements, red replaced white in 1973–76

close together far in the west of Germany on the Dutch border. They are at sufficient distance from the East/West German border to afford useful warning against impending air attack, and to avoid or delay being over-run or neutralised by the rapid advance of the Soviet rolling front, whilst permitting the attack and reconnaissance aircraft to operate in close co-ordination with the forward elements of NATO ground forces, with immediate access from HQTWOATAF.Curiously only Wildenrath had RHAG and all Phantom emergency landings were made there.

RAFG introduced the Phantom and Buccaneer simultaneously, the latter in the long range strike/attack role, and the arrival of the Harrier filled the close-support gap. AVM Foxley-Norris, C-in-C RAFG/TWOATAF at the time, wrote of the Phantoms, Harriers and Buccaneers: 'Their greatly superior performance much improved the operational effectiveness of the Command.'

No 14 Sqn disbanded at Wildenrath as a Canberra interdictor unit on 30 June 1970, and reformed the same day as RAFG's first Phantom FBSA squadron. The first Phantom FGR.2s delivered to the unit included XT914, XV411 and XV439. On 31 December 1969, No 17 Sqn

disbanded as a Canberra PR.7 photo-reconnaissance unit at Wildenrath. No 17 (Designate) Sqn (FBSA-Phantom), amongst whose first Phantoms was XT901, began to form at Wildenrath on 1 July 1970, reforming on 1 September. After a short training period, it moved to Bruggen where it officially reformed on 16 October 1970, dropping the caveat (Designate), and became semi-operational. In January 1971, after No 2 (AC) Sqn had disbanded at Laarbruch as a Hunter PR.10 photo-reconnaissance unit, No 2 (Designate) Sqn (AC-Phantom) formed at Bruggen, where it began to work up before moving to Laarbruch in April 1971. The unit's first FGR.2 was XV485. As the first British Phantom tactical-reconnaissance squadron, it pioneered the use of the EMI-developed reconnaissance pod, whose multi-sensor capability made the Phantom substantially more effective than the Hunter and Canberra PR aircraft. Like No 41 Sqn in No 38 Group, attack was No 2 Sqn's secondary role.

No 31 Sqn was the last RAFG FBSA Phantom squadron to form. After sixteen years as a Canberra PR.7 unit at Laarbuch, No 31 Sqn disbanded on Friday, 5 March 1971, although its last Canberra did not leave until October 1971. No 31 (Designate) Sqn (FBSA-Phantom) formed at Bruggen in June 1971 under Wg Cdr J C Sprent. However, in April 1971 Sqn Ldr Graham

FGR.2 XV498 of No 17 Sqn, devoid of AIM-7E-2s to reveal the ejector launching racks and fin slots, but carrying CBLS, an SUU-23/A, two wing tanks, and a blue Sparrow drill round (carried for CG reasons)

No 31 Sqn FGR.2s, Bruggen. In April 1971, No 31 Sqn chose markings reflecting its new role: a gold five-pointed star (mullet), medium green laurel and red bow on a white disc over green and yellow checks

FAR LEFT
At Bruggen, No 31 Sqn groundcrew load an FGR.2's Sergeant Fletcher wing tank. Groundcrew's names were stencilled on the squadron's FGR.2s from Exercise ROYAL FLUSH *in July 1976*

LEFT
At Decimomannu during APC, No 31 Sqn groundcrew pose with 600 US gal centreline tank, with adapter pylon, the largest store carried by UK Phantoms. Here, the insignia's laurel is a medium green ring

Gibb, a Flight Commander and Deputy CO, and his pilot, Flt Lt David Pollington, arrived at Bruggen two months ahead of the others to prepare accommodation. When No 2 Sqn moved to Laarbruch, No 31 Sqn took over their hangar, No 4, 'nicely situated at the end of the airfield well away from the other two resident squadrons, 14 and 17', recalled Dave Pollington. 'Perhaps it was the situation or the fact that the then Wg Cdr Sprent stated at a guest night that 14 and 17 together came to 31! but we never seemed to get on well with the other squadrons.'

Most of No 31 Sqn's original aircrew came from the No 9 Course at No 228 OCU, with a few from the No 8 Course, including Gibb and Pollington, plus Flt Lts Horning, Dachtler, McDonald and Rixon who were transferred from Nos 14 and 17 Sqns, and Sqn Ldrs Robertson and Hodges as B Flight Commander and Navigator Leader respectively. But No 31 Sqn did not get the 30 aircrew it needed to carry out its role effectively for three years, mainly due to the repercussions of the Spey availability problems which halted training at No 228 OCU. However, the squadron's strength was increased to 24 by OCU staff, including Flt Lts Nattress and Flynn as QWI and QFI respectively. Personnel shortages also affected groundcrews for similar reasons. The first Phantoms arrived in June 1971, but Bruggen was Tacevaled and this delayed work-up and flying training until the third week in July.

Although located in No 4 Hangar, servicing at Bruggen was semi-centralized. All rectification was done a mile away in No 2 Hangar, imposing a considerable strain on groundcrews and administration. The squadron could not fully meet its commitments until it became semi-autonomous about a year after formation with an increased number of groundcrew under Sqn Ldr Loveday. Moreover, as the last squadron to form at Bruggen, the virtual lack of married quarters within easy distance of the base was an unwelcome pressure. No squadron can expect to move from formation to operational status without encountering problems, and it is precisely for the purpose of identifying and solving such problems and for integrating the administration, servicing and operational elements into a coherent, efficient whole that the work-up period is designated.

No 31 Sqn officially reformed on 7 October 1971 at a parade at Bruggen outside the squadron's hangar. The Queen's colours were paraded, the Central Band of the RAF played, and ACM Sir Harold Martin, C-in-C RAFG, presented the squadron colours. The squadron officially took up residence operationally the next day.

The squadron continued to train intensively for all aspects of its operational roles, nuclear strike, interdiction, tactical ground attack, and close

No 31 Sqn FGR.2 on APC at Deci awaiting its crew, carrying CBLS for practice weapons, but 1,000 lb (454 kg) bombs, SNEB and cannon were also expended

TOP LEFT
No 31 Sqn groundcrew prepare FGR.2 XV393 for flight during APC at Deci; one repacks the brake chute. The squadron's star, white on a blue disc, appeared on the fin of some Phantoms

OPPOSITE
No 31 Sqn Phantoms with differing insignia styles at Deci during APC. A single-tone star was carried until April 1976 when a yellow and deep yellow star was applied to FGR.2s participating in ROYAL FLUSH

support, and deployed to Decimomannu in March–April 1972 for its first APC, training with missiles and bombs, having worked up on the Vliehors and Nordhorn ranges. The squadron was also tasked with all-weather interception and armed (fighter) reconnaissance in secondary capacities. For air-to-air combat experience and simulated weapons practice, the squadron flew against the Lightnings of Nos 19 and 92 Sqns based at Gutersloh, and for live firings used Jindivik drone targets. Initially, the squadron's Phantoms were not equipped with reconnaissance equipment or controls to carry the EMI pod, but by 1974 some had been equipped. Following trials conducted by a No 31 Sqn Phantom FGR.2

(XV491) in 1972, the in-flight refuelling probes were de-activated on RAFG Phantoms, because there was little use for them in FBSA roles; aircrews in RAFG have not been in-flight refuelling qualified. Throughout 1972, except when on detachment, the squadron mounted nuclear strike QRA, the role which absorbed most of the training effort during this period. The air and groundcrews' sense of achievement and pride in creating an operational squadron was nurtured by achieving good results and assessments in Tacevals, despite the difficulties under which the squadron initially operated.

In August 1974, Wg Cdr Tom Stonor took over command of No 31 Sqn, remaining until the squadron disbanded as a Phantom unit. He wrote of the squadron's roles:

It was one of the dual capable/strike attack squadrons of TWOATAF. The strike missions were straightforward in that they involved singleton operations by an aircraft armed with a nuclear weapon and missiles for self defence. The attack missions were divided into three types: Counter Air, Interdiction, and Close Air Support/Battlefield Interdiction.

The Counter Air missions invariably involved four or more aircraft armed with General Purpose (iron) bombs, and the attacks were directed at the enemy's air capability – aircraft on the ground, support and POL facilities, even runways. The weapon delivery technique involved toss-bombing, low angle dive, and lay down.

Interdiction missions were directed at the enemy's logistic and communications lines, the aim being to stop the ground movements of armoured and soft skinned vehicles. Attacks were generally concentrated at 'choke points' (bridges, gullies, tunnels, etc). Armament included GP bombs, CBU and cannon, and the attacks invariably required a 'pop up', low angle dive attack, not only for the purpose of acquiring the target, but also in order to achieve an element of weapon penetration and also ground separation to enable fusing of the bombs.

Close Air Support involved missions in support of the army in the area of the FEBA, and attacks were co-ordinated by ASOCs and directed by FACs who were in direct contact with the aircraft. Acquisition of targets was more difficult in that they were invariably well camouflaged and inevitably moving. The success of these missions depended naturally on the skill of the FAC, and also on the effectiveness of ground-to-air communications – sometimes a problem. Armament and attack techniques were similar to those used for interdiction.

In all these missions, the armament included missiles for self defence purposes, and the squadron occasionally practised air defence tactics and techniques under the control of GCI controllers. All missions were flown using Hi-Lo-Hi or Lo-Lo profiles and penetration to the target and weapon delivery were both at low level – always. That is why high angle bombing techniques were never practised. En route to the target, aircraft flew in either 'card' or 'escort' formation. 'Card' is the best tactical low level formation but it requires practice and experience to fly and therefore 'escort' was favoured if there was a new boy in the formation; he would fly as No 2. Both formations provided for crosscover and

mutual support, and also ensured maximum difficulty for visual acquisition by enemy AD fighters; with both visual look-out and radar scan, the formation cleared a corridor ahead of itself – very effective.'

The Phantom FGR.2s of Nos 14, 17 and 31 Sqns were tasked with nuclear strike, maintaining in rotation QRA Phantoms on 24-hour immediate readiness with nuclear stores, the crew in the cockpit, ready to respond when the first indications of nuclear attack developed. They were isolated. Only authorized personnel could approach. If the crew left the cockpit, another had to replace them immediately. They formed the forward edge of NATO's nuclear deterrent, a role taken over by Buccaneers and Jaguars, and by Tornados from 1984. In wartime they would have been called upon to deliver tactical nuclear strikes to halt the Warsaw Pact advance. They used various US nuclear weapons. The Phantom could carry one B28 nuclear free-fall strategic or tactical bomb, yielding 1.4-28 MT in strategic form, or three B43, B57 or B61. The B43 is a tactical or strategic, free-fall or parachute-retarded bomb, with a low-altitude release 'lay-down' surface burst capability, and yielding in the KT-MT range, with several options. The tactical B57 yields 10–20 KT, while the B61 yields 100–500 KT in tactical form, and in the MT range in strategic form.

Stores carried on a typical Hi-Lo-Lo-Hi tactical nuclear mission at full range would have been four AIM-7E-2, one 500 lb B57 on station 5, and two 370 US gal wing tanks, in addition to full internal tanks. The Phantom crew would use maximum take-off power and military power acceleration to clear the base rapidly, then initiate a steep climb at military power, sustaining an average of Mach 0.8, to reach the optimum cruise altitude of some 33,100 ft at about 55 nm and seven min flying time out. The pilot would cruise at this altitude, climbing gradually to 34,500 feet, and maintaining an average Mach 0.87, dropping the tanks when empty. At 290 nm out, after 0.58 hr, the pilot would drop to sea level, dash to the target at about 550 nm at Mach 0.80, and expend the weapon at about 1 hr 30 min out. He would dash from the target, initiate a steep military power climb to optimum cruise altitude for his new weight of 39,400 ft, and cruise at Mach 0.86, climbing to 40,600 ft until reaching base. The total mission time would have been just over 2 hours.

The EMI reconnaissance pod is a sophisticated equipment developed specifically for the RAF's Phantom FGR.2 to enable an RF-4's tasks to be performed while retaining weapons capability and performance. The pod gave comprehensive cover in all weathers by day and night and overcame camouflage and concealment to a large extent by employing various types of sensors at low level to suit changing light and weather conditions. To

Typical RS-700 IRLS imagery shows the 'hot' (white) details of a port area, at 10.00 hr after heavy rain, revealing storage tank levels, the oil tanker's engine area, pipelines, piers, barges and even sea vegetation

eliminate the need for crews to fly at very low altitudes in poor weather and light conditions in a hostile environment, high-definition side-looking radar (SLR) and infrared linescan (IRLS) equipment is fitted which can be used by day and night. The 'recon gap' between the response regions of a visual camera and radar is bridged by the IRLS which provides a broader response than other sensors and gathers intelligence unobtainable by them. The pod's IRLS is completely passive and can operate effectively in all weathers, and requires no illumination, natural or artificial. It can therefore collect data without persons in the target area being aware of surveillance, a significant tactical advantage. The pod's cameras gave wide coverage. An automatic in-flight film processor was fitted and film casettes could be ejected in flight to allow information to be available to ground commanders rapidly. To amplify visual information, the Phantom FGR.2 was equipped with a UHF voice communications radio to provide instant contact with ground bases and commanders, so that a strike could be called in rapidly; it also had an observer's voice recorder. The Phantom FGR.2 is equipped with terrain-following and mapping radar, linked to an autopilot, to avoid the hazards of low flying, especially at night.

The pod was accepted for service in 1970. Carried on the centreline pylon, it can be fitted and removed quickly, greatly increasing the aircraft's role flexibility, and permitting the optimum use of aircraft to meet changing requirements, while offensive stores can be carried at the same time. The pod can be carried in conjunction with a strike camera on station 4. Not all FGR.2s had the equipment to use the pod, and the RN's FG.1s did not use it.

The pod carried five optical cameras, one vertical, one forward and two oblique F95, and one F135, supplied by Aeronautical and General Instruments, and Vinten. The cameras operate simultaneously for 360° coverage and have quick wind mechanisms to ensure that no ground cover is lost. A data converter notes the precise position, speed and heading for any of the recordings (inertial platform). The F135 is a low-level, high speed day or night camera which has two lenses to take high quality stereo pictures, one lens normally set at 4° forward, the other 4° aft, each covering

57×57 mm side by side on 126 mm film. For visual photography at night, four F135 are used in conjunction with an electronic flash carried in a specialised wing tank, fired by a synchronising pulse produced when the cameras' shutters operate. For special tasks, an F95 oblique camera with a 12 inch lens, or an F126 medium altitude vertical camera can be fitted. The F126's automatic exposure control caters for changing light conditions, while image movement compensation permits sharp pictures up to Mach 1.3 at 1,520 m altitude.

The Royal Radar Establishment and EMI collaborated in the development of two Linescan SLR types for TSR-2's pod, an X-band equipment for reconnaissance and navigation, and a high definition Q(Ka)-band equipment for reconnaissance. The second type was developed for the Phantom pod, designated Type P391. The main units are the transmitter/receiver, modulator, recorder, power units, control unit, and port and starboard aerials for transmission. A medium range tactical system, it operates by day or night in ground mapping, moving target indication and photographic recording modes. It is not used as a navigation aid and therefore a rapid-processing and display unit is not fitted as standard to the FGR.2. The system's radar scans successive strips of terrain extending several miles at right angles to the flight path. Cover varies with altitude. The radar mapping information from each strip is presented on a display tube and converted by Linescan system into images on a roll of 12.7 cm film which is moving past the tube at a rate proportional to the aircraft's ground speed. The film is processed at base.

The pod uses the Texas Instruments RS-700 series IRLS. All bodies radiate thermal energy by day and night in the IR waveband, .72 to 100 microns, just above the visual spectrum, as a function of their absolute temperature emissivity. IRLS detects anything which produces heat energy, and can therefore be presented on a thermal linescan picture. RS-700 is sensitive to the varying patterns on the terrain overflown in the 8 to 14 micron IR region. In this region, most earth and earth-like materials have a radiant energy nearly proportional to their absolute temperature, but man-made objects have a different radiometric temperature to their actual temperature, and can therefore be distinguished. This natural phenomenon is exploited by RS-700.

The infrared radiation from successive strips of terrain across the optical path is focused by a mirror and photocell system, which is sensitive to IR frequencies, on to detectors which convert it into electrical signals. These are processed by video electronics and converted by light-emitting diodes (LED) to light for film recording. A comprehensive IR image is built up line by line by the Linescan on a continuous strip of film to produce a profile of a target's natural temperature radiation, showing detailed variations in terrain and man-made surface objects. The processed information in the video recorder can either be retrieved at base or transmitted during flight.

The RS-700 imagery can easily distinguish between a decoy and an actual target due to the radiation signature identified with each, and it can detect and penetrate camouflage and concealment systems. Most camouflage systems use man-made devices which are detectable in the IR region, and camouflage or smoke cannot conceal heat. The RS-700 can detect the 'shadow' (latent image) of a recently moved object because different amounts of energy have been absorbed by the background. Power sources, ship's engine compartments, command stations, fuel storage facilities and vehicle or aircraft activity are detectable (engines continue to emit IR energy for hours after operation has ceased). Personnel groupings and supplies are detectable against natural backgrounds. This information permits the strategic evaluation of *materiél*, the identification of vulnerable target areas, and assessment of activity.

Of lightweight modular construction, servicing and repair of the IRLS are rapid and simple. It has a built-in test equipment (BITE). The pod has its own air conditioning, with two cooling ducts for the IRLS either side behind the pod's nose. RS-700 has a high/velocity height performance, providing low-level survival. It has manual and automatic level control. The RS-700 can be roll stabilized up to $+/-30°$ about nadir, eliminating the effects of roll manouevres during reconnaissance. Oblique slew allows up to $+/-25°$ offset from nadir, providing stand-off profile data from targets of special interest.

As Phantom tac-recce units, RAFG's No 2 Sqn and No 38 Group's No 41 Sqn participated with great success in the reconnaissance competition ROYAL FLUSH. The Bruggen Phantom FBSA squadrons competed with particular success for the Salmond Trophy which is awarded annually to the RAFG squadron achieving the highest scores in bombing and navigation exercises during a week of intensive competition. No 14 Sqn won it in 1972. In 1973 the squadrons took the first three places: out of a possible total of 1,680 points, No 31 Sqn scored 1,102, No 14 1,028 and No 17 1,002. In both 1975 and 1976 No 14 Sqn came first, and No 17 Sqn second. Phantom, Jaguar, Harrier and Buccaneer squadrons all competed, and in 1976 nine squadrons took part. First presented in 1930 by AVM Sir Geoffrey Salmond, AOC RAF India, 1927–31, the Trophy was awarded annually to Army Co-operation squadrons in RAF India until the outbreak of war in 1939. After the war, the Trophy as allocated to Bomber Command but was passed to RAFG for internal competition between the command's assigned operational squadrons, as the symbol of their combat proficiency.

The normal range of overseas deployments, such as for APC, existed, while Bruggen's Phantoms frequently deployed to other TWOATAF bases and aircraft from other TWOATAF forces regularly operated from Bruggen to refine inter-operability and conduct mutual training. Some operational deployments were further afield, involving considerable organisation. For instance, No 31 Sqn went on an exchange visit to Eskisehir, a Turkish fighter base about 100 miles south-east of Istanbul, in NATO's Southern Region.

While the RAFG Bruggen and Laarbruch Phantom squadrons were involved in larger exercises covering all RAFG, No 11 Group, TWOATAF or even NATO, individual stations were also subjected to annual tactical evaluations by a multi-national team, sprung without notice to keep stations at a high state of readiness at all times. The teams assess all aspects of the operational effectiveness of bases and their units, and discover deficiencies, and report to the C-in-C RAFG, or C-in-C Group, and SACEUR upon assigned units. All NATO units are evaluated to the same standards against as realistic a war scenario as possible, including NBC, and units react as they would in war, within peacetime safety constraints. Thus, a station must react as a whole.

Not only do Tacevals provide invaluable training, the more valid for being spontaneous and almost total, but they display the muscle in deterrence.

Having re-equipped with Buccaneers, Phantoms and Harriers in the strike, attack, close-support and tac-recce roles in the early 1970s, RAFG replaced the FBSA Phantoms with the next generation of tactical strike aircraft, Jaguar, in 1975–76, following which the Phantoms thus released re-equipped RAFG's Lightning air defence squadrons. In accordance with HM Government's continuing commitment to NATO in Europe, most front-line Jaguar squadrons were to be deployed to RAFG at Bruggen to re-equip the three Phantom squadrons forming the RAFG main strike/attack force, and No 2 Sqn's tactical reconnaissance capability at Laarbruch. However, Nos 6 and 54 Sqns (ex-Phantom) again took precedence in re-equipment in order to monitor problems within Strike Command. By Spring 1974, the first RAFG squadrons were forming at Bruggen. In each case the Jaguar squadron designated to take over the squadron number plate

Phantoms and Jaguars of No 2 Sqn all with similarly-equipped recce pods and RWR. Phantom pods were Light Aircraft Grey; some wore shark mouths

and tasks worked-up alongside the Phantom unit, which disbanded when the Jaguar squadron was declared operational, the last Phantom not being re-allocated until then. The Phantom aircrews were re-assigned to Phantom and Lightning air defence duties or converted to Jaguars.

No 14 (Designate) Sqn (FBSA-Jaguar), which formed in April 1975, was the first RAFG unit to receive Jaguars, its first (T.2, XX836) arriving on 7 April 1975. The Phantom unit ceased operations on 30 November 1975. The Jaguar unit dropped the caveat and became operational next day. No 17 (Designate) Sqn (Jaguar) formed at Bruggen on 1 September 1974, the second Jaguar unit in the progressive change-over. No 17 Sqn (FBSA-Phantom) disbanded on 30 January 1976, when the squadron standard was formally handed over to No 17 Sqn (Jaguar). No 31 Sqn was the last British FBSA-Phantom squadron to disband. No 31 (Designate) Sqn (Jaguar) formed at Bruggen in January 1976, after No 17 Sqn's initial aircrew and aircraft requirements had been completed, and began a daily flying training programme the next month. While the Jaguar is a very capable aircraft for ground attack, opinions in some quarters hold that the Phantom was a far more capable aircraft. It did not amuse the Jaguar crews when they found bowls of milk left in front of their aircraft during the night by No 31 Sqn Phantom crews! The Phantom unit disbanded in June 1976, and No 31 Sqn became fully operational on Jaguar in December 1976. Jaguar GR.1 deliveries to No 2 (Designate) Sqn (AC-Jaguar) began in February 1976. Equipped with specially developed reconnaissance pods similar in concept to the

FGR2 (XT901/'J') of No 17 Sqn on display at Bruggen in September 1971 carrying 4 × 1,000 lb (454 kg) retarded bombs

Phantom's, the Jaguars worked-up alongside the Phantom squadron, supplanting it in October 1976.

The Jaguar was derided as a fighting aircraft at the time and the transition to this new aircraft appeared to represent a step backwards in overall mission capability. But the 'Jag' undoubtedly brought several advantages, such as advanced maintenance features and an up-to-date nav/attack system. Wg Cdr Tom Stonor (No 31 Sqn's CO) compared the two aircraft thus:

As a fighting machine, the Phantom was excellent. It was robust, it had three separate hydraulic systems, and (literally) 'tons of poke'. With its in-built missile system and second pair of eyes, it presented a formidable opponent to any Warsaw Pact AD fighter. I remember well the knocks and jibes that the Jaguar squadrons received. However, to be fair to the Jaguar, in my time as Station Commander of Coltishall, I came to recognize its talents and advantages: tiny and difficult to see at low-level; no 'smoke trail'; the excellent view from the cockpit and HUD; so easy to low-fly compared with a Phantom; wonderful aiming and delivery system compared to the Phantom; sensitive controls in comparison with the Phantom. After all, the Phantom wasn't designed to be a low-level aircraft, the Jaguar was. That being said, I missed the 'beefiness' of the Phantom, I certainly missed the missiles, and I missed the navigator: the only pilots who berate navigators are those who haven't flown with them. A good 'fighter navigator' is worth his weight in gold and he'll probably save your life and his several times in a shooting war.

Chapter 11
Air Defence of the United Kingdom

In an emergency or a war, as in World War II, the British Isles would serve as a key forward base for operations in Europe. A high proportion of NATO land and air forces reinforcements from across the Atlantic would either be based in or stage through the UK. Normally some 40 per cent of SACEUR's offensive aircraft are based in the UK, and installations vital to the conduct of operations in Europe and the NATO EASTLANT and CHANNEL maritime areas are similarly located. It would also be the main base for the UK's own effort in continental reinforcement and maritime tasks. The UK is therefore, regardless of nuclear assets, a high priority target for Soviet attacks and effective defence against air attack is essential to maintaining the credibility of NATO's deterrent policy. In recognition of this importance, the UK Air Defence Region (UKADR) is a major subordinate NATO command under SACEUR, commanded by the C-in-C UK Air Force (CINCUKAIR), the NATO appointment of the AOC-in-C, RAF.

In UKADR the threat is from long range bombers rather than from fighters, and a stand-off threat in particular. For instance, the Tu-22M *Backfire* operating from bases in North-West Russia, can, with inflight refuelling, approach the UKADR from any direction at high or low-level. It can carry two nuclear or conventional AS-6 *Kingfish* or AS-4 *Kitchen* ASM, both of which can be launched from roughly 400 nm (740 km) from a target, depending on altitude. The conventional attack threat is also considerable. From bases in Western Russia the Su-24 *Fencer* can carry a significantly greater weapons load than its predecessors in a Hi-Lo-Hi profile in all weathers to the UK, and, from forward bases in East Germany, could carry out larger scale low-level attacks on the UK. Both types could be

escorted by MiG-23 *Flogger* fighters, and ECM would degrade the UKADR's radar and defence systems.

The classic air defence system is layered to maximize the chances of intercepting hostile aircraft: air defence fighters at long and medium range, then area-defence SAMs, then point-defence SAMs. Defence of the UKADR is based on initial interception at maximum range. The objective is to detect a threat using airborne early warning (AEW) aircraft and NATO ground radars on the approach to UKADR in order to be able to vector interceptors into position for early attacks.

The air defence of the UK is currently entrusted to four (five until 1983) Phantom and two Lightning front-line squadrons, about 80 aircraft. A second-line force, available in emergency, is provided by the Phantoms of No 228 OCU and about 70 Hawks. In the UKADR, the Phantom is primarily a long range interceptor, which means a maritime environment. To meet the threat beyond stand-off range, the Phantoms must be either out on Combat Air Patrol (CAP) or scrambled from Quick Reaction Alert (QRA), perhaps from forward operating bases, particularly for the North and Northwest approaches. Tanker aircraft are essential to maintain CAP and carry out QRA. In NATO's Central Region, in contrast, the Phantoms of RAFG have to operate in a closer environment, probably against fighters, and low-level attackers. The Lightnings of Nos 5 and 11 Sqn are essentially short-range, area-defence interceptors. They would be supplemented in an emergency by the two squadrons of AIM-9L-armed Hawks from RAF Brawdy. The area-defence SAMs are the Bloodhound 2s of No 85 Sqn. Since 1982–83, these have been located at strategic points down the east coast and are directed by the same operations control centres as the fighters. Each Bloodhound detachment is allocated a missile engagement zone. The Rapiers of the RAF Regt are all-weather point-defence SAMs for close-range targets, and protect airfields and installations.

UKADR is divided into geographical air defence sectors, in each of which tactical air defence is managed by a sector controller. The UKADR interceptors are based in three tiers, the North-controlled by Buchan, and the Centre and South, both controlled by the Neatishead Operations Control Centre. The Northern squadrons are Nos 43 and 111 at Leuchars, Fife, with Phantom FG.1s. The Central squadrons are Nos 29 and 64 (No 228 OCU) at Coningsby, Lincolnshire, with Phantom FGR.2s and Nos 5 and 11 at Binbrook, with Lightning F.3/F.6. The Southern Sector has only one squadron, No 56 with Phantom FGR.2s at Wattisham, Suffolk, but had two until March 1983 when No 23 Sqn disbanded at Wattisham, reforming in the Falklands.

Each sector is responsible for the tactical control and battle management of the air defence resources within the sector, which, in addition to fighter, Bloodhound and Rapier assets, includes AEW and tanker aircraft allocated to that sector. Each sector controller can use these assets as the situation demands, and will always seek to match the threat. Tactics are governed by the availability of aircraft. Allocation of tanker and AEW aircraft to a sector and any re-allocation of any assets is the responsibility of the Air Defence Commander (ADC) who operates from the Air Defence Operations Centre (ADOC) at HQ Strike Command, High Wycombe. The sole line of information to interceptor squadrons is from the sector controller, who controls aircraft directly when they are airborne. This is the starting point. In war there would be considerable redeployment, and sector boundaries are not inviolate. Phantoms operating in support of SACLANT can be deployed to the Southwest, while Stornoway, on Lewis, can act as a fighter FOB, and Leuchars, the most vital air defence base, could be reinforced by Southern squadrons, but the ADC has limited assets and must deploy and allocate them in such a way as to maintain a balanced capability.

Each sector has independent Interceptor Alert Forces (IAF) to maintain QRA (Interceptor). Each squadron in rotation takes QRA(I). When a base holds QRA, it is manned 24 hours a day throughout the two to six week period, with two fully armed aircraft held at ten minutes readiness. Only the pilot's master switch and trigger pressure are required for firing the missiles. Scrambled aircraft are immediately replaced on the line. The four aircrew members remain in the 'Q-sheds' – the Hardened Aircraft Shelters (HAS) which house the QRA fighters – for 24 hours, and the

No 43 Sqn FG.1 (XV 575/'M') at Chivenor, 7 August 1971, without unit emblem. Colours are (BS381C references): Dark Green 641, Dark Sea Grey 638, Light Aircraft Grey 627

OPPOSITE TOP
No 43 Sqn FG.1 (XV 573/'L') at Leuchars. RAF Phantom squadron colours have been carried on the nose by Nos 2, 14, 23, 29, 31, 41 and 111 and on the intake cheeks by Nos 17, 19, 43, 56 and 92 Sqns

RIGHT
No 43 Sqn FG.1 with a Lightning F.1A to the left. From 1969, No 43 Sqn operated as part of the Leuchars Lightning swing, until joined by No 111 Sqn with Phantoms in 1975. Note the nitrogen cylinders for the tyres

BELOW RIGHT
No 43 Sqn's FG.1s carry its Fighting Cock in a white disc on the fin, and black and white checks. About 1972, RAF Phantom tail stripes varied; swept, unswept, some red/white/blue, others red/blue and some white bordered

seven groundcrew for a week. A third crew waits at home. Every second is vital in the interception and identification of a potentially hostile intruder before it can fly within stand-off range. The declared time of ten minutes to take-off is normally bettered by several minutes.

The Southern sector squadrons are tasked with intercepting aircraft coming from the Baltic and central European areas, and with the air defence of the Southwest and Western approaches, in addition to providing a 'backing' force for the Northern squadrons. Nos 29 and 64 Sqns at Coningsby essentially cover East Anglia and the Home counties from attack. In war it would be from the Baltic and NATO's Central Region that the heaviest threat would come, in terms of aircraft numbers and frequency.

No 43 Sqn was the first RAF air defence squadron to form in the UKADR, in 1969, and remained the only one until late 1974. No 43 Sqn

formally disbanded as a Hunter FGA9 unit in Aden on 14 October 1967, ceasing active operations on 7 November. Beginning to fly from Leuchars in July 1969, No 43 Sqn reformed at Leuchars on 1 September 1969 under Wg Cdr I R 'Hank' Martin as the RAF's first Phantom FG.1 unit and first Phantom air defence unit, a double first which further extended the squadron's record number of firsts in operating types. No 43 Sqn was effectively the substitute for the unformed second RN operational Phantom FG.1 squadron. Its aircraft were FG.1s taken over from the RN's order, and its first aircrews were trained on No 767 Sqn's Phantom FG.1s at Yeovilton, rather than at No 228 OCU which used FGR.2s and was geared primarily for strike/attack. Most subsequent aircrews were trained by No 767 Sqn until August 1972 when the Phantom Training Flight took over the task at Leuchars. When the PTF disbanded in May 1978, No 228 OCU assumed the task, having concentrated upon air defence since 1974–75.

On 19 September 1969, No 43 Sqn's standard

was handed over from RAF College Cranwell at the official reformation ceremony. During September 1969, No 43 Sqn's four pilots and three navigators flew 41 sorties. The squadron continued an intensive operational work-up, with further aircrew arriving, and was declared fully operational on 1 July 1970.

No 43 Sqn was tasked with the air defence of the Northern Sector of the UKADR, with an assignment to SACLANT for the Tactical Air Support of Maritime Operations (TASMO). This involves maritime air defence to cover any RN or NATO task forces in the North Sea, in conjunction with tankers, by flying CAPs and intercepts, involving long sorties to distant patrol lines. No 43 Sqn worked as part of the Leuchars

An FG.1 of No 43 Sqn, in company with two USAF F-4Cs of the 57th Fighter Interceptor Squadron from Iceland, intercept a Soviet Tu-20 Bear long-range maritime reconnaissance bomber. The Northern UKADR receives more trade than any other NATO sector

Lightning air defence force, with Nos 11 and 23 Sqns, until joined by No 111 Sqn, the RAF's second Phantom air defence unit, in November 1975. Leuchars, in 1969, was scheduled to become the main base in the UK for the Phantom FG.1, both RAF and RN. It was to house all Strike Command's air defence squadrons eventually, with two further Phantoms squadrons to form there in 1970–71, the Lightning squadrons based there then deploying to Binbrook. However, the plans were revised.

No 43 Sqn mounted IAF for the first time with Phantoms on 23 March 1970. The following month, it intercepted and shadowed Soviet aircraft in the Faroes area during the Soviet Naval Spring Exercises, a task which emphasized the capabilities of the Phantom's weapon system and ability to operate at extended ranges from base. In November 1970, No 43 Sqn made its first interception of a Soviet *Bear* from IAF, a task which has since dominated the squadron's activities. Shortly before this interception, eight of the squadron's Phantoms had deployed to Luqa, Malta and from there to Akrotiri for APC. The squadron has since deployed overseas at least two or three times each year.

No 43 Sqn was the RAF's first Phantom air defence squadron, and as such was in the forefront of developing tactics and procedures, designed to optimize use of the radar and heavy armament; air combat techniques were developed to suit the Phantom's greatly advanced capability but poorer handling compared to previous British fighters. The crews progressively built up experience and developed interception techniques to match the advanced performance of the Phantoms and its new concept weapons system. Trials were carried out in a wide range of conditions which simulated those likely to be encountered in war. After careful analysis of the results, the squadron prepared basic guidelines for the use of the Phantom's radar interception modes which proved invaluable to later air defence Phantom squadrons. The RAF flew Meteors, Hunters, Javelins and Lightnings in pairs, and in RAF Phantom operations the basic number is also two, a fighting pair, after which there is no co-ordination in air combat. However, the RAF does not operate the USN's 'loose deuce'. Air combat techniques are developed by drawing upon the experiences and development of other nations, and by the analysis of actual wars, but this is very much a circular process. Nevertheless, air combat procedures are contained in standard NATO documents.

In recognition of No 43 Sqn's development work, ACM Sir Andrew Humphrey, C-in-C Strike Command presented the Wilkinson Sword Battle of Britain Memorial Sword for 1972 to No 43 Sqn at HQ Strike Command on Wednesday, 7 February 1973. The sword, presented to the RAF

in October 1970, is awarded annually to the unit adjudged to have made the most valuable contribution to the development of operational tactics.

No 43 Sqn was also tasked with providing the Strike Command solo aerobatic display Phantom from its formation until the end of 1978, and again from the start of the 1981 season, principally because of the emphasis placed upon performance by the air defence role. This is a diverse task. For instance, FG.1 XV579/R demonstrated at the RAF Binbrook Open Day in July 1974, displayed individually at the Annual International Air Day at RAF St Mawgan, Cornwall on 6 August 1974, and was the squadron's representative at the American Bicentennial celebrations on 4 July 1976 at RAF Mildenhall, Suffolk. Crews are allocated for a season on the basis of their flying skill; in 1976, Sqn Ldr Ian MacFayden and Flt Lt Norman Browne were the crew. XV579/R, with this crew, displayed on the weekend of 5/6 June 1976 at Leuchars when No 43 Sqn celebrated its sixtieth anniversary with Open Days and a gathering of past and present squadron members.

As the Jaguar replaced the Phantom FGR.2 in the FBSA roles in Nos 6, 54 and 41 Sqns in No 38 Group, freeing the Phantom for air defence duties, the RAF gradually replaced the Lightnings of Nos 23, 29, 56 and 111 Sqns with the more effective, more appropriate two-seat Phantom in the air defence role in the UK between 1974 and 1976. Further Phantoms became available as the Jaguar replaced the Phantoms in Nos 2, 14, 17 and 31 Sqns in RAFG in 1975–76. Each of the disbanded Lightning squadrons reforming on Phantoms worked-up at Coningsby in turn as a position became available, moving to an operational base vacated by the next Lightning unit to disband. After UK requirements were near completion, RAFG's Lightning interceptor squadrons, Nos 19 and 92, re-equipped with Phantom FGR.2s in 1977. The tactics and procedures developed by No 43 Sqn provided a ready source for the new AD-Phantom squadrons, assisting operational work-up. One Lightning squadron, No 74 Sqn, had disbanded in Singapore in 1971, as a result of the withdrawal of the British presence in the Far East, and was not reformed. Nos 5 and 11 Sqns continue to operate Lightnings.

The first RAF Strike Command FGR.2 air defence squadron, No 111 (Designate) Sqn (AD-Phantom) formed on Monday, 1 July 1974 as a No 11 Group Lodger Unit at Coningsby, beginning the run-down of the Lightning in the air defence role. On 30 September 1974, No 111 Sqn (AD-Lightning) disbanded at Wattisham, and the squadron standard was handed over at a ceremony there to No 111 (Designate) Sqn, which dropped the caveat (Designate) and was retitled No 111

Sqn the following day, 1 October. Many of No 111 Sqn's aircraft and some of its aircrews and ground crews came from No 54 Sqn, a Coningsby-based Phantom FGR.2 ground attack unit, which had disbanded on 29 March 1974; No 111 Sqn effectively took its place at Coningsby. No 111 Sqn became fully operational in early 1974. On 1 October 1974, a second Phantom FGR.2 squadron, No 29, had formed at Coningsby, the two squadrons briefly forming the Coningsby air defence force. However, on 3 November 1974, No 111 Sqn transferred to Leuchars, replacing No 23 Sqn which had disbanded there as a Lightning air defence unit on 31 October 1974, in turn reforming at Coningsby as a Phantom FGR.2 unit in the place vacated by No 111 Sqn.

The Phantoms at Leuchars are kept at a high state of readiness at all times. Either No 111 Sqn or No 43 Sqn have a pair of fully armed Phantoms at ten minutes notice to take-off every hour of every day and night all year round. At times of heavy Soviet air activity, there have been occasions when almost all the base's aircraft have been armed and despatched on QRA assignments one by one. The Phantoms fly sorties of up to four hours' duration with Victor tanker support. Under Wg Cdr Don Read, CO between October 1978

Crew board FGR.2 of No 111 Sqn, whose insignia is three black sea axes crosswise on a black-outlined yellow cross over two red crossed swords, on a white disc. The lightning flash is black, edged yellow

No 111 Sqn FG.1s, the RWR fairings bearing the unit colours, black, edged yellow. Unusually, F had ILS but not RWR, concurrent modifications; it may be ex-PTF. No 111 Sqn re-equipped with FG.1s after the RN paid-off Ark Royal

Highly sculptural study of a Phantom FG.1 from No 892
Sqn being prepared for launch from the carrier HMS Ark
Royal

*King (foreground) and Queen: two Phantom FG.1s from
No 892 Sqn appropriately decorated for the Royal Naval
Review in September 1977*

A Phantom FGR.2 (XV432/'L') of No 54 Sqn at RAF Coningsby in the early 1970s wearing 'Type A' markings. The historic landmark of Tattershall Castle is visible in the background, behind a 6 Sqn aircraft (left)

Sharkmouthed Phantom FGR.2 of No 56 Sqn looks ready for anything

Phantom FG.1 (XT595, the YF-4K1 prototype) in use as an instructional airframe at RAF Coningsby. Never on RAF charge, this aircraft was delivered to the MoD(PE) in 1968

ABOVE RIGHT Leuchars-based Phantom FG.1 (XT863/'G') of No 111 ('Treble One') Sqn on display at RAF Greenham Common in 1983. This aircraft served consistently with No 892 Sqn, FAA, until November 1978. It was transferred directly to Treble One

The fin of a No 29 Sqn FGR.2 showing RWR and ILS antenna

RIGHT Taken at Wattisham in June 1980, this toned-down Phantom FGR.2 (XV474/'F') is on the strength of No 23 Sqn at the time of writing, based at RAF Stanley in the Falkland Islands

This 'Alcock and Brown' Phantom FGR.2 flew the Atlantic in 1979 to mark the 60th anniversary of the world's first non-stop transatlantic flight – and just about everything else. One of the two specially painted F-4Ms attended the International Air Tattoo at RAF Greenham Common

Falklands: a Phantom FGR.2 of No 23 Sqn departs from RAF Stanley in a blaze of reheat

*Phantom FG.1 (XT597, A&AAE) all dressed-up for the
F-4 25th Anniversary Meet at RAF Greenham Common
in 1983·*

*Floodlit Phantom FGR.2 of No 29 Sqn at RAF
Coningsby in January 1979*

and March 1980, No 111 Sqn made an outstanding number of interceptions of Soviet aircraft. The average per week was at least two, but in one week in April 1980 the squadron recorded an incredible one hundred interceptions. 'This squadron has done more interceptions than all other QRA squadrons put together since I have been in command,' commented Read, 'Anything whose track is not known which enters NATO airspace, we intercept.'

No 43 Sqn has operated Phantom FG.1s since its formation. In August–September 1972, No 892 Sqn, RN moved to Leuchars from Yeovilton, and the Phantom Training Flight was established to support No 892 Sqn and No 43 Sqn; both No 892 Sqn and the PTF operated FG.1s. No 111 Sqn initially operated FGR.2s, but subsequently re-equipped with FG.1s. Leuchars thus standardized on the FG.1 for engineering support purposes; it has also been the only RAF FG.1 base. There is no difference between the RAF's FGR.2 and FG.1 in terms of capability in the air defence role. No 111 Sqn was able to fully re-equip with the FG.1 following the cessation of RN Phantom flying. Although No 12 Sqn, RAF reformed at RAF Honington in 1979 on the Buccaneer S.2C and S.2D from *Ark Royal*'s disbanded No 809 Sqn, RN, no new RAF Phantom air defence squadron was formed from No 892 Sqn's FG.1s, as some had expected. Instead, after servicing, modification up to RAF standard, and the removal of certain equipment, such as fast reheat, basically for

engineering support reasons, and a thorough inspection for corrosion, most were issued to No 43 Sqn. No 43 Sqn transferred FG.1s to No 111 Sqn to allow No 111 Sqn's FGR.2s to be released to make up deficiencies in other RAF FGR.2 units, as well as standardizing Leuchars on the FG.1. However, some ex-RN FG.1s were issued directly to No 111 Sqn, and some went directly into store. Since September 1979, by which time the re-allocation was virtually complete, No 43 Sqn has had an aircraft establishment of fifteen FG.1s, with 20 crews, and has operated a mixture of original FG.1s from its early years complemented by FG.1s from the disbanded No 892 Sqn and PTF.

Unlike the other air defence Phantom squadrons which formed and worked-up at Coningsby as Lodger Units before moving, the second to form, No 29 Sqn, remained based there. No 29 (Designate) Sqn (AD-Phantom) formed at Coningsby on 1 October 1974 under Wg Cmdr Lavender AFC, who had relinquished command of No 6 Sqn (FBSA-Phantom) when it disbanded at Coningsby the previous day. No 29 Sqn took over the position vacated by No 6 Sqn at Coningsby. No 29 Sqn's first aircrews consisted of a small number of pilots and navigators from No 6 Sqn, Lightning air defence pilots, and pilots from a large variety of other roles, although most navigators subsequently came from the disbanding RAFG strike/attack squadrons. On 31 December 1974, No 29 Sqn (AD-Lightning) disbanded at

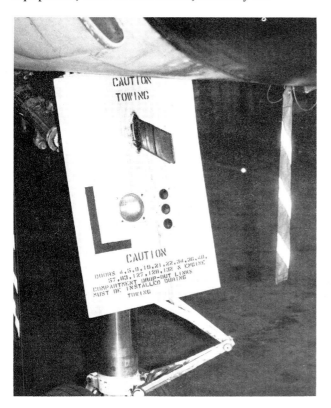

LEFT
No 111 Sqn FG.1's torque link, communications antenna, single taxi light (common to FG.1 and FGR.2), and three approach lights applied only to RN FG.1s

No 111 Sqn FG.1's stabilator slat and hinge point, and the remains of the quadrant applied to RN FG.1s to enable catapult crews to check that the stabilator was set at the correct angle for launch

Loading a Sky Flash onto a No 29 Sqn FGR.2; three fins are fitted afterwards. No 29 Sqn's badge is three red Xs, a red, black-detailed eagle over a black, yellow-detailed buzzard on a red-edged white shield

Wattisham. At a ceremonial parade there, commanded by the outgoing CO, Wg Cdr John D C Hawtin, and reviewed by Air Cdr J P Curtiss, MBIM, SASO No 11 Group, the squadron number plate and standard were handed over to the Phantom unit, which was retitled No 29 Sqn on 1 January 1974. No 29 Sqn was declared fully operational in the air defence role in May 1975, and joined the IAF alongside No 111 Sqn at Coningsby, charged with the defence of the UKADR. No 111 Sqn moved from Coningsby in November 1975 but subsequent air defence Phantom squadrons forming there bolstered the base's interceptor assets during the late phases of their work-ups, while No 228 OCU in the shadow guise of No 64 Sqn is able to act as a second air defence squadron at Coningsby in an emergency.

No 23 (Designate) Sqn (AD-Phantom) formed at Coningsby on 6 October 1975, under Wg Cdr W J Wratten AFC, in the place being vacated by No 111 Sqn. No 23 Sqn (AD-Lightning) disbanded at Leuchars on 31 October 1975, and the following day the Phantom unit took over the squadron number plate and standard at Coningsby. To mark the change over, Lightning XP753 and Phantom XV396/A flew together over Leuchars and then Coningsby, both bearing the squadron's eagle insignia. Several of No 111 Sqn's first crews were from FBSA-Phantom squadrons, others from Lightning air defence squadrons; as

the work-up period to operational status intensified, the respect of the 'ex-Mud Movers' for the 'Scopies' began to grow. The CO declared No 23 Sqn as limited operational on 20 February 1976, and five days later the squadron flew to Wattisham, its operational station: the number of hours flown that day propitiously totalled 23. The Phantoms' arrival was spectacular: eight roared in over Wattisham, and split into two flights of four, each of which made a pass over the airfield before breaking off to land. The eight Phantoms, mainly ex-No 14 Sqn, were XV422/C, the CO's mount and fitted with dual controls and RWR; XV490/G; XV496/H; XV434/J; XV421/B; XV432/D; XV465/E; and, also with dual controls, XT912/K.

As part of the squadron's final work-up to operational status, anti-fast patrol boat missions and air combat training (ACT) were practised. On 14 May 1976, the AOC No 11 Group declared the squadron as fully operational. No 23 Sqn's first APC was held in Malta in November 1976, during which its Phantoms became the first RAF fighters to intercept Soviet-built *Blinders*, in Libyan air force markings, flying from Eastern European air bases. Next year, the squadron became the first

FGR.2 XV396 of No 23 Sqn, whose eagle is red, edged white with black detail, and tail band is red and dark blue squares edged white. FGR.2 nose gear doors carry the serials numerals in black

No 23 Sqn FGR.2, XV490. Pylons, undercarriage legs, wheels, wheel wells, and undercarriage doors are gloss white; the doors have red edges. Radomes were dull matt/semi-gloss black-brown, and now 'Barley Grey'

AD-Phantom unit to go on APC to Akrotiri. No 23 Sqn's air defence tasks specifically included Hi-Medium-Lo profiles against fast and slow targets, visual identification, shadowing, shepherding, maritime support and ECM. QRA activity at Wattisham as a Phantom squadron was less hectic than it had been at Leuchars as a Lightning squadron. On the night of 26/27 January 1978, the first Phantom scramble from Wattisham by the unit which resulted in the successful interception of a Soviet aircraft was launched. No 23 Sqn disbanded in the UK on 30 March 1983, the occasion marked by a flypast of nine Phantoms over Wattisham. It reformed simultaneously in the Falklands, taking over the Phantom FGR.2s of the RAF Phantom Detachment flown out with No 29 Sqn the previous October. The re-allocation of No 23 Sqn's Phantoms in the UK, six to No 56 Sqn at Wattisham, had begun some months earlier in an effort to maintain a balanced capability following the deployment of elements of No 29 Sqn to Ascension and the Falklands during the 1982 Falklands war.

No 56 (Designate) Sqn (AD-Phantom) formed at Coningsby on 31 March 1976, taking over No 23 Sqn's position. It became the last UKADR Phantom squadron to form. Four FGR.2s had appeared at Coningsby in No 56 Sqn markings at the beginning of March: XT909/Y, XV489/F from No 31 Sqn; XV497/G from No 17 Sqn; and

XV470/C from No 2 Sqn. No 56 Sqn (AD-
Lightning) disbanded at Wattisham on 28 June
1976, handing over the squadron standard and
number plate to the Phantom unit which was
retitled No 56 Sqn (AD-Phantom) next day.
Appropriately, No 56 Sqn celebrated its Diamond
Jubilee the same month. No 56 Sqn moved from
Coningsby on 8 July 1976 to replace Lightnings at
Wattisham and join No 23 Sqn to form the
Wattisham Phantom air defence force. It became
fully operational on 13 September 1976.

The work-up of a squadron to full combat ready
status is a hard school for both ground and
aircrews. Air combat, for the AD-Phantom
squadrons, played a major part in the work-up, the
aircrews training to shoot down aircraft thousands
of feet above or below their Phantoms with the
'snap-down/up' facility. Interception of high and
low, fast and slow targets by day or night, in or
beyond visual range, often in an ECM
environment, and including visual identifications at
night, became routine. The ground crews
concentrated upon producing finely tuned radars
and fully operational weapons systems, and
training to cope with several simultaneous turn-
arounds, often in full NBC protective clothing.
Inflight refuelling training was a vital part of the
work-up; for instance, Nos 29 and 111 Sqns
jointly trained with the then new Victor K.2

*No 23 Sqn FGR.2 in the grey low-visibility air defence
scheme, which is semi-matt (eggshell) rather than matt like
the later tactical finish, the drag chute has done its job*

*No 23 Sqn FGR.2. The three greys are (Federal Standard
595A/Methuen): Barley 36314/23(C-D)2; Light Aircraft
Grey 365357/22(C-D)1; Medium Sea Grey 36270/22D3.
Roundels are Pale Red 32356/11A5 and Pale Blue
35450/23A4*

BELOW
*No 23 Sqn FGR.2 in tactical finish with its drag chute
deployed*

tankers of No 232 OCU from RAF Marham, under Wg Cdr J S B Price, although during operations they were supported by Marham's Nos 55 and 57 Sqns.

The responsibility, high cockpit work-load and demanding flying make it essential that Phantom pilots and navigators are among the best of the RAF's aircrews, many with experience of other types. Wg Cdr Read, for instance, CO of No 111 Sqn in 1978–80, was a navigator who had flown Meteors, Vulcans, and Canberras, and was transferred in 1980 to MoD Central Staff Plans. His two No 111 Sqn flight commanders, Sqn Ldr Euan Black and Sqn Ldr Cliff Spink had extensive Lightning air defence experience as well as many Phantom hours, while Black had also served a tour on Canadian CF-101 Voodoos, at Chatham AFB, New Brunswick. Phantom aircrews are versatile: Sqn Ldr George Lee of No 43 Sqn first won the World Gliding Championship in 1976 and has successfully defended his title.

The aircrew tour on a Phantom unit is normally three years, but it is two and a half for squadron COs. A number of exchange tours are designated on a standing programme, although not on a one for one basis; one German, two USAF, one USMC, and one Canadian aircrews are spread between the No 11 Group squadron. Typically, No 43 Sqn has a US aircrew, No 56 Sqn a US and a German crew, and No 29 Sqn a Canadian

crew. Exchanges to the USA are not necessarily type orientated, particularly as US aircraft manufacturers 'buy places' for foreign crews on their new types in the belief that the crew will become advocates of the aircraft in their own country, influentially if they reach decision-making positions! Exchanges in RAFG of aircrews include Vitenhahen and Bremgarten. There are also regular detachments to foreign bases or squadrons to sharpen interoperability, giving the other bases practice and undertaking mutual training.

Phantoms in the UK are purely for UKADR air defence tasks, but two squadrons, Nos 29 and 43, are tasked with maritime air defence, the later since 1970, and are thus assigned to SACLANT. No 29 Sqn, formerly under the command of SACEUR, was assigned to SACLANT on 1 January 1980, the change meaning that the squadron's role was primarily the air defence of maritime forces, with the secondary but still very important role of the air defence of the UK. However, all Phantom squadrons would be assigned to SACEUR in a war, and Nos 29 and 43 are likely to remain in the UK in the event of a major war involving NATO, although they could deploy elsewhere; in fact, No 29 Sqn deployed to Ascension and the Falklands in 1982–83. Although No 43 Sqn uses FG.1s and No 29 Sqn FGR.2s, there is no difference in capability. The mark used is primarily a function of basing. Other Phantom squadrons have a maritime air defence capability.

The only difference between maritime and land air defence is procedure, in that the fighter aircrew must observe naval fleet practices, such as control, and missile and gun arcs: 'once you've hacked the procedures and you're sitting in the cockpit, there is no difference,' commented one navigator. 'It is the AD system which drives the position.' Unlike the layered land system, the sea AD system evolved to counter a 360° threat. Arcs in the perimeter are allocated to fighters, such as Phantoms, others to guns and missiles. As in the. UKADR, the primary air threat to a fleet is from long-range and stand-off bombers against which Phantoms fly CAPs, but the threat differs between Faslane (Northern Scotland) and Germany, for instance, and again in the Western Approaches.

The RAF's Phantoms now fulfill the same function of fleet defence as *Ark Royal*'s No 892 Sqn Phantoms did between 1970–78. A paper requirement for certain 'carrier capability' equipment has existed to permit land-based RAF Phantoms to reinforce NATO carriers. However, RAF Phantom FG.1s and FGR.2s as normal standard have no carrier capability (an exception was the PTF's FG.1s). It would be possible, but impractical, for an RAF FG.1 or FGR.2 to land and take-off from a carrier as long as USS *Nimitz*.

There has been co-operation with the USAFE in the UK, particularly with the F-5Es of the 227th Tactical Fighter Training Aggressor Sqn and there is a great deal of co-operation in Germany with other NATO squadrons. However, no USAFE aircraft in the UK are in the air defence role and all USAFE F-4s in the UK are allocated to other roles. In the event of war, however, if SACEUR based USAFE AD squadrons from Germany in the UK, they would integrate with RAF AD squadrons, and contingency plans for such integration exist. Air defence procedures are contained in NATO documents, promulgated by CINCUKAIR, and are therefore available to all USAF forces, and thus USAFE forces could swiftly integrate into the UKADR if allocated.

The Phantom is still a magnificent weapons system. Although now dating, it remains a very capable aircraft in the air defence role, particularly for the UKADR where fighters are less of a threat. It has been continually improved, with updated radar and digital weapons control system, ECM, RWR, and other retrofitted equipment. It can carry as many weapons and use them as effectively as the most modern aircraft, such as the F-14, F-15 and F-18. The F-15 is a superior fighter, and wins in a straight combat, although the Phantom can win by confusing it. Tornado F.2 has greater weapons capability and endurance and will be much more capable in the UKADR air defence role, as would the comparable F-14.

The results of two early 1970s development programmes by Westinghouse were combined to create the improved AWG-10A, -11A and -12A. The UK customer is Ferranti acting for the UK Government. The first modification programme, initiated in 1971, was a reliability and maintainability improvement programme, and the second involves the substitution of a modern digital computer and improved displays for the analogue computer delivered with the equipment. The work has been closely related to Sky Flash's introduction, to improve the effectiveness of weapon delivery. Six completely new LRUs are added, seven deleted and nineteen modified in varying degrees. Only three remain unchanged. A new optical sight is incorporated and one air-to-air and three air-to-ground modes are added to the basic system's ten. Improved maintenance capability results from the new digital BITE mode. The modifications increased the systems' close air-to-air combat capability, primarily as a result of increased computer speed and accuracy, the use of a digital computer enabling the pulse-Doppler radar to be fully exploited. In 1975, the modified systems were hailed as 'the most advanced weapons control systems available to the Free World.'

For the air defence role with which the Phantom was tasked from 1974, a much larger number of missiles was needed than the stocks of AIM-7E-2 procured for self-defence in the FBSA roles. The Air Staff also sought to improve the Phantom's operational effectiveness by taking advantage of technological progress, and accordingly issued an Air Staff Target in January 1972 for an improved MRAAM. In the 1970s, it was considered that the missiles required for fighter defence against the foreseeable air threat must exploit the aircraft's inherent flexibility and performance, where it is most cost-effective to build performance into the missile rather than the aircraft.

Feasibility studies conducted by British industry in collaboration with RAE concluded that an AIM-7 with repackaged control and power sections and using the mono-pulse seeker head developed by Marconi and the radar proximity fuse developed by EMI would be the most cost-effective and quickest solution to the AST. This was designated Project XJ521, and formed the basis for an Air Staff Requirement issued in January 1973. This recognized the need to

No 111 Sqn FGR.2, recently redeployed from tactical duties, at Coningsby in 1974 displaying its comprehensive AD armament: medium range AIM-7E-2s, short range AIM-9Ds, and close range SUU-23/A with 100 of its 1,200 20 mm rounds

No 56 Sqn FGR.2 armed with Sky Flash, externally identical to the AIM-7E-2, except for the black proximity fuse antenna strips on its forebody

optimise future MRAAM performance against the air threat to the UK and its maritime forces, assessed as primarily a low-level, possibly stand-off threat. The ASR called for a high kill capability and full engagement capability at all altitudes in clear and ECM environments and against closely spaced groups of targets, and for snap-down/up capability, and for improvements in specific characteristics of AIM-7E-2. The AIM-7E-2 airframe was selected because the new missile had to be compatible with the Phantom's semi-recessed AIM-7 installation, and had to be in service in the shortest possible time. Project definition was completed in July 1973. HS Dynamics (now BAeD) was selected as the prime contractor with MSDS and EMI as subcontractors. HSD negotiated a licence with Raytheon for manufacture of the AIM-7E-2 airframe. The project was approved to enter full production on 1 December 1973.

The trials programme, almost equally divided between R&D and service evaluation firings, was conducted between November 1975 and December 1977 at the Pacific Missile Test Centre (PMTC), Point Magu, Ca., and the Naval Test Centre (NTC), China Lake, in collaboration with the USN. UKMoD hired two USN F-4Js, equipped with AN/AWG-10A MCS, for the trials. One of the pilots was Wg Cdr B W Lavender AFC, ex-

Nos 6 and 29 Sqns CO. The overall test results were outstandingly good. Of the 22 pre-production missiles launched, sixteen resulted in target kills, half direct hits. The proximity fuse had a 100 per cent success rate. No warheads were fitted, the warhead section housing telemetry equipment. The targets, QF-86, QF-4, BQM-34 and QT-35, represented a range of hostile aircraft, some enhanced to represent the radar echoing area of a specific type of target, others to produce severe radar glint, to realistically test the accuracy of the missile's guidance. Firings were also made in exacting ECM and target manoeuvring conditions, including multiple targets, and low-flying snap-down attacks.

Production deliveries began in 1977 and Sky Flash achieved full operational status in 1979. On 15 August 1979, a No 29 Sqn RAF Phantom FGR.2 successfully carried out the first UK firing of Sky Flash over the Aberporth closed test range. Flying at 20,000 ft at 350 kt, it shot down a radio-controlled Meteor drone which was flying at a lower altitude at 400 kt. In September 1980, No 23 Sqn was involved in the successful Sky Flash

The AIM-9D (illustrated), has been superceded by the all-aspect AIM-9L, distinguished by double-delta forward fins. This weathered, grey No 56 Sqn FGR.2 carries an F-15 'kill', rare for an F-4!

firing trials in the UK. Sky Flash is used concurrently with AIM-7E-2, of which large stocks remain, and equips Tornado F.2.

Like Sparrow, Sky Flash is a semi-active radar guided, medium range, boost and coast missile with moving wings and fixed fins. It is designed for all-weather, all-round attack against subsonic, supersonic, and close evading targets, and for multiple target attacks, from very low to very high altitudes. It can be carried and launched at supersonic and subsonic speeds. It has a snap-down capability against evading targets at low level in high clutter conditions and a snap-up capability against high flying targets from low launch. It has ECCM capability and is effective in ECM and other countermeasures environments.

A comparison of all known Phantom combat air kills up to early 1983 shows that AIM-9 is the most successful weapon with 96 victories, followed by AIM-7 with 64, cannon with $22\frac{1}{2}$, and AIM-4 Falcon with four; a further 91 victories fell to undetermined weapons. The third generation of AIM-9 Sidewinder, the AIM-9L, began to supercede the AIM-9D on UK Phantoms in the late 1970s. It is a considerable improvement over earlier, tail-only attack, easily distracted models, from which it differs in having an all aspect attack capability. Several internal changes significantly increase the firing envelope, including a new all-

aspect IR homing head using AM-FN conical scan, providing increased seeker sensitivity and tracking stability. An internal, Argon coolant pressure tank (TMU-72B) is provided for the seeker, although USN and UK Phantoms have a coolant container in the launcher, unlike USAF F-4s. A new active optical laser fuse (DSU-15B), coupled with the 25 lb (11.4 kg) WDU-17B annular blast fragmentation warhead, increases lethality. Externally, it has reconfigured control surfaces, which, together with the larger firing envelope, enhance dogfight capability. Trials gave AIM-9L a 90 per cent success rate when fired within its launch parameters, an assessment confirmed by the RN's Sea Harriers in the bad weather conditions of the 1982 Falklands war. Bodenseewerk is the prime contractor for a West German/Norwegian/Italian/British consortium to licence produce the AIM-9L. BAeD, Bolton Division has produced the guidance and control units and other sections. Bodensewerk delivers the assemblies to clients, including the RAF, who do the integration.

Phantom aircrews posted to squadrons directly

from No 228 OCU are given about a further 30
hours on the Phantom to enable them to acquire
the expertise and precision of fully operational
crews. They practise interceptions at all altitudes
from 45,000 to 250 ft, or, formerly in FBSA
squadrons, ground attack profiles and escort
formations, before being declared operational
several weeks later, and after which they can go on
QRA. A navigator may not be declared fully
operational for some months after posting to a
squadron. His tasks are vital. In addition to
navigation, he is responsible for briefing and de-
briefing, pre-flight pilot and navigator cockpit
checks, systems monitoring, CAP management, air
and sea target identification, single and multi-
target intercepts, and ECM. If heavy enemy ECM
were to jam ground radars, he would have to use
his radar to effect interception. Perhaps more than
these, a second pair of eyes and a second brain
enhances the survivability of the aircrew markedly.
Fully experienced aircrews continue to practise air
combat techniques regularly, and the inevitable
rivalry between the aircrews aids in keeping
standards high.

Major air defence exercises are held about every
three months. They have a high degree of realism
to actual war. 'Enemy' aircraft are supplied by
NATO nations, the Aggressors, and other RAF
squadrons. The exercises include fighter control
and direction procedures, ECM from attackers and
defenders, air combat and inflight refuelling.
During April 1980, Exercise ELDER FOREST
took place, the largest flying exercise staged since
World War II, during which simulated enemy
aircraft probed the air defences of the entire
UKADR, and attacked every major UKADGE
installation and base.

Each Phantom squadron goes out to Akrotiri,
Cyprus each year for air-to-air gunnery at
Armament Practice Camp, which lasts between
four and six weeks. Cyprus has ideal, clear
conditions for ACM and interceptions and is close
to extensive over sea ranges. APC covers not only
live cannon firing, but also provides training in
out-of-area deployments in support of NATO
commitments. Targets are towed 300 ft behind a
Canberra, and each Phantom pilot flies cine-
camera sorties until he consistently demonstrates
he has the required safety parameters of range and
angle-off. The squadron QWI tests the pilot with

*An F-4J launches a Sky Flash in a successful snap-
down attack on a BQ-33 target drone during the Point
Mugu trials*

*Sky Flash's semi-active monopulse radar seeker greatly
improved its performance over AIM-7E-2, especially
against accompanied or ECM-screened targets. Its radar
proximity fuse detects a target in lethal range and fires the
warhead*

No 56 Sqn's checks are red and white, its emblem a black-edged yellow phoenix rising from black-edged, orange and red shaded fire. A navigator's rear-view mirror has been added to AD Phantoms

live rounds against the target banner before the pilot flies six academic shoots to gain SACEUR qualification, based on a percentage of hits made against rounds fired. No 23 Sqn was the first AD-Phantom squadron to do an APC at Akrotiri, in August 1978. Regular missile firing practice is undertaken off the North Wales and the North-East Scottish coasts. The annual Missile Practice Camp at RAF Valley, the Strike Command Air Missile Establishment, permits each crew to fire a live AAM on the Aberporth range.

There are a number of Trophies awarded in recognition of achievements in training. The Seed Trophy is awarded annually to the air defence squadron achieving the best results in air-to-air gunnery during APC. The first Trophy was awarded to No 111 Sqn in 1979 for a score of over 25 per cent against the banner. No 43 Sqn, during APC in May–June 1979, achieved the highest score against the target ever attained by a Phantom squadron, winning the Trophy, with Nos 23 and 111 Sqns second and third. The d'Acre Trophy is awarded annually by AOC No 11 Group, RAF Strike Command to the squadron which has made the most significant contribution to overall air defence efficiency during the year, including missile and gun firing at APC, flight safety, aircraft recognition, response to alerts, and overall aircraft serviceability. No 43 Sqn won it in 1977. In May 1980, it was announced that No 23 Sqn had won the d'Acre Trophy for the fourth time, having won in in 1967, 1969 and 1975 when flying Lightnings. The Aberporth Trophy is awarded annually to the squadron achieving the best results in overall conduct at missile camp. No 43 Sqn

won it in 1976. In 1980, when the squadron was at missile practice NBC camp at Valley, it was announced that No 29 Sqn had been awarded the Aberporth Trophy for 1979–80. In May 1981, No 29 Sqn was also awarded the Sky Flash Trophy, mainly due to the work of the ground crews. This is awarded for the best performance for the operational turn round of a squadron's aircraft.

While overseas and UK deployments for APC, exercises and affiliation training are a regular part of a squadron's activities, other deployments may be made for specific purposes. For instance, in April 1977, No 23 Sqn deployed to a USAF dispersed field, RAF Wethersfield, 30 miles from Wattisham, to permit runway resurfacing to be carried out at Wattisham. It operated from Wethersfield until returning to Wattisham on 16 November 1977. No 43 Sqn deployed to Kinloss in April 1979 while Leuchars' runways were refurbished, although it redeployed to Akrotiri for a six-week APC at the end of the month.

Currently the usual range of rapid redeployment arrangements exist as contingency plans, both in the UK and in support of NATO and British out-of-area commitments, in which Phantoms would be deployed as appropriate. No particular squadrons are assigned to a rapid redeployment force. Stornoway in the Hebrides is available as an FOB for maritime support of Northern UKADR QRA operations, and Phantoms operating in

No 56 Sqn FGR.2 with muted badge on the nose and checks on the RWR fairing, and red code on the rudder. Typically, RWR's front and rear antenna, and V/UHF antenna on top, are matt light or dark brown/brown-black, and ILS localiser/glide path blades gloss white with black leading edges

Another No 56 Sqn FGR.2 (XV492), devoid of all markings except for SACLANT insignia on intake and serial

support of SACLANT can be deployed to bases in Southwest England. Other bases can be used in an emergency Southwest.

The Falkland Islands

Early in the 1982 Falklands War, a Phantom squadron, No 29, was selected to deploy in support of operations. The RAF wanted and received little publicity during the War. This gave the impression that it was largely an RN/RM/Army affair: the RAF's role was vital. Wideawake airfield on Ascension, off the West coast of Africa, was an essential link for the forces en route and deployed to the Falklands, 8,000 miles from the UK. Ascension and the sea routes to the Falklands were logical targets for the Argentinians. The threat of the carrier *Veinticinco de Mayo* launching strikes against Ascension or British warships and supply vessels en route to the Falklands could not be discounted. Long range maritime surveillance of sealanes, a capability demonstrated by the Argentinians, and reconnaissance of Ascension had to be discouraged. The possibility of a commando raid flown in by Hercules to Ascension could not be entirely dismissed. Therefore, elements of No 29 Sqn, at least three Phantoms, deployed to

Wideawake to provide air defence and maritime support, and to form the nucleus of an AD unit to be maintained both on Ascension and on the Falklands. The choice of No 29 Sqn was logical, given its maritime support orientation. The reconquest of the Falklands themselves brought the War with Argentina to an end before No 29 Sqn could deploy to the Falklands.

In October 1982, No 29 Sqn's Phantoms replaced the Sea Harriers of No 809 NAS, from HMS *Illustrious*, as the Falklands air defence element, introducing a more appropriate, greatly improved capability, an ironic reflection upon the P.1154 saga. The Phantoms are charged with the air defence of the 200-mile total exclusion zone, and maritime support, but flights have been made along the edge of Argentinian air space. A few Hercules tankers are based at Stanley directly in support of AD operations, vital to give the ability to patrol for several hours and cover a large sector of the protection zone in one sortie. The threat is partly stand-off from Argentina's Super Etendards with Exocet missiles. Argentina also has Lockheed Electras for maritime patrol, Trackers for strike direction, and a strong force of Mirages and Daggers. The Phantoms can carry the versatile SUU-23/A, so they have an air-to-ground strafe capability, and could be used against fast patrol boats or amphibious craft. No 1 Sqn's Harrier GR.3s remain at Stanley for close support, armed with AIM-9L for self-defence, although it was assumed the squadron would return to the UK after the Phantoms arrived. The Harriers can disperse to other sites. No 29 Sqn also retained a detachment on Ascension, and Phantom numbers can be floated between the UK, Ascension and the Falklands, or supplemented at short notice.

Stanley became the major airbase from the liberation, with Sea Harriers and Harriers operating from it before the runway was rebuilt and Hercules operations began. Stanley is the most heavily defended RAF base anywhere, because the Argentinians have not renounced the use of force to retake the Falklands. It is protected by RAF Regt Blindfire and Rapier units. Rapid deployment reinforcement capability and regular exercises make it more formidable.

RIGHT
*A No 23 Sqn FGR.2 at RAF Stanley in the Falklands, with the Falklands Arms featuring a white hornless ram on green tussac grass in the blue upper half, and two blue navy bands (sea) and a gold sailing ship (*Desire, *discover of the islands), with five red stars on the mainsail (*Southern Cross*) in the white lower half of the badge*

FGR.2s of No 23 Sqn on Operational Readiness at RAF Stanley. In June 1983, it was announced that a new, permanent airport is to be built on the Falklands

Conditions are primitive, despite great improvements in the first nine months of service, and life is difficult and rough. Aircrews, groundcrews and staff work seven days a week, living in Nissen huts with continuous CAPs and QRAs, the alerts called by megaphone, reminiscent of 1940s airfields. Port Stanley's runway and facilities required considerable work to operate Phantoms. The day it was recaptured, the Royal Engineers began to repair and lengthen the runway by 2,000 ft to 6,100 ft. The runway was constructed of AM2 reinforced runway matting to enable Phantoms to operate from it for about three

years. The runway was completed a few days before the first Phantom arrived, in an astonishing four months, the last AM2 slabs being slotted in just before it landed. Several sets of RHAG were installed at Stanley with either rapid or gradual deceleration, to shorten the landing run, minimise the wear on brakes, a logistic benefit, and to speed up the operational turnaround. They can be used in either direction, and the Phantoms always land with them.

The first Phantom in, XV468 was ferried from Coningsby via Ascension. It was flown by No 29 Sqn's CO, Wg Cdr Ian MacFayden, and his navigator, Sqn Ldr Peter Simpson. MacFayden is no stranger to long range maritime operations, being an ex-No 43 Sqn pilot. The 4,000 mile flight from Ascension took 8 hours 45 minutes. The Phantom was refuelled by Victor K.2 tankers out of Ascension seven times, to give a safety margin. It performed a victory roll before touching down at Stanley on 17 October 1982, and being pulled up inside 700 feet by the RHAG. Re-armed and refuelled, it was handed over to Flt Lt Andy Maddox and his navigator Lt Peter Grey, who took-off to fly the Phantom's first sortie from Stanley. It was the first of an undisclosed number of Phantoms deployed to Stanley, others including

An FGR.2 of No 23 Sqn with AIM-9Ls, replenished its tanks from a Hercules tanker off the Falklands above the South Atlantic

XV402, XV419, XV423, XV426, XV464, XV466, XV474, and XV484. Predictably, on 18 October 1982, the USSR condemned the deployment, charging the UK that it was part of a plan to build up a major South Atlantic military base.

But the UKADR could not afford to loose a squadron, so No 29 Sqn was called the Phantom Detachment (No 29 Sqn continuing to run in the UK as well as the Falklands). The way it was manned was changed too, personnel rotating from all UK Phantom squadrons to spread the load throughout No 11 Group, and because the living conditions were poor. Aircrew do a five month door-to-door tour, effectively four months. However, the Phan Det represented a burden on UKADR which it could not sustain without major changes to NATO commitments, and effectively meant cancelling a UKADR squadron. Therefore, in early 1983 it was decided to establish a squadron number plate, No 23, in the Falklands, but to continue to rotate air and ground crews from all UK squadrons, while No 29 Sqn moved back fully to Coningsby, and No 23 Sqn disbanded in the UK. Thus, the Phan Det was redesignated No 23 Sqn on 30 March 1983, with the same Phantoms, and No 23 Sqn officially disbanded at Wattisham the same day.

This position had been stated in the Services' post-Falklands requests for replacement and new equipment. As a result, UKMoD entered into negotiations with the US Government for the purchase of at least eight ex-USN F-4s, to replace those deployed in the Falklands. The decision to purchase 'at least 12 F-4Js to form a squadron for the air defence of the UK to replace the squadron of Phantom FGR.2s committed to the South Atlantic' was announced in the White Paper *The Falklands Campaign: The Lessons*, published on 14 December 1982. In early 1983, the US Department of Defense released more specific details, although negotiations had to be finalized. The RAF was to receive fifteen ex-USN F-4Js from the US Government at a cost of $51 million (£33 million), a unit cost of £2.2 million, not far from that of the original F-4K and M!

The selection of the F-4J was logical. The F-4K and M were based upon the J, and its airframe and radar are compatible with those of the F-4K and M to a greater degree than those of other variants. It is essentially an air defence aircraft, which meets RAF requirements. It is also available, because it had largely been replaced in the USN by the F-14 by 1982, serving only in the Pacific Fleet. But the F-4Js lack commonality with the UK Phantoms in many respects. The RAF does not operate any J79-powered aircraft, but there was no possibility of re-equipping the F-4Js with Speys; nor with the PW1120 turbofan which Pratt & Whitney proposed as a replacement for J79s in F-4s in 1983, meeting interest from several

operators. Wheels, brakes, tyres and several systems are, however, identical, and the F-4J has the AWG-10A MCS. The F-4Js are based together for logistic and engineering support purposes, but are run on the same basis in other respects as the F-4K and M, with supplies from the USN or direct from McDonnell Douglas, and with no USAFE involvement. To distinguish them, they are designated Phantom F-4J(UK), and are solely AD. They form one AD squadron, thus restoring UKADR to its strength prior to No 29 Sqn's overseas deployment. The decision upon which squadron deployed them was taken at a very high level, involving RAF AD plans into the 1990s.

Phantoms will continue to serve as front-line air defence fighters with the RAF into the 1990s, but the sophisticated and integrated European air defence system envisaged for that period is likely to render them obsolete by reason of incompatibility. The UKADR Phantom force will be run down from 1986 with the introduction of Tornado F.2; the Phantoms may then be re-assigned to FBSA roles.

Under NATO's 'trip wire' policy, the UKADGE system had been oriented towards the defence of the UK's nuclear retaliatory V-bomber capability in the 1960s. It had been realised by the mid-1970s that it would be unable to meet the range of threats forecast for the 1980s and 1990s, and was inappropriate for conventional war against such aircraft as the Tu-22M. A programme was initiated to provide less vulnerable radars giving all-round cover at medium and high altitudes over the UK land mass and its immediate approaches and specialist surface-wave radars to give low-level cover, improved ECM and ECCM capability, and an extensively modernized, more secure communications system. An advanced digitised, highly-automated air defence system, the improved UKADGE will provide a real-time recognition air picture at ADOC and all SOC and Control and Reporting Centres to increase the flexibility of directing interceptions. The UKADGE information system feeds into MoD's secure, survivable integrated communications system, UNITER, and will be integrated with the NATO system, the UKADGE will be fully upgraded by the late 1980s. In an effort to increase the UKADR's deterent value immediately, all combat aircraft bases were hardened to cope with any enemy aircraft which breeches the defences; tactical and AD aircraft operate from HAS, while larger aircraft rely on dispersal for protection.

A White Paper published on 25 June 1981 stated: 'Air defence ground radar and communications systems are being extensively modernised. Stocks of modern air-to-air missiles are to be more than doubled and surface-to-air missile covers improved. . . . It is however

'Somewhere in Britain . . . 'aircrews scramble to their QRA Phantom FGR.2s

essential to provide more United Kingdom-based fighters. Two Phantom squadrons will be retained instead of being phased out as Tornado F.2 comes in. For local air defence, a further 36 (making 73 in all) of our Hawk advanced trainer aircraft will be equipped with Sidewinder air-to-air missiles. We are also considering whether to switch to the air defence configuration the last 20 Tornadoes in the strike (GR.1) version.' On 1 July 1982, Mr John Nott announced in the Commons that a total of 70 Tornado F.2s were on order.

The air defence Tornado F.2 is due to enter RAF service in 1986. Nos 23 and 56 Sqns are to be retained with Phantoms, at Wattisham and possibly the Falklands, probably assigned to SACLANT, to bolster the Tornado AD force,

while a decision was subsequently taken in early 1983 that Nos 19 and 92 Sqns in RAFG will also be run-on. This is not a real increase, but a result of a 1974–79 Labour Government decision, perpetuated by the following Conservative administration, to slow down Tornado deliveries by a third to spread the cost over more years. The Tornadoes and Phantoms together will, however, increase the UKADR's fighter assets to over 120; of these, the usual proportion will be unserviceable at any given time. There is limited provision for replacements for aircraft which would be lost in the event of war.

Chapter 12
Royal Air Force Germany: Air Defence

RAFG's national commitment is the responsibility for maintaining the integrity of the Northern half of West Germany's national air space, which includes the Air Defence Identification Zone which is a buffer zone along the East/West German border, the corridors to Berlin and an area of the North Sea out to meet the UKADR. RAFG's air defence forces are also assigned to the operational control of SACEUR to support NATO exercises and operations.

Since the 1960s, RAFG has had two air defence units. In 1965, Nos 19 and 92 Sqn equipped with Lightnings moved from RAF Leconfield to Geilinkirchen, and replaced RAFG's Javelin FAW.9 squadrons, Nos 5 and 11. Nos 19 and 92 Sqns were RAFG's first supersonic fighter unit. In January 1968, they moved to Gutersloh, 80 miles (130 km) from the East German border, for greater effectiveness.

Shortly after the FBSA Phantom squadrons disbanded, Nos 19 and 92 (Designate) Sqns (AD-Phantom), formed at Wildenrath on 30 December 1976 and 1 January 1977 respectively. They were based upon nucleii of experienced Phantom aircrews and two or three first tour navigators. Their COs were Wg Cdrs A J Bendell AFC and D C Ferguson AFC, respectively. The Lightning-equipped Nos 19 and 92 Sqns continued to operate from Gutersloh in the interim period while the Phantom squadrons worked up to operational state.

No 92 (Designate) Sqn's official history for January 1977 declares: 'The squadron to a man is enthusiastic to prove its worth as a front-line unit and also to ensure that the traditional spirit and excellence of No 92 Sqn is maintained.' At a parade at RAF Gutersloh on Friday, 1 April 1977, No 92 Sqn's standard was officially handed over to the Phantom squadron. It dropped the caveat and

took over No 92 Sqn's commitment to NATO. The Lightning squadrons simultaneously ceased operations.

Nos 19 and 92 Sqns are responsible for providing air intercept and CAP cover for the British air defence sector of West German air space. Whereas in the UK Air Defence Region the Phantom's role is stand-off bomber-type interception at long range, in RAFG, where the primary threat is from low-level, fast strike aircraft, the Phantom's role is low altitude defence below the NIKE belt, behind the HAWK belt, and in front of the SHORAD (Bloodhound and Rapier) belt. The airspace is very cramped, but identification in war would not be a problem. A mass of aircraft detected on radar flying from the East is likely to be the enemy, and, if the IFF fails to respond, they can be shot down beyond visual range. The squadrons' tasks involve some overseas operations, the TWOATAF sector meeting the UKADR over the North Sea.

The Phantoms fly CAPs in pairs. They fly parallel race track patterns with one aircraft's radar always scanning in the direction from which an intruder into West German air space might come. At CAP height, their pulse Doppler radar cover extends from ground level up, and their AIM-7s or Sky Flash can destroy an enemy from zero to

Phantom FGR.2s of No 19 (closest) and 92 Sqn

No 92 Sqn FGR.2 armed with an SUU-23/A. The insignia is an orange cobra with a brown branch and leaves on a white disc, and red and yellow checks

70,000 ft. Thus, they do not have to fly very high, and can exploit their excellent low level acceleration, an especially valuable asset because the threat is primarily low-level.

In Beyond Visual Range (BVR) interception, the fighter is vectored on to a target aircraft by ground-based controllers or AEW until the target is acquired by the fighter's radar, at up to 40 miles. The fighter closes fast to AIM launch range; the AIM is activated and launches when it has acquired the target. The fighter bathes the target in its radar beams – 'illuminates' it – for the AIM's semi-active homing, simultaneously accelerating to high supersonic speed in order to have velocity to convert into energy for manoeuvre to avoid retaliatory AAMs from the target.

Nos 19 and 92 Sqns maintain on rotation at Wildenrath a 24-hour, all-year round QRA(I), the Battle Flight or 'Fire Brigade', of two Phantoms able to be airborne generally well within the

No 92 Sqn FGR.2 landing with brake chute deployed. Another FGR.2's drogue can be seen about to deploy the chute

BELOW
Fully-armed No 19 Sqn FGR.2 equipped with RWR. No 19 Sqn's insignia is a red and green inverted dolphin on a white oval in a black and yellow laurel, and white and light blue checks

OPPOSITE
No 19 Sqn Phantom FGR.2 with AIM-9D, AIM-7E-2 and SUU-23/A and a No 3 Sqn GR.3

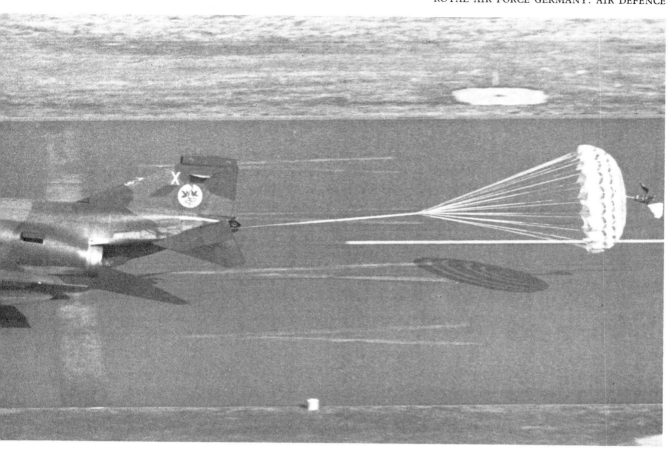

*No 19 Sqn FGR.2 outside its HAS at Wildenrath.
RAFG's tone-down and hardening programme and the
introduction of Blindfire equipped Rapier missile batteries,
considerably improved its ability to survive a pre-emptive
strike*

stipulated five minutes. Its task is to intercept
suspicious aircraft detected on ground or AEW
radar, interrogate them and intervene as required
in order to preserve the integrity of West German
air space and provide constant evidence of an
efficient deterrence force. Crews on QRA(I) are
permanently and uncomfortably kitted up ready to
go on command for twelve-hour shifts. Only
weather of exceptional severity might prevent the
launching of a QRA(I) Phantom, and that decision
rests with the Sector Controller. The Phantoms
are kept in HAS, well out of view.

On 25 May 1982, a No 92 Sqn Phantom
FGR.2, as a result of a chain of errors linking up,
accidentally loosed-off a live AIM-9 during
exercises and shot down Jaguar GR.1 XX963 of
No 14 Sqn at Wesel, West Germany. Ironically,
the Jaguar pilot, Steve Griggs, was an ex-No 31
Sqn Phantom pilot. He ejected successfully.

Nos 19 and 92 Sqns train and exercise
continuously in West German and Dutch air

*No 19 Sqn ground crew load an AIM-9D onto an
FGR.2's LAU-7/A launcher. After loading, the AIM-9Ds
caps are removed and the launchers' noses (on the ground)
are fitted. The all-aspect AIM-9L has replaced the D*

space, often with other NATO aircraft, in
preparation for their critical role in NATO's front
line. They use German and Dutch ranges, but,
like UK-based Phantom units, they undertake
specific training abroad, annually deploying for
five or six weeks APC on Cyprus, and Dissimilar
Air Combat Training (DACT) at Decimomannu,
and to the UK ranges for missile firing.

The lack of ECM on RAFG aircraft was a
serious deficiency. ECM is particularly essential
for survival in the tight, fast, close, low-level
combat environment over Europe. As the saying
goes: 'Without ECM, nobody does it'. Phantoms
began to receive Radar Warning Receiver System
(RWR) pods in 1975, followed by Buccaneers,
then Jaguars from 1979. Most Phantoms had
RWR by 1978. The system developed for British
Phantoms and RAF Buccaneers is the Marconi
ARI 18228, developed specifically for two-seat
aircraft, which have the capability of dealing with
high cockpit workloads, from the ARI 18223 for
single-seat aircraft, such as Jaguar. Both use the
same frequency band coverage of 2 to 20 GHz (E
to J band) and the same antennae on the fins.
Whereas ARI 18223 identifies only the most
serious threat, the Phantom's RWR simultaneously
shows the directions from the aircraft of several
threats on a small circular cathode ray display
tube.

In the mid-1970s a drastic hardening and tone
down programme took place within RAFG. The
major part of the programme involved building
hardened aircraft shelters (HAS), hardening vital
base installations and providing an improved
communications system. The Phantoms return to
the HAS immediately after a sortie in a well
practised operational turn around procedure and
can be refuelled, re-armed and serviced inside
HAS which have built-in power supplies. Engines
can be started and pre-take-off checks run within
HAS. Positioned so that no one bomb run can hit
all HAS in any area, no two face the same
direction.

All front-line aircraft were repainted in a low-
visibility, matt scheme. The Phantom FGR.2
entered RAF service in 1969 in the FBSA/tac-
recce roles and was therefore delivered in standard
RAF low-level tactical camouflage, Dark Green
and Dark Sea Grey uppersurface disruptive
pattern, and Light Aircraft Grey undersurfaces.
No 43 Sqn (AD-Phantom) followed suit. The
radome was Black and there was extensive natural
metal aft. During the general toning of tactical
aircraft from 1971–72 matt colours supplanted the
original gloss and Type B roundels were applied
by deleting White from the original Type A
Red/White/Blue roundels when aircraft underwent
major overhauls.

From 1974, the FGR.2 moved to air defence,
retaining toned-down tactical camouflage, but this

*Phantom FGR.2 XV418, one of the first two sprayed in
the low-visibility greys, was issued to No 19 Sqn in 1978.
The other flew with Nos 23 and 56 Sqns, UKADR. The
tanks remain in the old scheme*

became increasingly inappropriate for the
Phantom's task, primarily long-range interception
in the UKADR, although more suitable for
operations over forested terrain in Europe.
Maximum concealment is essential to reduce the
chances of visual contact during air interception or
combat, especially if radar lock is broken or in
fleeting fights, because of the highly effective
airborne radars now deployed, while HAS obviates
the need for grey/green schemes at base.

The RAF's home interceptor force Lightnings
were highly visible natural metal, and a grey/green
scheme was applied from 1975, followed by a two-
tone grey scheme. The Phantoms, already
camouflaged, were less urgent. In 1978, Phantom
FGR.2s XV418 and XV474 evaluated an overall
matt Light Aircraft Grey scheme with diminutive
roundels for RAFG at Wildenrath, and Strike
Command with Nos 23 then 56 Sqns, respectively.
Following further studies, Mr P J Barley of the
RAE Farnborough formulated a standard Phantom
scheme of three semi-matt (eggshell) greys. Two,
Light Aircraft Grey 627 and Medium Sea Grey
637, were standard BS381C colours, the former
for the undersurfaces as before, the latter for the
upper inboard wing panels. The third, named
Barley Grey after its inventor, covers the rest of
the aircraft, including the radome, and is two parts
627 and one part Black.

The camouflage effect is produced by subtly
combining light and medium greys to give a
uniform appearance by reducing contrasts. Grey is
a neutral colour which will reflect any surrounding
colour if the correct degree of brilliance is selected,
a chameleon effect. A single grey would reflect
light in different strengths from different areas of
the airframe, producing visible shadows and
contrasts.

Chapter 13
Royal Navy

On 4 October 1968, No 892 Sqn, RN decommissioned at Royal Naval Air Station Yeovilton as a D.H. Sea Vixen unit. The squadron was recommissioned at Yeovilton by the Flag Officer Naval Air Command (FONAC), Vice Admiral H R B Janvrin CB, DSC, on 31 March 1969 as the RN's Phantom FG.1 Operation Unit (Fixed Wing Squadron), in accordance with a commissioning order dated 12 March 1969. It was commanded by Lt Cdr Brian Davies AFC, RN. The commissioning ceremony began at 1030 hours, after which Davies led a formation flypast of Phantoms and Sea Vixens to mark the end of an era. It was the fifth No 892 Sqn to commission, the first having commissioned in July 1942. No 892 Sqn was considered at the time to be the last RN fixed-wing squadron, and adopted the last letter of the Classical Greek alphabet, *Omega*, as its insignia, in recognition of this.

The squadron formed from a nucleus of crews and aircraft from No 700P Sqn. These crews had trained in the USA and, with IFTU experience, were well qualified to work the RN Phantom up to operational pitch. For instance, Lt Hugh Drake had been an exchange officer with the USN in an F-4 training squadron between July 1966 and April 1968, after five years on Sea Vixens.

The squadron was tasked with fleet air defence, attack and close support, requiring a wide variety of skills and a carefully scheduled work-up. The squadron began with air defence training in April 1969, practising the procedures, routines and skills of interception at all altitudes, ACM and in-flight refuelling with the RAF Marham's Victor tankers.

On 10 April 1969, it was announced that the squadron was entering three competitors in the *Daily Mail* Transatlantic Air Race to be held during the week of 4–11 May 1969, 50 years after the first heavier-than-air direct West to East

transatlantic flight by Alcock and Whitten-Brown. The race comprised a number of classes, with the award of a money prize for the winner of each. The prizes were awarded for the fastest time overall from the top of the Post Officer Tower in the centre of London to the top of the Empire State Building in New York for East-West flights, and vice-versa for West-East flights. Competitors used helicopters, boats and other forms of transport to get between the two buildings and the various airfields around New York and London at which they took-off and landed.

Preparations for the race had begun several months before, under the direction of Capt R D Lygo RN, who was to be *Ark Royal*'s next captain. No 892 Sqn made high altitude level flights at speeds over Mach 1 far out over the Atlantic to establish fuel consumption figures, and practised inflight refuelling with the Victor K.1As of the Marham-based No 55 Sqn which would provide in-flight refuelling support for the race.

The race project was codenamed *Royal Blue*, and the three Phantoms entered were coded Royal Blue 1, 2 and 3. The three Phantoms departed from Yeovilton individually between 0900 and 1000 hours on 24 April 1969 to fly to New York to prepare for the race. Their base was Floyd Bennett Naval Air Station which was about 15 minutes by motorcycle and Wessex helicopter from the starting line at the top of the Empire State Building. The Phantoms landing field in the UK was BAC's airfield at Wisley, Surrey, where the observers, who were the official race entrants, would immediately transfer to a Wessex which would fly them to the foot of the Post Office Tower in about 10 minutes.

It was estimated that the flight from Floyd Bennett to Wisley would take about 5 hours. The record stood at 5 hours 29 min 14 sec, established

The 1969 Transatlantic Air Race winner, Lt Cdr
Goddard scrambles from XT858 at BAC Wisley before it
has stopped rolling. Seconds later, he dropped from the
wing and sprinted to the waiting Wessex helicopter

XT861's tyre bursts under braking as Lt Hickling lands
rapidly at Wisley on 7 May 1969, 4 hr 53 min after
leaving Floyd Bennet. Between them, the RN and RAF
made the nine fastest race times

Lt Cdr Borrowman in 004 of No 892 Sqn during training
for the 1969 air race. UK Phantom ejection seats are semi-
gloss black, with black and yellow striped firing grips, matt
buff or green headrests and parachute and survival packs,
and dull green, buff or grey harnesses

The three No 892 Sqn 1969 air race crews, left to right: Lt Cdr Goddard, Lt Waterhouse, Lt Cdr Borrowman, Lt Cdr Davies, Lt Hickling and Lt Drake, during training at Yeovilton. XT862 004 was not used

by a USAF KC-135 tanker in 1958. The plan was that each Phantom would climb at military power from Floyd Bennett and accelerate to 1,100 mph at 45,000 ft. The first inflight refuelling from a Victor K.1A would take place 60 miles South of Nova Scotia. Then the Phantom would fly at supersonic speed to a second refuelling South of Newfoundland. It would then cruise at high subsonic speed, about 535 kt IAS, at 40–50,000 ft over the 1,100 mile mid-Atlantic stretch before the last refuelling 400 miles West of Ireland. The Phantom would then fly at supersonic speed round Eire, drop to high subsonic speed for the dash up the Bristol Channel, and go straight into Wisley. Careful fuel management was essential, and each Victor rendezvous required accurate navigation, although those on the West were aided by the frigate HMS *Nubian*.

On 4 May 1969, the first day of the race, Phantom FG.1 XT860/002, flown by Lt Cdr Douglas Borrowman with Lt Paul Waterhouse as observer and official entrant, flew from Floyd Bennet to Wisley in 5 hours 3 min 18 sec, beating the previous record convincingly. Waterhouse took 5 hours 30 min 21 sec between the start and finish points. 002 had been delayed by technical problems with refuelling and only had a 9 kt tail wind, while it had encountered abnormally warm air at 40,000 ft, which increased fuel consumption.

On 7 May 1969, Lt Alan Hickling with Lt Hugh Drake as the entrant flew XT861/003 from Floyd Bennett to Wisley in 4 hours 53 min 10 sec despite radio problems which delayed the first refuelling by four minutes, and bursting the port main wheel tyre on landing. Drake made it tower-to-tower in 5 hours 19 min 16.9 sec.

On the last day of the race, 11 May 1969, the third Phantom FG.1, XT858/001, flown by Lt Cdr Brian Davies, the squadron CO, and Lt Cdr

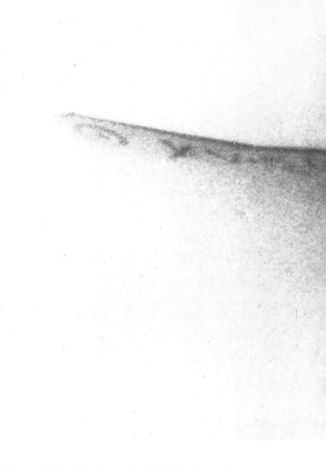

High speed, low level pass by XT858, the 1969 race winner, setting a new record to claim the £5,000 Daily Mail prize, the Alcock and Brown Trophy, and £1,000 for the fastest west-east time

Peter Goddard, No 892 Sqn's senior observer and the race entrant, established the new record at 4 hours 46 min 57 sec. Goddard took 5 hours 11 min 22 sec between the start and finish lines, the fastest time in the class, and fastest in the race, thus winning the 'Blue Riband' and £6,000 in prize money. Davies, favoured with a 23 kt tail wind, used the other crews' experience to achieve higher air speeds without reducing the safety margins, and averaged a true air speed of 1,100 mph to Lundy Island.

Davies' and Goddard's new point-to-point New York–London record was ratified on 22 September

1969. On 10 December 1969, at an informal ceremony at Yeovilton, Mr R A S Ames, Secretary General of the Royal Aero Club, presented the *Aéronautique Internationale Record de Diplome* to Davies and Certificates of Performance to Borrowman and Hickling for having set short-lived records.

In June 1969, No 892 Sqn began training in their secondary role, attack, as part of their role would be the close-support of amphibious landings. They would use the same weapons as No 38 Group Phantoms, SNEB, retarded bombs, and BL755, but were not equipped to carry the SUU-23/A. In autumn, the squadron undertook a programme of mirror deck landing practice at Yeovilton and deck landing practice 'touch and goes' on *Eagle*. Carrier Borne Ground Liaison

(Army) Group, Section 55 was to be located aboard *Ark Royal*, as normal practice, and No 892 Sqn next concentrated upon air control exercises with the Army on Salisbury Plain. During these they first practiced with SNEB rockets.

In September 1969, Rolls-Royce presented on loan a Silver Shadow to No 892 Sqn to commemorate the company's long association with the RN. The presentation was a publicity success, and the car was later embarked on *Ark Royal* for 'showing the flag' in foreign ports. It was very popular with the squadron, but it received Category 4 damage in August 1970.

The squadron's work-up was advanced but the schedule would be impeded if operational carrier training could not be undertaken. *Ark Royal* would not be ready for flying operations until

March 1970 and *Eagle* could not operate Phantoms
for sustained periods. Therefore, preparations
were made in September, to carry out operational
carrier practice aboard USS *Saratoga* (CV-60), a
US Sixth Fleet carrier which operated F-4Js, in
the Mediterranean, where, as a bonus, the weather
was ideal. Selected No 892 Sqn crews went to
RAE Bedford for catapult launches on field
facilities in September, and support facilities were
airlifted out to CV-60 on 8 October when she was
in Argostili Bay, Greece.

Four No 892 Sqn Phantom FG.1s were to
embark on CV-60 for a week of operational
training between 17 and 23 October 1969, the first
time that RN Phantoms had been embarked for
operations at sea. *Saratoga* departed from Argostili
Bay for Valetta, Malta on 10 October. The first
RN Phantom, flown by No 892 Sqn's CO, Davies,
embarked on 12 October, but the other three were
delayed by poor weather. *Saratoga* anchored at
Naples for a three day port visit, departing on 17
October to commence operations in the
Tyrrehenian Sea. The remaining No 892 Sqn
Phantoms embarked on 17 October. The four RN
Phantoms were XV567/011, XV568/012,
XV569/013, and XV570/014. They had 'USS
SARATOGA' on their aft fuselage, like USN F-4s.

However, *Saratoga* was directed by the
Commander Sixth Fleet to conduct contingency
operations in the Eastern Mediterranean during
the period 17 October to 9 November 1969 in
response to the crisis in Lebanon and the coup in
Libya, which gave an unexpected impetus to No
892 Sqn's operational schedule. The RN
Phantoms flew air defence sorties with VF-103's
F-4Js, tactical missions with the task group and
inflight refuelling operations with US aircraft
during their six-day exercise, which was formally
part of routine bilateral training exercises.
However, following blast and heat damage to CV-
60's deck from the Spey's at take-off, launches had
to be made at reduced weights, and flights were
consequently shorter. The British aircrews carried
out 61 launches and all were declared carrier
qualified on the Phantom FG.1.

A further advantage of *Saratoga* was that she
had become the first carrier to put the Automatic
Carrier Landing System (ACLS) AN/SPN-42 into
operation on 3 June 1969, the first 'hands-off'
landing being made on 8 June 1969 by a VF-103
F-4J. *Ark Royal* would have the less sophisticated
SPN-35, the USN's back-up system, but aircrews
required experience of ACLS, while they would
also be cross-decking with USN SPN-42 equipped
carriers. ACLS permitted fully automatic,
automatic to half a mile, pilot flying cross-point
indicator, and normal controlled approach final
until within visual range modes.

In November 1969, No 849B Sqn's Gannet
AEW.3s, which would embark on *Ark Royal*, and

*XV567/011 of No 892 Sqn ready to launch from USS
Saratoga's port catapult during operational trials in
October 1969, the first time that Phantom FG.1s had been
embarked for an extended period*

RIGHT
*Devoid of pylons and AIM-7s, one of four No 892 Sqn
Phantoms embarked on Saratoga in October 1969 comes in
over the carrier's stern. All oleos are at full unladen
extension: sink rate could be as high as 24 ft (7.3 m) per
sec*

FAR RIGHT
*Well-stencilled No 892 Sqn FG.1 XV569, towed by a
tractor aboard Saratoga, October 1969. Note the nosewheel
steering power unit above the torque link. Behind are an
RA-5C Vigilante of Reconnaissance Attack Wing 1 and
an HU-2/HH-2 Seasprite*

No 892 Sqn's Phantom began to work-up
together, practising procedures for CAPs and
interception control. Training intensified in
January 1970 with a rigorous programme of high
and low altitude interceptions and live firing
practice on Salisbury Plain in the close support
role. For several days in February 1970, the
Phantoms and the F-8E(FN) Crusaders of Flotilles
12F and 14F, French *Aviation Embarqué*, from
Landivisiau, Brittany, trained together, practising
visual identification and air combat manoeuvering
off Lands End. Many exchanges took place
between the Crusader squadrons and No 892 Sqn
while the Phantoms were based at Yeovilton, but
there was no cross-decking.

On 23 March 1970 the Flag Officer Naval
Flying Training, Rear Admiral C K Roberts
DSO, made the operational readiness inspection
(ORI) of the squadron at Yeovilton. The squadron
flew 46 hours during the inspection, and
afterwards received this signal: 'Throughout your
ORI there was an aura of calm, meticulous
professionalism. 30 sorties were programmed and
32 were flown. A satisfactory result by any
standard, particularly for a first of type squadron.
Omega may be your insignia but you earn an
Alpha for this inspection.'

A month earlier, HMS *Ark Royal* had
recommissioned. The decision in 1967 to give her
a major refit and reconstruction at Devonport was
taken for three reasons: to enable her to operate
the Phantom; to extend her useful life until the
mid-1970s; and to improve her crew's
accommodation. It had earlier been intended that
Eagle would also be converted to operate a
Phantom squadron. She was in several respects
better suited than *Ark Royal*, with a fully angled
flight deck incorporated in her 1959–64
reconstruction and more hull life. However, the
decision to fully modify only *Ark Royal* to embark
Phantoms operationally and to modify *Eagle* only
for their operation in emergency or for short
detachments was political. Moreover, *Eagle* had
just completed a refit. As a result, only one
operational naval Phantom squadron was formed,
No 892, and the Phantoms for the unformed
second squadron were passed to the RAF.

Edward Heath's new Conservative Government
of 1969 was expected by many to revise the
Labour Government's plans for withdrawal from
the Far East and the Gulf, and to reconsider
phasing out carriers. However, the Supplementary
Statement on Defence of 28 October 1970 only
stated that *Eagle* would serve until 1972, operating
Sea Vixens and Buccaneers, but her life would not

Ark Royal *refitting at Devonport, showing the large
extension for the fully-angled deck, enlarged island for new
ESM fit, and new lattice mast forwards for two Type 965
air warning/search radars. She had Types 982 aircraft
direction, 983 height finder and 993 tactical radars*

be extended in view of the manpower problems and the cost of refit, while *Ark Royal* would serve until the late 1970s, but would not be replaced.

Aircraft embarked in *Ark Royal*, the Paper continued, would be on FAA charge and mainly flown by RN aircrew but RAF aircrew would be seconded as required. Although some adjustments would be made to the run-down of FAA officers and ratings, recruitment for fixed-wing flying would not be re-opened. Maximum use was to be made of planned facilities for FAA fixed-wing aircraft for maintenance and support. *Ark Royal*'s Phantoms and Buccaneers would complement the support provided by shore-based aircraft to naval forces at sea until the late 1970s, after which improved weapon systems, such as Exocet, would enter service, along with new helicopter ASW or V/STOL through-deck carriers. In the interim, the Paper concluded, *Ark Royal* would 'alleviate the shortfall in the weapon capability of the Fleet', and would be a substantial reinforcement of NATO's maritime strength.

It has been standard NATO practice to operate carriers as a pair, and the RN could justify retaining only one carrier by operating with the USN. *Ark Royal* in fact was a welcome and very capable addition to NATO's maritime strength.

Ark Royal had paid-off at Devonport on 5 October 1966. The reconstruction, begun in March 1967 and completed in January 1970, cost £32.5 million. She was given a fully angled flight deck, $8\frac{1}{2}°$ off the centre line, by adding large extensions at the forward and after ends, considerably increasing the flight deck forward on the port side. The angled deck obviates the need for crash barriers to prevent aircraft which fail to hook from hurtling into aircraft parked forward. It also permits greater flexibility in launch operations. A fully angled flight deck was essential for the Phantom, which landed faster and at higher weights than previous FAA aircraft. However, new crash barriers were also specified for Phantom emergency landings.

Ark Royal was fitted with two improved BS4 steam catapults. A port bow catapult was retained, but the starboard unit was removed, and the deck extensions permitted a new 199 foot waist catapult to be fitted for the Phantom, with increased launch speed to allow operation in almost nil wind over deck (WOD) conditions. American Van Zelm bridle arrestors were installed in the catapults. Catching the bridle, the wire strop which attached aircraft to the catapult shoe, for re-use was a

Ark Royal's hangars from her lift. The lower hangar accommodated eight Buccaneers, the upper eight Phantoms, six Sea Kings and three Gannets. The hanger sides and decks were armoured with steel plate

The upper hangar: wing and nose folding is essential to maximize the space available

significant economy measure and virtually eliminated a logistics problem. The bridle was now expended only when time-expired. The Spey's afterburner thrust and heat, exacerbated by the angle created by the FG.1's 40-inch extensible nose leg, could turn deck plates viscid in 15 seconds at full power. Therefore, the whole launch deck area was strengthened and special 8 foot high water-cooled jet blast deflector plates and water-cooled deck panels were fitted behind both catapults. New direct acting, water-spray arresting gear was fitted with several wires with increased energy absorption to take the Phantoms.

New features were required to operate, accommodate, service and support *Ark Royal*'s new aircraft. Her lower hangar accommodated eight Buccaneers, and her upper hangar eight Phantoms, six Sea Kings and three Gannets; until it became an additional store, the upper hangar extension housed two Wessex. The upper hangar decks were strengthened to take the heavier loads. The remaining aircraft, four Phantoms, six Buccaneers, and one Gannet, generally the serviceable ones, had to be parked on deck. There

was more space than before for parking aircraft at Fly 1 in front of the island and at port aft as a result of extending the forward and after decks and removing the starboard catapult, but space remained very restricted. New workshops and store facilities were installed to cope with servicing and stores requirements. *Ark Royal* carried 1,600 tons of AVCAT for her CAG, of which some 300 tons was used daily.

The AN/SPN-35-CCA (Carrier Controlled Approach) radar was fitted, with the Phantom in mind and TACAN, an intrinsic part of Phantom CAP operations. A substantial part of the cost of the refit was absorbed by a new radar and electronic surveillance measures (ESM) fit. *Ark Royal*'s remaining gun armament was removed. Seacats were scheduled to be fitted but were not installed. Phantoms and Buccaneers were her sole defence.

Yeovilton was No 892 Sqn's land-base until September 1972 when it moved to Leuchars where its aeroplanes were held by the RN Detachment. For a period in 1975, Lossiemouth was used. 003 carries CBTE

These additions and improvements permitted *Ark Royal* to operate her new CAG to its full potential. Although the reconstruction gave her ten more years of hull life, her machinery was old, and she spent considerable time under repair and maintenance during her last commissions. A second refit was undertaken at Devonport between July 1973 and April 1974. At 1976 prices, she cost £17.1 million to operate, including aircraft.

Ark Royal's refit and the offensive and defensive weapons capability of her CAG made her the most flexible and potent warship the RN has ever commissioned. Her CAG's component units and numbers remained the same between recommissioning in 1970 and paying off in 1978. Her CAG comprised twelve Phantom FG.1s, fourteen Buccaneer S.2s, four Gannet AEW.3s, seven ASW Sea King HAS.1s, later 3s, and two SAR Wessex and a COD Gannet, representing a

balance between defensive and offensive types. This enabled the carrier to defend herself and the fleet against almost all forms of attack while at sea, and to seek and destroy enemy forces at great distances at will, and to support operations ashore. The paramount advantage the conventional CAG offers is intense multi-role capability. It can undertake almost all military aviation tasks, from ASR through CAP to nuclear strike, operating against targets afloat, submerged, on the ground and in the air over land or sea, and at ranges beyond the reach of land-based aircraft.

Lt Michael S Seider USN, an exchange pilot with No 892 Sqn, wrote of *Ark Royal*:

Though small by (USN) standards, she has many of the capabilities of (USN) super carriers. However, the limited size of her flight deck and hangar areas severely curtails continuous operational readiness for she cannot launch and recover aircraft at the same time. The

A routine pre-launch scene aboard Ark Royal.
Phantoms always parked to port, Buccaneers to starboard.
The lightest aircraft were launched first and the heaviest
last

RIGHT
FG.1 013 coupled to a tractor. An auxiliary is alongside
Ark Royal. *Note overpainted code, lack of nose door code,*
and Silver Jubilee red/white/blue flash – the unit's badge
replaced '77' in 1978

location of lifts, at center deck rather than at deck edge,
eliminates movement of aircraft on deck when either of
them is down. The ship is of 1940 design and wasn't
intended for the operation of heavy jets like Phantoms
and Buccaneers. *Ark* can truly be called an aircraft
handler's nightmare. For all her drawbacks, though, the
carrier can still launch tactical air support and nuclear
strikes. Her updated, AWG-11-equipped Phantoms are
a match for any airborne fleet threat and the level of
training of aircrews would be the envy of any (USN) air
wing commander.

The Gannet AEW.3s of No 849 Sqn B Flt were
a vital component of the CAG. More flexible and
less vulnerable than ships, they could detect
hostile air and shipping threats at ranges well
beyond that of ship's radar, which was limited by
the horizon, providing timely warning, and direct
strikes against shipping. Gannets had Thorn-EMI
ASV-19 Maritime Reconnaissance Systems,
providing extended area surveillance in high sea
states of all surface targets, including even
submarine periscopes. They could maintain long-
range shipping plots for relay to *Ark Royal*'s radar
displays. The Gannets were also responsible for
CAP and associated fighter control. They could
detect hostile aircraft and direct the Phantoms
onto them, well beyond the stand-off range of
anti-shipping missiles like Exocet. The squadron
was based at Lossiemouth from November 1970.

The Buccaneer S.2Cs and S.2Ds of No 809 Sqn
provided attack and strike capability against targets
ashore and afloat, including low-level strike/attack,

air-to-ground missile or rocket attack, close support for ground forces, and (S.2D) Martel-assisted penetration. They also provided long-range photo-recce, air-to-air refuelling for Phantoms and other Buccaneers, maritime search, and night illumination. For logistics reasons, No 809 Sqn was based at RAF Honington alongside the RAF's Buccaneers when not embarked.

In April and May 1970, three No 892 Sqn Phantoms joined the four A & AEE Phantoms in *Ark Royal*'s intensive flying trials. These took place mainly in the Lyme Bay area off Dorset.

An unenviable task in wet weather: bow catapult FDO signals to the aircraft director that the nosewheel has passed the 'hold-back' gear. Phantom nosewheels are steerable, but the pilot cannot see obstructions

'Badgers' connect the 'hold-back'. Fixed to the deck, it is connected to the FG.1 by a dumb-bell shaped bar which breaks at a precise strain, around 95,000 lb (43,083 kg), achieved by full thrust plus the catapult's release

LEFT
007 immediately on arrival at the bow catapult. The FDO, extreme left, signals for the nose oleo to be fully extended, operated by an air engineer under the wing, extreme right. 'Badgers' prepare the launch gear

159

After they have checked the bridle, 'Badger One' clears out his team before handing the aircraft over the FDO to launch. 'Badgers' are marine engineers designated as catapult crews, named from their black and white waist coats

There, on 3 May, both radio and radar contact was lost with XV566 while it was under radar control as a target for low level interception. It had crashed into the sea and both crew were killed, No 892 Sqn's first loss. *Ark Royal*'s CAG, including No 892 Sqn's full complement of twelve Phantoms, embarked on 12 June 1970 for a work-up at sea, beginning in the Moray Firth area and continuing in the South-West Approaches in July. The aircrews became accustomed to the movement, swirling eddies, smoke and fumes of the carrier deck, a very different environment to Yeovilton's runway, in preparation for embarking operationally. The CAG disembarked at the end of the work-up, re-embarking on 4 September. Late that month, the carrier took part in the NATO autumn exercise NORTHERN WEDDING, the CAG's first major operational involvement. Catapult and arrestor problems were revealed by intensive flying between 4 and 10 October and the CAG disembarked again while *Ark Royal* underwent repair.

It had been intended that *Ark Royal* would deploy to the Far East in support of the British withdrawal from Singapore but, as a result of policy re-alignment, she was committed to NATO for Atlantic and Mediterranean deployments. On 19 October, she sailed for the Mediterranean, her full CAG officially embarking on an operational basis the following day. This was the first of four major embarkations by the CAG between 1970 and 1978. It lasted until 26 July 1973, following which *Ark Royal* underwent a refit. The second extended between May 1974 and mid-November 1975, and the third between February 1976 and 15 October 1976 after which *Ark Royal* underwent maintenance and repair using parts cannibalised from *Eagle*. The CAG's last embarkation was between June 1977 and 27 November 1978.

In addition, there were several temporary disembarkations by the CAG, for periods of one, two or three months while the carrier was in port for leave, or maintenance. During these periods,

No 892 Sqn continued training from Yeovilton, then from Leuchars from September 1972, or from dispersed bases; for instance, No 892 Sqn spent summer 1974 training in the Bristol Channel area when *Ark Royal* was in port for several weeks. There were also short disembarkations by CAG aircraft. As examples, for three weeks from 5 October 1974, while *Ark Royal* undertook self-maintenance in Valetta, Malta, her Phantoms and Buccaneers disembarked to Luqa, and while she was in Portsmouth drydock in late June 1975, three No 892 Sqn Phantoms were seconded to USS *Nimitz* (CVN-68), the world's largest warship. When on Western Atlantic deployments, *Ark Royal* was based at Fort Lauderdale and used other USN facilities. For a week until 1 July 1971, while the carrier put into Mayport, Florida, several Phantoms deployed to US Naval Air Station Cecil Field, Jacksonville; again, while she was in Mayport for six weeks from late May 1975 her fixed-wing aircraft deployed to USNAS; and when she was in Norfolk Navy Yard, Virginia in April 1975, two No 892 Sqn Phantoms flew across to California.

004 at full oleo extension seconds before launch. The two catapult bridle members check the tension. Its SAR Wessex checks the port ailerons, flaps, etc. Note the waist catapult 'howdah' plus catapult ready lights

In 1971, Phantom XT872/007 made what was believed to be the longest ever re-embarkation flight made by an aircraft at sea. When *Ark Royal* put out from Devonport on 2 June, 007 was unserviceable and did not embark. On 6 June, it flew from Yeovilton to rejoin *Ark Royal*, cruising 1,700 miles away, south west of the Azores. It was flown by Lt D Hill, RN with Lt M Grainger-Holcomber, RN as observer (who had earlier bent the squadron's Rolls). It refuelled in flight from Buccaneer 034 of No 809 Sqn, flown by Lt R Withey, RN with observer Lt J Fitzgerald, over Lajes in the Azores. On arrival in the carrier the CO Capt J O Roberts, RN presented the crew with a very long French loaf as survival rations and a very large ball of string as an extra navigation aid. No 892 Sqn improved upon this performance in 1975. *Ark Royal* left behind an unserviceable Phantom when she sailed

007 being boosted off the bow catapult. From the bow 'howdah' – left, raised above flight deck level – a petty officer engineer controlled catapult firing but the launch procedure was entirely run by the FDO, one per catapult

In ideal flying conditions there was little difference between the catapults. In poor conditions – very heavy aircraft, poor wind, speed and steam – the longer waist catapult launched most aircraft. Note fuselage top anti-slip patches

FAR LEFT
001 on full reheat on the waist catapult. The FDO, with launch flag raised, checks FLYCO ready lights, catapult ready lights, the aircraft's configuration and the deck's rise and fall before launching the aircraft

LEFT
003 prepares to leave the bow catapult; 002 waits for the bow catapult; 010 on the waist catapult will be launched when the bow is clear. The launch cycle was always split between the catapults

from Norfolk Navy Yard for the Atlantic Fleet Weapons Range (AFWR) on 21 April. She sailed for Rio de Janeiro in early May, and the Phantom flew some 2,500 miles, a nine-hour flight involving several inflight refuellings, to rejoin *Ark Royal* as she steamed towards the equator.

After short disembarkations, flying exercises were conducted in the Channel or en route; after long disembarkations, work-ups were undertaken in the Moray Firth, Lyme Bay or the South West Approaches, followed by an ORI. No 892 Sqn undertook a continual, rigorous schedule of training whether embarked or shore-based. *Ark Royal* exercised on the AFWR when on WESTLANT deployments, her Phantoms being able to expend AAMs and bombs. In the Mediterranean, her aircraft exercised over the Sardinian weapon ranges, for the first time in November 1970; in late October 1974, her CAG also took part in live bombing practice with the Italian Fleet. During her last deployment, to the Mediterranean in October and November 1978, in eight weeks her Phantoms and Buccaneers expended nearly 60,000 lb of bombs and her Phantoms fired fourteen AAMs during practices.

From 1966, with the announcement of the run-down of the carrier force, the RN had a hard task recruiting fixed-wing aircrews, and the effective run-down of aircrews began. At the same time, the RAF began supplying aircrews, as between the Wars. FAA fixed-wing recruitment was terminated in 1968, and the last pilot training course was completed in July 1970 at RAF Linton-on-Ouse, and the last observer/navigator course soon after. Following the disbanding of No 767 Sqn and the Fighter School at Yeovilton in August 1972, all new Phantom crews came from the RAF's Phantom Training Flight at Leuchars. By 1974, there were only seventeen Phantom qualified pilots in the Royal Navy, many serving their third tour with No 892 Sqn. In consequence, the RN aircrews were very experienced, the Air Warfare Instructor in 1974, Lt Owen 'Nutty' Walters, RN for instance, being among those who had learnt to fly F-4s at Norfolk, Virginia, before joining No 892 Sqn. The number of RAF Phantom and Buccaneer aircrews on *Ark Royal* gradually increased until it was over 50 per cent by the time RN fixed-wing flying ceased in November 1978. For a short period at the change-over, RN aircrew were given the opportunity to join the RAF; few did.

Although No 892 Sqn's RN aircrews were all experienced in carrier operations, most RAF crews were entirely new to deck conditions. And *Ark Royal* was smaller than the USN carriers from which the F-4 had been designed to operate. 'Think what the life of a (USN) squadron commander would be like if half of his flyers were USAF-exchange types trying to land on an

003 prepares to launch from the bow catapult. During launch operations, the shorter bow catapult tended to launch the lightest aircraft in each batch

004 at full thrust on the waist catapult; another Phantom waits for the bow catapult: catapult crews survive between them in pain from noise, they brave the heat and violent buffeting of each launch

002, carrying ten bombs on CBTEs, departs at full thrust

013 seconds after launch. No 892 Sqn FG.1s bore white three-digit codes on their noses. The last two digits were repeated on the trailing edge flaps in white, and black on the nose gear door

'Essex'-class carrier', wrote Lt Michael Seider, a USN-exchange pilot with No 892 Sqn. Training in launches and recoveries for the new RAF crews was thorough, commencing in the simulator, and continuing on runway facilities with launches and Deck Landing Practice before proceeding to 'touch and goes' on *Ark Royal* when in Home waters, while work-ups were necessary to qualify new crews. No 892 Sqn's roles required all-weather and night flying, particularly demanding from a carrier in fast, heavy jets. However, as Lt Seider recalled:

There is a surprising lack of 'color' on the squadron's carrier approaches. This is primarily because of the training received and the fact that the Royal Navy has very stringent rules on night flying.

A pilot must have 40 day cats and traps before he is allowed to 'dusk fly' . . . During 'duskers' there must be a clear horizon. After you become dusk-qualified, you are eligible to launch in the black, again provided there is a clear horizon and divert field. Fully qualified night flyers are able to launch in any weather without a bingo field. The squadron has three ace crews considered non-diversion night qualified and an additional three, night-diversion qualified.

To fly at night, a crew must have had a day launch the same day or a night sortie the previous night . . . *Ark*'s carrier controlled approach system uses SPN-35 equipment, the normal back-up on (USN) ships, but the quality of control is excellent.

Ark's operations guide permits a maximum of eight aircraft airborne at night, due primarily to deck spotting problems. There simply isn't enough room to park more

airplanes on the bow without fouling the landing area. The area aft is so narrow that aircraft cannot be parked there at night. Deck lighting is similar to (USN carrier's) with red droplights and a center-line string with mid-deck T arrangement. White floodlighting is kept to a bare minimum. The critical factor in landing on *Ark* is line-up. The landing area is only 86 feet wide with a 10-foot off-centre engagement.

It is not appropriate, given the integrated nature of a CAG, to treat No 892 Sqn's operations entirely separately, nor, despite its base not being geographically fixed, to follow the CAG's movements in detail. *Ark Royal* operated between the extremes of climate, from the Arctic circle to the Equator. In July 1971, tropical trials of No 892 Sqn's Phantoms were successfully conducted aboard *Ark Royal* off Florida, in which the Naval Air Department, RAE Bedford and Rolls-Royce participated. The benefits of the high lift devices and long nose gear were evident during launches in the hot, still air. Then, in late September/early October 1971, she operated in the other extreme during Exercise ROYAL KNIGHT in NATO's Northern flank, the North Sea, Norwegian Sea and North Cape Areas, beyond the Arctic circle.

Ark Royal's roles included convoy escort, shipping and land strikes, ASW, air support for amphibious landings, air superiority, and Task Force air defence. She took part in regular and special NATO and national exercises designed to test her capabilities and ability to operate with NATO land, sea and air elements. Following the

Bow catapult crew prepare their launch gear as the waist catapult is launched. The aircraft director (right) signals the next aircraft onto the bow catapult. As the catapult launch areas overlapped, launches were synchronized

OPPOSITE
012 descends on Ark Royal. *No 892 Sqn's insignia was a black* Omega *in a white 'kite' and a red flash. Its FG.1s carried* Ark Royal's *code 'R' in white. Underwing and fuselage serials were black*

RIGHT
002 comes in over Ark Royal's *round-down, seen from an SAR Wessex, on the beam in position to launch divers to rescue the crew of an aircraft which went over the side. No 892 Sqn's safety record was superlative*

FAR RIGHT
001 landing-on, viewed from the bombard weapons park. 010 is parked in 'Fly 4', where two Phantoms at various readiness states could park without affecting land-ons

No 892 Sqn Phantom is halted by Ark Royal's *direct acting rotary hydraulic arrestor gear, installed for the Phantom. Arrestor wires were raised 4 in (102 mm) from the deck for recovery. The FG.1s hook is stressed to 4.8G*

tropical trials in 1971, the Phantoms were cross-decked with USN F-4s and were found compatible. RN Phantoms, Buccaneers and helicopters, as had Scimitars and Sea Vixens before them, cross-decked to US carriers on numerous occasions, while USN and USMC aircraft cross-decked to *Ark Royal*. Her control and operations procedures and systems had to be compatible with those of USN carriers: NATO operates carriers in pairs or trios as the focus of a Task Force, and cross-decking, cross-tanking (inflight refuelling) and cross-controlling were essential and regular parts of joint operations. In war, rendering a carrier's deck unserviceable not only prevents it launching aircraft, but forces its airborne aircraft to find another deck, divert to a land base or ditch. Moreover, with saturation attacks on carriers, tactics the Soviets would employ, and intense air operations continuing uninterrupted for several days, cross-operations give essential flexibility.

As an example of cross-operations, between 6 and 23 March 1975, *Ark Royal* took part in NATO's Operation LANDTREADEX 2-75 with USS *Independence* (CV-62) and *Enterprise* (CV-65) off the coast of Florida. 'A highpoint of LANDTREADEX for the Air Department,' CV-62's 1975 Command History records, 'was the cross-decking operation with HMS *Ark Royal*.' Two Phantom FG.1s, two Buccaneer S.2s, and one Gannet AEW.3 were successfully recovered and launched on *Independence*, while Cmdr James Flatley III, Commander Carrier Air Wing Seven led one VF-102 and one VF-33 F-4J, two VA-65 A-6s, and a VA-12 and a VA-66 A-7 aboard *Ark Royal*. In addition, several British and American crewmen cross-decked for supporting roles in the operation.

NATO maritime exercises are constructed to simulate the conditions of war closely. In Exercise TEAMWORK 76 in mid-September 1976, *Ark Royal* launched 130 Phantom sorties alone. During

A USN LTV A-7 Corsair from VA-46 refuels a No 892 Sqn Phantom FG.1. Cross-tanking ensures that aircrews are familiar with USN procedures, and increases operational flexibility

her deployment to the Caribbean and the USA
between February 1976 and 16 July 1976, she
made almost 2,000 aircraft launches and 2,700
helicopter sorties during three major exercises and
normal training. As an indication of the intensity
of flying operations during NATO exercises,
Independence teamed with *Ark Royal* conducted
'60 continuous hours of air operations from 0600
17 March to 1800 20 March' during
LANDTREADEX 2-75.

Ark Royal also engaged in mock carrier against
carrier battles, such as SOLID SHIELD fought
with USS *John F Kennedy* (CV-67) off Florida in
May 1976. These provided invaluable experience
and lessons in both offensive and defensive
operations – search, strike, CAP, interception and
radar – for both carriers. For instance, between 11
and 14 November 1971, *Ark Royal* and
Independence conducted DOUBLE EDGE in the
Mediterranean, the latter's 1971 Command
History statings: '. . . the two carriers launched
search and attack missions against each other after
which cross-tanking, cross-decking and cross-
controlling were practised.'

Some exercises, such as DOUBLE EDGE,
included several operational elements, those
involving several NATO nations invariably being
multi-faceted. Between 4 and 12 October 1976,
Ark Royal took part in Exercise DISPLAY

LEFT
A 'zapped' (see fin) Phantom FG.1, of No 892 Sqn aboard the USS Independence

No 892 Sqn Phantom FG.1 (XT8721/'001'), at full burner and cleared for launch on the port catapult of USS Independence *(CV-62) in November 1975 during Exercise Ocean Safari*

DETERMINATION, a regular event, in the Mediterranean teamed with *Nimitz* (CVN-68) and *America* (CV-66) and the French carrier *Clemenceau*, and operating with ships of the Greek, Italian, Portuguese and Turkish navies. *America*'s 1976 Command History records that the carriers 'conducted convoy escort duties, simulated close air support for amphibious operations and simulated strikes against military targets.' The only aircraft cross-decked were F-8E(FN) Crusaders of Flotille 12F from *Clemenceau* to *Nimitz*, because *Clemenceau* was not equipped to operate US or RN Phantoms.

Air support for amphibious operations was a major part of *Ark Royal*'s commitments, and she

took part in several NATO and national amphibious exercises. In the event of war, reinforcements would be shipped by sea directly to Europe from the UK or the USA, involving both convoy escort and close air support for landings. Typical was a British combined Services amphibious exercise, SALLY FORTH 73, held in the Orkneys between 8 and 16 July 1973. No 892 Sqn's Phantoms and No 809 Sqn's Buccaneers supported landings by Wessex and landing craft from the assault ship HMS *Intrepid* and the logistics landing ship *Sir Geraint*. The forces opposing the landings were supported by Pumas and Hunters of No 38 Group, Strike Command, RAF.

For a more ambitious amphibious support scenario, NATO's Exercise NORTHERN MERGER, 16 to 27 September 1974, *Ark Royal* was paired with *America* (CVA-66) to provide air support to the NATO task force and amphibious landings. Despite extremely adverse weather conditions, *America*'s CVW-8 conducted a demanding schedule of operations without a single incident, while *Ark Royal*'s Phantoms and Buccaneers contributed air support and strike by day and night, most of the Phantom aircrews flying 30 hours during the exercise. The weather was more of a limiting factor than aircraft availability and the Phantom's airframe and radar reliability was excellent under the tremendous tempo and pressure of operations. No 892 Sqn did not fly a Phantom with an unserviceable radar, but availability was never seriously reduced by this policy.

As a result of the RAF taking over RN fixed-wing flying support in 1972, No 892 Sqn ended its long association with Yeovilton, last declaring there on 5 September, and took up residence at RAF Leuchars, declaring there on 19 September. The RAF took over from FONAC responsibility for parenting No 892 Sqn, providing training, maintenance and hangaring facilities and assistance when it was shore-based, and worldwide support when embarked. The RN's permanent establishment at Leuchars was titled the RN Detachment Leuchars and, although sharing facilities and MUs, had its own hangar at Leuchars.

Aside from the RN's long association with the base, Leuchars was selected as No 892 Sqn's new base in order to standardise the base on the Phantom FG.1 for engineering and administrative support. Naval fighter training also ceased in August 1972, No 767 Sqn disbanding at Yeovilton and the Phantom Training Flight, under RAF control, forming at Leuchars instead with FG.1s. Leuchars was the base of the RAF's maritime Phantom FG.1 squadron, No 43; in November 1975, a second RAF squadron moved there, No 111, converting to FG.1s. When RN fixed-wing

flying ceased, the RN Phantom FG.1s were to go to these squadrons.

The RN Phan Det Leu was responsible for No 892 Sqn's reserve Phantoms and for preparing them to operational issue standard, and for the squadron's entire complement when disembarked, but was not responsible for the PTF's aircraft, which were on RAF charge, although used by the RN for refresher training. For instance, XT860 was prepared to issue standard by the Detachment and issued to No 892 Sqn on 15 December 1975 in rotation with XT863 which had been sent to HSA Holme-on-Spalding Moor on 11 November 1975 for an MoD update. XT863 was passed to the RN Detachment on 13 May 1976, but went to No 23 MU for a surface finish on 27 May, returning to the Detachment on 10 June for preparation to issue standard and holding in reserve for No 892 Sqn, to whom it was again issued on 18 August 1976. Preparatory to No 892 Sqn disbanding, the Phantoms held by the Detachment were transferred to the RAF in 1978, XT860 on 15 March and XT867 on 20 April. No 892 Sqn's last two reserve Phantoms, XV587 and

LEFT
No 892 Sqn Phantom FG.1 about to touch down on USS Nimitz *(CVN-68). An F-4J of VF-31 of* Saragota's *air group is in the background*

Phantom XT864 inches from the deck of USS Nimitz

XV592, left Yeovilton, their forward base, in early November for conversion to the RAF's air defence variant and were taken off RN records on 7 December 1978. However, one other, XT868, was lost when it crashed at the RAF Abingdon air display on 12 May 1978; following an enquiry by the Naval Accident Investigation Unit, it was struck off RN records on 20 December 1978.

The six COs who commanded No 892 Sqn during its fifth commission were all Naval Officers. Lt Cdr Davies, the first, was relieved on 2 October 1970 by Lt Cdr N N Kerr, under whom the squadron embarked in *Ark Royal* on an operational basis; Kerr had been nominated in August 1970. Lt Cdr C R Hunneyball, nominated in January 1972, took over on 7 July 1972, just before the squadron moved to leuchars, while his relief, Lt Cdr W 'Bill' L T Peppe was nominated in April 1973 and took command on 7 January 1974, in preparation for No 892 Sqn's second major embarkation. The next CO, Lt Cdr Hugh S Drake, was nominated in July 1975 and took command on 10 December 1975, aged 38. Joining the RN in 1953 as an artificer apprentice, he was promoted to Naval Air Cadet from petty officer in January 1960, and, as a sub-lieutenant, began operational flying in 1961 as a Sea Vixen observer with No 890 Sqn from *Ark Royal*. Then,

as a lieutenant, he was an instructor with No 766 Sqn at Yeovilton. He carried the Home Air Command Colour at Sir Winston Churchill's state funeral in January 1964. He again flew from *Ark Royal* on Sea Vixens in 1964–66 before being posted on exchange to a USN F-4 training squadron. He joined No 892 Sqn in April 1969, participated in the Air Race, and served for eight months before going to *Ark Royal*'s operations section on promotion to lieutenant commander. He served with No 892 Sqn as senior observer in 1972–74 and returned as CO after serving as operations officer at RNAS Portland. Lt Cdr John E Ellis, an observer, became CO on 4 October 1977.

The decision that No 892 Sqn would disband in December 1978 was made known in late 1976. *Ark Royal*'s future had been officially under consideration since June 1972, when fixed-wing carrier flying would have ceased under previous Government policy. Her machinery was old, breakdowns more frequent, repairs more difficult and *Eagle* provided only limited spares. Moreover, as planned, the RAF was gradually taking over the

RN Phantom FG.1 lining-up on USS Independence. *In the foreground, two F-4Js and a North American RA-5C*

roles of the FAA's Buccaneers and Phantoms, while the major British defence effort was increasingly devoted to Europe. Finally, the V/STOL ASW carriers were scheduled to enter service in the early 1980s. It was decided to pay off *Ark Royal* in late 1978; clearly, her squadrons would then be surplus, and would disband, and the RAF absorb their aircraft.

At the end of a farewell cruise of the Mediterranean, *Ark Royal* catapulted off her Phantoms and Buccaneers for the last time on 27 November 1978. The last aircraft off was Phantom XT870/012 – which had been issued to No 892 Sqn when it had formed – flown by Flt Lt Murdo Macleod, RAF with Lt Denis McCallum, RN, No 892 Sqn's Deputy Air Engineering Officer, in the observer's seat on his first catapult launch. No 892 Sqn's Phantoms – XT859, XT863, XT864, XT865, XT870, XT872, Xv567, XV568, XV586, XV589, XV590, and XV591 – flew directly to RAF St Athan where they were handed over to RAF charge the same day. Of these, as representative examples, XT859 had 1,450 and XT863 had 1,485 airframe hours on 1 July 1978. These twelve aircraft were the last operational Phantoms removed from RN records, on 11 December 1978. No 892 Sqn officially ceased to be part of *Ark Royal*'s CAG on 15 December 1978,

simultaneously decommissioning at Leuchars by an order dated 1 December 1978.

As a result of the decision to phase out the carrier force, reinforced by the determination to withdraw from East of Suez, of the 50 production Phantom FG.1s purchased, the RAF received nineteen, XT873-876 and XV571-885, which were delivered directly to RAF Aldergrove. Of these, the RAF lent the RN five, XT873, XT875, XT876, XV572, and XV579, for training purposes for varying periods between 1968 and 1972; XT876 was lost in RN service. Like the two YF-4Ks, XT955 and XT596, F-4K1 and 2, XT597 and XT598, were used for trials and did not enter service. Of the remaining 29 FG.1s taken on RN charge directly, one, XT858, only served briefly for trials with No 700P Sqn before being transferred to the Ministry of Technology in 1968. Seven, XT862, XT868, XT869, XT871, XV565, XV566 and XV588 were written off; XT857, XT861, XT866 and XV569 were transferred to the RAF's PTF in 1972, and XV570 in 1973; the remaining sixteen were transferred in 1978.

USS Independence's flight deck crews marshal an F-4K onto its parking slot. There was much more room aboard US carriers

Chapter 14
That Phantoms May Fly

Introducing a new aircraft type to service requires the organisation and establishment of massive support and facilities at all levels from flight line through maintenance units to stores depots. The Phantom, as an American aircraft, albeit with much UK content, required specific arrangements to be made. Under the terms of the February 1965 arrangement with the USA, the UK had entered into 'a co-operative logistics supply support agreement' under which the UK was given equal priority with the US forces for the supply of spares, modification kits, repair and overhaul services, and engineering support. Supplies are direct from the US Navy or McDonnell Douglas. However, after delivery of the Phantoms, the manufacturer's responsibility for major servicing, heavy modification programmes and the production of certain spares was passed to HSA (later BAe) at Brough, as sister design firm, in accordance with 1966 agreement. Flight testing after overhaul or modification was carried out at Holme-on-Spalding Moor, Brough's test field, until it closed in mid-1983. HSA technicians also undertook the embodiment of modifications and corrective repairs at maintenance units and NASU.

At the same time as the Phantom entered UK service, RAF and RN support services were being rationalized, centralized and cut, which affected the responsibilities of the maintenance units. In line with the planned termination of naval fixed-wing flying from 1972, the responsibility for naval air stores for the RN's Phantom FG.1 passed to RAF Support Command in early 1969. Following the decision in 1970 to extend RN fixed-wing flying and keep *Ark Royal* into the late 1970s, it was nevertheless decided that all support and maintenance for the RN Phantom would pass to the RAF from August 1972 as planned, although aircraft would remain on naval charge.

No 767 Sqn FG.1 in NASU's hangar. The aft fuselage section and the radar have been removed, the leading edge BLC duct can be seen and the Nos 5 and 6 fuel cell cover lies on the wing

TOP RIGHT
No 767 Sqn FG.1s in NASU. Technicians also trained on No 767 Sqn. After Daedalus' *20-week course, trainees underwent three months supervised training at Yeovilton's Technical Training Department and School, then on a second-line squadron. After examination, they could sign for work*

OPPOSITE
No 767 Sqn FG.1s in NASU. Yeovilton parented Nos 700P, 767 and 892 Sqns, and NASU, the RN's heavy repair squad, received onto charge, serviced and prepared for issue the RN's FG.1s, and carried out some modification programmes

No 892 Sqn Phantoms, 003 with CBTEs, outside Ark Royal's *hangar at RAF Leuchars, where the RN Detachment serviced, repaired, prepared and held No 892 Sqn's Phantoms after the RAF took over parenting the squadron from Yeovilton*

The RN Phantom Detachment (No 892 Sqn) was established at RAF Leuchars, to simplify organisation and engineering support. It was the base of the RAF's maritime air defence Phantom squadron, No 43, which also flew FG.1s, and would be the base for a second from the mid-1970s, to whom No 892 Sqn's FG.1s would be passed. No 23 MU, Aldergrove handled some major servicing, surface finishing and modification tasks on RN FG.1s from 1969, with assistance from St Athan later, and, after the RN's Phantoms moved to Leuchars, carried out the receipt and pre-embarkation checks for the RN Detachment's aircraft. The work done on the ex-RN FG.1s in 1978–79 upon transfer to the RAF entailed the removal of certain equipment such as fast reheat, purely for engineering support, and a thorough check for corrosion before acceptance and transfer of service. By 1983 all FG.1s had been brought up to FGR.2 standard, and all had been modified to take the SUU-23/A.

Yeovilton, the base of Nos 700P and 767 Sqns, was responsible for 'parenting' No 892 Sqn until support was entirely passed to the RAF.One of the responsibilities of FONAC is providing 'parenting' shore facilities for front-line carrier squadrons and ships' flights, involving hangaring aircraft and assisting with and maintaining the standards of flying training and maintenance ashore. Yeovilton's Technical Training Department held Short Aircraft Maintenance Courses (SAMCOs) for technical officers and ratings on Phantoms. Normally, SAMCOs are held at HMS *Daedalus* or at the aircraft company concerned, but it was decided that it would be preferable to give this training at Yeovilton where the RN Phantom was based.

The Naval Air Support Unit (NASU) at Yeovilton began handling Phantoms as soon as they were delivered from St Louis, preparing them to issue standard. NASU's primary task was modernization, rectification and repair jobs which were beyond the squadron's scope, but NASU relied upon skilled civilian tradesmen from BAe/HSA to perform certain tasks and embody HSA modifications. The modernization task covered the electrical, mechanical and weapon systems, and demanded a very high and varied level of expertise. In one eighteen month period up to mid-1972, NASU handled 28 Phantoms, twelve Sea Vixens and three Wessex. Aircraft could be with NASU for several weeks and a replacement was provided to the squadron if possible. For instance, when No 892 Sqn's FG.1 XV590 became unserviceable, XT871 was issued to replace it on 16 April 1971. It was not always possible to move aircraft back to Yeovilton for repair. In early 1972 one Phantom was repaired by NASU in Scotland, and another shortly afterwards at Lee-on-Solent. NASU also had a 'dope shop' but RN Phantoms also used No 23 MU for surface finishing.

RAF Support Command's motto – UT AQUILAE VOLENT: That Eagles May Fly – is apt. The Command's maintenance units between them have the capability to undertake the servicing, repair and modification of most structural, mechanical and electrical items held in supply depots or returned as unserviceable. The primary role of RAF St Athan, Support Command, is to provide the engineering facilities required for the major servicing of operational aircraft. Supply sponsored engineering commitments include the deep overhaul, servicing and repair of airframe, structural, mechanical and electrical components. The engineering organization consists of three wings, Engineering Co-ordination and Development, General Engineering, and Aircraft Engineering. St Athan undertakes the design and manufacturing required by the maintenance roles.

The Aircraft Engineering Wing undertakes extensive servicing and frequently the embodiment of major modifications. It comprises several squadrons each handling different aircraft types, and an Aircraft Surface Finishing Facility, which resprayed the Phantoms in the grey scheme. A mixed civilian and service manned squadron is responsible for servicing Phantoms. It completed its one hundredth Phantom major service in July 1981. As the emphasis is on front-line aircraft, programmes are based on fixed turn around times of minimum duration. A small team of pilots and navigators at St Athan test fly and ferry

production aircraft after major servicing.

No 431 MU

The build-up for Phantom operations began around 1969 for No 431 MU, but this tasking is only a small portion of its wide responsibilities in Europe. Controlled by RAFG, No 431 MU is administratively supported by RAF Bruggen, where it occupies a 38-acre site. In the event of tension in Europe, it would deploy personnel and equipment around RAFG's four main bases. The MU has three squadrons, and an HQ Flt which plans, co-ordinates and supports activities. A Supply Squadron procures and stores spares and equipment. The Mechanical Transport and General Engineering Squadron has two flights: MT Flt, tasked with freight and specialist transportation, and GEF, which covers carpentry, welding, spraying, signwriting, machining, etc., making components which are unavailable and templates using damaged parts or manufacturer's drawings.

The Aircraft Engineering Squadron (AES) has three flights, AEF, Support (SF) and Propulsion (Prop Ft). SF provides teams for RAF and Army aircraft salvage and recovery in NW Europe when beyond the parent unit's second-line facilities, and are RAFG's specialists at moving Cat 4 and 5 aircraft by road, mostly to manufacturers for Cat 4 repair. SF's crash recovery team is on permanent standby, normally undertaking Cat 3 repairs of transportable components. The MU's first recorded Phantom crash recovery was of XV479 from near Karup. Five more were recovered up to 1982: XV427 in August 1973; XV431 in October 1974 from Bruggen; XV441 in November 1974 from Marsbree, Holland; XV483 in July 1978 from Drenke, West Germany, and XV418 from Lohne, West Germany in July 1980. SF develops, and trains RAF personnel in aircraft battle repair procedures. AEF undertakes damage categorization and survey, repair scheme preparation, Cat 3 and 4 repairs and programmed modifications for RAFG and Army aircraft in NW Europe, and servicing assistance to RAFG units.

Prop Flt provides fault diagnosis and rectification, deep second-line servicing and testing of uninstalled RAFG Speys, Adours and, from 1 September 1983, RB.199s, and receipt from and

In February 1973, RAFG Phantom FGR.2 XV487 caught fire when reheat was selected on ground runs, damaging the whole tail section. No 431 MU, Bruggen, repaired FGR.2 XV487's fin ribs, reskinned the fin and replaced the rudder, stabilator and tail cone assembly. The reskinned fin and rudder is shown, before final respray

XV465's port tail, after engine failure during pre-take-off reheat selection. Ruptured fuel pipes caught fire, badly burning the engine bay and electrical looms and components, rippling and distorting heatshields, and weakening ribs, stringers and skin. No 431 MU repaired it

despatch to units and manufacturers of all such engines, ECU modules and jet pipes. The engine bay converted for Spey servicing became operational around June 1970; an uninstalled Spey running facility was built. The Spey Bay's initial work was receiving new units into stock, but by late 1970 and throughout 1971 issues to and receipts from squadrons totalled six per month. A regular MT Flt shuttle service was required to and from Rolls-Royce. Providing the basic workload in the bay were several deep strip ECUs. Not being of modular design, a Spey can take up to six months to strip and repair. Few serious problems have arisen. The workload was fairly constant until early 1981 when the Defence Moratorium's financial constraints showed up as fewer ECUs being issued to and returned by the squadrons. In August 1981, there was an increase in unserviceable ECUs requiring repair. The bay coped, but early in January 1982 the rate demanded overtime working until February.

No 431 MU's first Phantom tasks were begun during November 1970, by AEF, consisting of modifying the radio installation and replacing the US-type fatigue meter with a standard UK-design, modifications carried out fleet-wide through 1971, taking about 350 manhours per aircraft. The first modified was XV411. Other modifications carried out in 1971 were fitting a gunsight recorder camera, oil collector tanks and an HP RPU indicator modification. The Phantom fleet was g-limited in July 1979 until all mainplanes had been X-rayed, heavily engaging SF's small non-destructive testing (NDT) team in August. Most modifications until early 1980 then involved work on the wings and fuselage to improve fatigue life, but XV470 had Camloc fasteners put on the engine bay doors and XV467 received a changed overheat warning system and modified firewire test plug attachment. The MU has since carried out no further Phantom modifications, although late in September 1983 a small team were requested to carry out a Cat 3 repair inside No 2 fuel cells, following damage found on XV475 during embodiment of a modification to the bay tank attachment by a St Athan Service Working Party. A spate of AEF servicing assistance to squadrons in 1972 dealt mainly with skin removal on the stabilators for an NDT check on the starboard upper outboard torque box. In November 1972, eight assistance tasks were started, and five in 1973. Servicing assistance was given with rivetting to Wildenrath's Structures Bay and ASF in 1980, and with skin repairs on XV480 and XV481, taking three weeks, in November 1981, and, in 1982, with minor structural repairs to two Phantoms at Wildenrath, taking 139 and (XT895) 399 manhours respectively. In February 1982, No 431 MU modified the Aero 1A fuel tank as a baggage carrier, improving on a USMC

modification. BAe Brough accepted it with minor improvements.

AEF's main Phantom involvement, however, has been Cat 3 repair to the airframe, the first begun on 24 January 1972. In 1970 GEF conducted trials of nimonic steels and titanium, then high technology materials, making the first successful welding in September 1970, allowing repairs to be made to smaller areas rather than replacing panels. Cat 3 work involves considerable planning and surveying of the task before starting repairs. After initial categorization by the aircraft assessor, usually the W/O i/c AEF, the aircraft surveyor, an SNCO, draws up a repair scheme. Liaison is maintained with the Phantom's design authority throughout a repair. Drawn from a pool, repair teams are not necessarily Phantom experienced, but team leaders probably will be. The Phantom has not suffered much structural damage. The flap-up stop bracket repair has become standardized due to the number carried out. Part of the machined frame Stn 414, the flap-up stop lugs crack or break and are replaced by items manufactured by GEF. Replacement of this becomes a squadron or ASF Wildenrath commitment.

Some No 431 MU repairs are made on site. On 11 February 1982, XV422 of No 92 Sqn made an emergency landing at Twenthe following bird strike damage to the starboard air intake. Visiting XV422 next day, No 431 MU's assessor and surveyor decided permanent repair on site was feasible. On 14 February, the surveyor flew to BAe Brough to arrange a repair drawing, returning two days later. Work strip started on the 15th, and, with overtime and weekend working, the repair was completed on schedule on the 28th.

Flight Safety

It is important to keep military aircraft accidents in perspective, and not to over-emphasize them. The Phantom has the potential of being a very safe and a very good fighting machine, borne out by its record. It has good self-defence and weapons capability, providing higher survival rates; it has lots of power and two engines, providing higher safety margins; and two people looking out and handling flying loads are better than one. The UK Phantom is in the better half, near of the top, of the RAF's safety record, but a lot of aircraft fall into this bracket. The F-4 type is controllable for safe return to base even if the hydraulics and control systems and powerplant are completely shot out on either side of the aircraft, which was proved in Vietnam.

The function of flight safety procedures, monitoring and organization is to minimize risk, but the job of the RAF and FAA is to prepare for war, and therefore risk cannot be eliminated, not even by flying gently. The RAF Inspectorate of

Flight Safety is responsible for RAF aircraft. The RN has a separate Directorate, with similar functions, accountable to the Director of Naval Air Warfare. In regard to crew safety, the Inspectorate of Flight Safety is involved in minimizing losses, human and material to practical limits, and monitors ejection seats, PLB, dinghies and ASR. The Phantom's record is very good.

Flight safety is a continual process, integral to overall training, flying and all aspects of aircraft operation, and not separate. Aircrew survival training is specific. Flight safety involves two basic aspects: the procedural action and the modification. It is a way of working to spot problems and apply solutions early, although some emerge suddenly and need rapid correction. The process is to monitor continually and to follow and identify trends and phases.

The US Phantoms have command ejection, but the British do not, and the British record is slightly better. Of 41 actual ejections up to mid-1983, only five were unsuccessful, four because the crew went out too late, and one because the pilot and navigator ejected too close together and one struck the other's canopy. An ejection is termed unsuccessful if the seat has fired but the man does not survive. In the UK Phantom, the pilot advises the navigator, or vice versa, of ejection over the intercom, but in the event of intercom failure, the navigator has an emergency battery-powered light operated by the pilot.

In terms of crew survival, the 'coat fastener' harnesses originally equipping the UK Phantom's ejection seats suffered from problems. If they were tapped, they could fly open, but if an ejectee was being dragged along by wind and current in the sea, he had to put his hands to his shoulders to release the harness, but having to overcome the hard strain from drag, which was doubled if, as was likely, only one side released, which then meant he was dragged along spiralling. The RAF identified the problems and gave appropriate training – including Land Rover and power boat simulation – and modified the harnesses, and eventually replaced them altogether.

In service terms, an accident is the result of any abnormal event. The results are categorised: Category 5 is a write-off or beyond economical repair (salvage); Category 4, extensive repair at the manufacturers; Category 3, repair by Service; Category 2, repair at operational base; Category 1, minor. At early 1983 the RAF Phantom accident write-off rate was seven out of 42 FG.1s (including one RN) and 22 out of 116 FGR.2s (a few more have been written off for test purposes). This rate is influenced by many external factors, and is indicative of the fact that low-level operation, such as ground attack, are definitely more hazardous than air defence, generally flown at higher altitudes. The low level environment imposes a greater work load on the crew and hence increases the risks of errors and fatigue. The aircraft flies through denser, bumpier, more turbulent air, and may undertake rapid, heavy or continual evasive or navigational maneouvres in carrying out attacks or in terrain following. Birds and other aircraft are also a considerable risk; for instance, in 1974 a Phantom on low-level exercise collided with a crop-spraying Pawnee, killing the civil pilot.

Some US experience is relevant. For instance, the USN, USAF and RAF all had wing-fold problems, while uncommanded control movement (UCM) is a problem on all aircraft where there is no direct link between the controls and the flying surfaces. UCM is a source for concern on the Phantom, but also on other RAF types such as Jaguar.

There have been a number of problems specific to the Phantom. The Spey headache resulted from the rapid development of an essentially civil engine to give military power and to provide augmented thrust. It had been intended to be a carbon fibre composite machine, but development problems and expense led to the rapid substitution of metals. As a result it suffered from imbalances and development problems continued in service when it was operating at higher temperatures than it had been designed for. The BLC also caused high turbine temperature. The result was a series of turbine-blade failures and related problems after about a year in service. These were spotted early on by normal monitoring. This did not affect aircraft front-line availability, although it restricted training severely. The main problem was replacement engines, and Rolls-Royce had difficulty keeping up with repairs. The problem had virtually been cleared up by mid-1972.

There was only one catastrophic engine failure, when FGR.2 XV441 of No 41 Sqn suffered an uncontained failure as a result of fifth stage compressor disc failure which split a fuel pipe. Most other engine failures have been successfully recovered. XV441 was taking-off from Bruggen. At 260–270 kt there was a loud bang from the left engine – eyewitnesses saw fire-sparks. There was no yaw – the Phantom has no assymetric problem. The pilot saw that the jet nozzle was closed and other engine indications were normal. Then, the left hand engine fire warning indicator lit. The pilot put the throttle to idle, the first action in any aircraft, then got the engine overheat warning. XV441's pilot then asked the navigator to read checks, but the intercom went dead. The controls began to harden up. Then, as the second warning caption, ENGINE FIRE went on, the pilot shut the engine down, but there was no change in the indications. The pilot pressed the navigator's emergency ejection-warning button. The navigator ejected successfully over Ruhrmund, Holland, and the pilot waited before the aircraft was over open country before ejecting, successfully.

There are three warning captions: overheat, referring to the back part of the engine; engine fire, referring to the front part; and engine warning, indicating catastrophic failure. The three lights are positioned above each other. Each engine has separate warnings; both engines' warnings are adjacent. Their original relationship on the panel was misleading and caused at least one pilot to shut down the wrong engine, so they were moved.

One of the features of the BLC problem, which is not strictly engine related, is that it was spotted early and a remedy applied, an excellent example of successful monitoring during routine servicing. If there is a leak in the BLC system, apart from degrading BLC performance, hot air can bleed at high pressure onto wiring and cause ignition and burning, degrading systems with possible serious consequences. There was one catastrophic failure on the UK Phantom, but the aircraft was not lost.

A much publicized aspect of aircraft safety is fatigue. General and heavy fatigue monitoring programmes are continuous on all aircraft types, and problems are identified early on the ground and solutions applied, which may or may not involve groundings or improving procedures – learning is constant. To a large extent, fatigue must be expected after several years' service, especially in powerful, high-performance aircraft operating in the tough low-level environment. There have been no disastrous fatigue problems on the UK Phantoms, except perhaps wing fold failure, and few of the problems are peculiar to the UK Phantom. The higher stress loads imposed by the Spey and vibration problems, however, may have contributed to certain conditions, including rear fuselage and wing joint cracking. RN Phantoms also suffered cracking of the main and forward keel webs. Stabilator hinges also cracked. This problem occurred on F-4s in general, and the method of repair used by BAe's Bitteswell factory so impressed McDonnell Douglas that they adopted it themselves.

The heavy metal fatigue monitoring programme is essential in order to detect fatigue on the ground at an early stage, and take action. For instance, fuel pipe fatigue was found by ground examination. The pipes were too thin, so they were replaced by pipes of heavier gauge metal. Fuel cell web failure through fatigue was also revealed by ground fatigue monitoring. This problem particularly affected the upper skin of No 4 tank, which was vulnerable. Inside the outer fuselage dorsal fairing, the fuel cell is under a thin, flat skin attached only at the perimeter and is therefore unstressed. As the cell emptied, and under hard manoeuvring, the skin flexed and ripped, endangering the cell. Failure of the cell would not necessarily cause a fire, but it would degrade the aircraft's operability. Action was taken, involving an extensive and expensive programme in the mid-1970s on RAF and RN FG.1s and FGR.2s to reskin the fuel cell with heavier gauge metal.

The USN, USMC, USAF and RAF encountered wing fold fatigue problems. FGR.2 XV417 of No 29 Sqn, flown by a Canadian pilot out of Coningsby, was lost on 23 July 1976 through wing fold failure. During air combat with two Dutch F-104s, part of XV417's wing outer panel fell off, seriously degrading performance. The pilot had gently turned towards the F-104s at 460 kt. He tightened the turn. At 5G there was a loud bang followed by uncontrolled roll to the right, but the pilot regained control at 30,000 ft and 360 kt by using considerable left stick and rudder. Then one outer panel fell off. The pilot lost control, so the crew ejected and the aircraft fell into the sea. The lower wing lock lug had failed, putting torsional pull on the hinge. Once torsion sets in, the wing simply twists. Almost the whole outer panel ripped off. The solution was to replace the original alloy lock lugs with stainless steel.

Acknowledgements

The co-operation of many people and organisations has been required to produce this book, and I want to express my gratitude to all of them, including those whose researches were inconclusive. Specific thanks are due to Media Services, Office of Information, Dept of the Navy, USN for permission to use material from 'Yank in the Royal Navy' by M S Seider, in *Naval Aviation News*, March 1975; to the members of No 31 Sqn RAF Association; to D A Rough for F-4K details; to Lt M S Lay RN, J K Flack of Aviation Photographs International, and R F Dorr for photographs; to the editor Dennis Baldry for his hard work, advice and faith; and to Julia Burns for assistance, advice and encouragement and for putting up with a phantom husband for too long. The following are notable among those who have assisted:

Aircraft and Armament Experimental Establishment, Boscombe
   Down (T Heffernan)
Associated Newspapers
The Dennis Baldry Collection
Bendix, Aircraft Brake and Strut Division (USA)
Bodenseewerk Gerätetechnik
British Aerospace:
   Aircraft Group, Scottish Division
   Aircraft Group, Warton Division (S Fielder, A F Johnson);
   Dynamics Group, Hatfield Division (S Raynes)
Chemring (E A Chapman)
Cossor Electronics (F R Berry)
Doulton Industrial Products (M Gollicker)
Dowty Electronics, Communications (F W Archer)
Dowty Group Services (C L Morris)
Dunlop (W B Williams)
Embassy of France to London (Capitaine de Frégate
   Gaucherand)
Embassy of the United States in London
Fairey Hydraulics
Fleet Air Arm Museum, RNAS Yeovilton (L F Lovell)
Fleet Air Arm Officers Association (Lt Cdr J Waterman RD
   RNR)
Fox Photos
General Electric (USA), Aircraft Equipment Division,
   Aerospace Control Systems Department (D Hogan);
   Armament Electrical Systems Department (C F Bushey)
Goodyear (P N Clark)
Graseby Dynamics
Hunting Engineering Management (G Rosie)
Irvin (Sidney Jackson)
Litton, Guidance and Control Systems
Marconi Avionics (M Moulton)
Martin-Baker Aircraft (B Limbrey)
McDonnell Douglas (G Norris, K F Stubberfield)

Ministry of Defence:
   Aeronautical Quality Assurance Directorate
   Air Historical Branch
   Directorate of Public Relations, RN
   Naval Historical Branch
   RAF Inspectorate of Recruiting (D Courtnage *et al*)
   RAF Inspectorate of Flight Safety
M L Aviation (J Fennimore)
National Air and Space Museum, Smithsonian Institute (USA)
   (W J Boyne, E Pupek)
Normalair-Garrett (S R Cheesman)
No 31 Sqn RAF Association (T P O'Halloran, W Smart, Air
   Cmdr T H Stonor BSc RAF)
Stephen Peltz
Plessey Electronics Systems
Rediffusion Simulation (J H Stewart)
Rolls-Royce (M Evans)
Rosemount Engineering (D J Goodsell)
Royal Aircraft Establishment, Bedford (R S Lawrie), and
   Farnborough
Royal Air Force:
   RAF Germany Command Public Relations (C Whitbread
   MIPR)
   Strike Command Public Relations (A Talbot *et al*)
   Units:
      No 2 Sqn (F/O H A Farrar-Hockley)
      No 6 Sqn (F/L P N J Applegarth)
      No 17 Sqn (F/O A R Hill)
      No 23 Sqn (F/L T J Farish BSc)
      No 41 Sqn (F/O L Palmer WRAF)
      No 43 Sqn (F/L M J Loveridge)
      No 92 Sqn (F/L J Turner BA)
      No 431 MU (W/C J M H Sabben BMet CEng MRAeS)
      RAF St Athan
Royal Navy Fleet Photographic Unit, HMS EXCELLENT,
   (Lt Cdr M H Larcombe)
The Tardis Collection
Texas Instruments (USA) (D L Porter)
Titanium Metal and Alloys
Triplex
Ian G Scott
Standard Telephone and Cables
United States Navy:
   Department of the Navy
      Naval Air Systems Command (NAVAIRSYSCON), Naval
      Air Systems (W J Armstrong)
      Office of Information, Still-Photography Branch (R A
      Carlisle)
      Office of the Chief of Naval Operations, Naval Aviation
      History (R A Grossnick)
Westinghouse Electric, (H D Lawton).

Abbreviations

Italics indicate specific use in Aircraft Notes.

A&AEE	Aeroplane and Armament Experimental Establishment
a/c	aircraft
AC	Alternating Current
ACM	Air Combat Manoeuvr(e/ing); Air Chief Marshal
ACT	Air Combat Training
AD; ADC; ADOC;	Air Defence; AD Commander; AD Operations Centre
AEW	Airborne Early Warning
AFB	Air Force Base (US)
AFC	Air Force Cross
Air Cmdr	Air Commodore
AN/123-4	JETDS (Joint Electronics Designation System) numbered communications equipment; letters as relevant:
	1 installation: A airborne, C air transportable;
	2 equipment: A infrared, C carrier, D radio, J electro-mechanical, P, R radar, S special, W armament;
	3 purpose: A auxiliary assembly, B bombing, G fire control, N navigation aids, Q special or combination of purposes, W control, X identification and recognition;
	4 model number, a suffix letter indicating modification, changes in voltage, phase or frequency.
AOC	Air Officer Commanding
APC	Armament Practice Camp
AW	Armstrong-Whitworth (AW.168/HS.168)
AWI	Air Weapons Instructor
ASW	Anti-Submarine Warfare
AVGAS	Aviation Gasoline
AVTUR	Aviation Turbine Fuel
AVM	Air Vice Marshal
BAC	British Aircraft Corporation
BAe; BAeD	British Aerospace; BAe Dynamics Group
BITE	Built-In Test Equipment
BLC	Boundary Layer Control
BAOR	British Army of the Rhine
CADC	Central Air Data Computer (ADC)
CAG	Carrier Air Group
CAP	Combat Air Patrol
Capt	Captain
Cat	Category (accident)

CBLS; CBTE	Carrier, Bomb, Light Stores; CB Triple Ejector (racks)
CBU	Cluster Bomb Unit
Cdr	Commander
CENTO	Central European Nations Treaty Organisation
ch	on service charge
CO	Commanding Officer
CV; CVA; CVN	Fleet Carrier; Attack Carrier; Nuclear Carrier (US)
cm	centimetre
C	Centigrade
CHANNEL	NATO Region, English Channel area
DAC; DACT	Dissimilar Air Combat; DAC Training
DC	Direct Current
del	delivered
EASTLANT	NATO Region, Eastern Atlantic
ECM	Electronic Countermeasures
ECCM	Electronic Counter-Countermeasures
ECP	Engineering Change Proposal
ERU	Ejector Release Unit
EW	Electronic Warfare
F.; F-	Fighter (UK; US)
FAA	Fleet Air Arm
FAC	Forward Air Control(ler)
FBSA	F.-Bomber, Strike, Attack (UK)
FDO	Flight Deck Officer (UK)
ff	first flight
FG/FGA	F, Ground-Attack (UK)
FGR	F, Reconnaissance (UK)
Flt Lt; F/L	Flight Lieutenant
FOB	Forward Operating Base
FONAC	Flag Officer Naval Air Command (UK)
FR	Inflight Refuelling
FS	Fuselage Section
ft	foot/feet
FY	Fiscal Year (US)
G	one gravity force
gal	gallon (1 US gal = ·83 Imperial)
GCI	Ground Controlled Interception
GP	General Purpose (bomb)
gpm	gallons per minute
Grp Capt	Group Captain
HAS	Hardened Aircraft Shelter
HE; HEMC	High Explosive; HE Medium Capacity (bomb)
HF	High Frequency

HMG/HM	Her Majesty's Government
HOSM	Holme-on-Spalding Moor
HP	High Pressure
HSA; HSD	Hawker Siddeley Aviation; HS Dynamics
HUD	Head-Up Display
Hz	Hertz
IAS	Indicated Air Speed
IFTU	Intensive Flying Trials Unit
INAS	Inertial Navigation and Attack
in	inch(es)
IR; IRLS	Infrared; IR Linescan
i/s	issue standard
km; km/hr	kilometre; km per hour
KT	Kiloton
kVA	Kilovolts alternating current
lb	pounds
LCOSS	Lead Computing Optical Sight System
lit	litre(s)
LRU	Line Replaceable Unit
Lt	Lieutenant
Lt Cdr	Lieutenant Commander
MCAIR	McDonnell Aircraft Corporation
mod/mod prog	modification; mod programme
MoD; MoD(PE)	Ministry of Defence; MoD (Procurement Executive)
Min Tech	Ministry of Technology
MPC	Missile Practice Camp
MRA	Major Replaceable Assemblies
MSDS	Marconi Space and Defence Systems
MU	Maintenance Unit
m	metre
mc	megacycle
MHz	Megahertz
mph	miles per hour
MT	Megaton
NACA	National Advisory Committee for Aeronautics
NAIU	Naval Accident Investigation Unit
NATO	North Atlantic Treaty Organisation
NASU	Naval Air Service Unit
NBC	Nuclear/Biological/Chemical warfare
NY	New York State, USA
OCU	Operational Conversion Unit
ORI	Operational Readiness Inspection
PCB	Plenum Chamber Burning
PR	Photographic Reconnaissance

RAE	Royal Aircraft Establishment
RAF	Royal Air Force
R&D	Research and Development
res	reserve aircraft
RHAG	Rotary/Runway Hydraulic Arrestor Gear
RN	Royal Navy
RN Det Leu	Royal Navy Detachment Leuchars
RNAS	Royal Naval Air Station
rpm	revolutions per minute
RWR	Rear Warning Radar/Receiver
S	Strike (UK)
SACEUR	Supreme Allied Commander Europe
SACLANT	Supreme Allied Commander Atlantic
SAM	Surface-to-Air Missile
SAR	Search and Rescue
SD	Specification Detail
SFC	Specific Fuel Consumption
SLR	Side-Looking Radar
SHORAD	Short Range Air Defences
SOCC	Sector Operations Control Centre
SOR	Struck Off Records (charge)
Sqn; Sqn Ldr	Squadron; Sqn Leader
SRAAM	Short Range Air-to-Air Missile
TACAN	Tactical Air Navigation System
temp	temporar(y/ily)
TER	Triple Ejector Rack
TFX	Tactical Fighter Experimental (US)
TSR	Tactical, Strike, Reconnaissance (UK)
UHF	Ultra High Frequency
UKADGE; UKADR	United Kingdom Air Defence Ground Environment; UKAD Region
USAF; USAFE	United States Air Force; USAF Europe
USMC	US Marine Corps
USNAS	US Naval Air Station
USN	US Navy
QFI/QWI	Qualified Flying/Weapons Instructor
V; VAC	Volt; Volt AC
VHF	Very High Frequency
V/STOL	Vertical/Short Take-Off and Landing
WESTLANT	NATO Region, Western Atlantic
Wg Cdr	Wing Commander
WOD	Wind Over Deck

Aircraft notes

These histories can not be complete, first for reasons of security and secondly, because they would be too extensive and confusing as aircraft periodically spend time out of service for various reasons (RN FG.1s provide examples). Further specific information can be found in the main text.

Phantom FG.1

Serial	C/no.	
XT595	1449	YF-4K1; trials a/c, no service; ff 27.6.66; trials; del USA 15.06.70; Min Tech/MoD(PE) ch; installation airframe RAF Coningsby; fuselage only RAF St Athan '82.
XT596	1527	YF-4K2; trials a/c, no service; ff 30.08.66; del USA 28.04.69; Min Tech/MoD(PE) ch; BAe HOSM '81; complete wing awaiting disposal RAF Carlisle '82.
XT597	1611	F-4K1; trials a/c, no service; ff 1.11.66; del USA 1.08.69; Min Tech/MoD(PE) ch; A&AEE '69, '70, 'A' Flt '74-.
XT598	1669	F-4Ks; trials a/c; no service; ff 21.03.67; del USA 6.01.68; Min Tech/MoD(PE) ch; to RAF; lost 23.11.78.
XT857	2097	F-4K2; trials a/c; ff 18.09.67; del USA 23.09.68; del Yeovilton, Min Tech ch 11.11.68;RAE Bedford trials, A&AEE *Eagle* trials '69 RN ch, NASU (removal) instruments, mods to i/s 2.10.70; No 767 Sqn (temp) 27.11.70; NASU (res; mods) 18.12.70; No 767 Sqn 8.02.71; Cat LC accident 15.04.71; NASU (mod prog; MARTSU) 10.06.71; No 767 Sqn 16.03.72; to RAF ch 1.08.72; SOR RN 10.08.72; *U* PTF to '78 (dual a/c); *C* No 11 Group.
XT858	2225	F-4K4; Spey trials a/c; ff 8.06.67; del USA (MCAIR del to Min Tech for R-R's Spey rectification trials) 11.07.67; del Yeovilton 29.04.68 (one of first to RN *see also* XT859, '860); RN ch 30.04.68; *724* No 700P Sqn 30.04.68; JBD trials (loan) RAE Bedford 1.-20.05.68; R-R Hucknall Spey trials continuation 20.05.68; SOR RN to Min Tech ch 26.07.68; continuation R-R trials; RAE Bedford trials '68–69; BAe Brough structures test, MoD(PE) *c.* '81–.
XT859	2279	Ff 19.01.68; del USA 25.04.68; del Yeovilton 29.04.68; RN ch 30.04.68; NASU 30.04.68; *725* No 700P Sqn 21.05.68; solo demonstrator Farnborough SBAC '68; *001* No 892 Sqn 31.03.69; *001* Atlantic race winner 11.05.69; NASU 14.04.70; No 23 MU (major service) 12.05.70; NASU (mods to i/s) 11.11.70; *155* No 767 Sqn 15.05.71; NASU (mods) 18.11.71; *155* No 767 Sqn

Serial	C/no.	
		23.03.72; No 23 MU 05.07.72; RN Det Leu/No 892 Sqn; No 23 MU (mods) 13.02.74; No 892 Sqn; RN Det Leu; HSA HOSM 20.03.75; RN Det Leu (hold) 17.12.75; No 892 Sqn 3.04.76; RN Det Leu (tank repair) 6.01.77; No 892 Sqn 23.03.77; RAF St Athan to RAF ch 27.11.78; SOR RN 11.12.78; *K* No 11 Group.
XT860	2336	Ff 2.02.68; del USA 25.04.68; del Yeovilton 29.04.68; RN ch 30.04.68; *726* No 700P Sqn 30.04.68; NASU 10.05.68; No 700P Sqn 27.05.68; *002* No 892 Sqn 31.03.69; *002* atlantic race 05.69; NASU 14.04.70; No 23 MU 21.07.70; NASU (mod prog) 28.04.71; No 892 Sqn (*Ark Royal*, replace XV570) 9.09.71; RN Det Leu 26.11.74; No 23 MU 23.04.75; RN Det Leu (prepare to i/s) 20.10.75; *006* No 892 Sqn (rotating with XT683) 15.12.75; RN Det Leu (tank top repairs; res) 26.04.77; Cat 3 (service) accident (stbd keel web cracked) Abingdon Camp 9.05.77; RN Det Leu; RAF St Athan, RAF ch, SOR RN 15.03.78; PTF 01.78.
XT861	2383	Ff 3.03.68; del USA 18.06.68; del Yeovilton 24.06.68; NASU (HSA mods), RN ch 24.06.68; No 700P Sqn 11.07.68; *003* No 892 Sqn 31.03.69; *003* atlantic race 05.69; No 767 Sqn 15.04.70; No 23 MU 1.03 – 29.09.71; NASU 30.09.71; No 767 Sqn 18.11.71; No 23 MU (mods), to RAF ch 1.08.72; SOR RN 10.08.72; *V* PTF to '78 (dual a/c); No 11 Group.
XT862	2426	Ff 29.03.68; del USA 18.06.68; del Yeovilton, NASU, RN ch 24.06.68; *722* No 700P Sqn 3.07.68; No 892 Sqn 31.03.69; No 767 Sqn 15.04.70; crashed 19.05.71 (Cat ZZ EW failure, crew recoeverd); SOR RN 15.06.71.
XT863	2463	Ff 9.04.68; del USA 1.07.68; del Yeovilton, NASU (HSA mods) 2.08.68; RN ch 5.08.68; No 700P Sqn 3.10.68; *150* No 767 Sqn 7.01.69; NASU (mod to i/s) 18.09.70; *150* No 767 Sqn 18.02.71; NASU 26.11.71; No 767 Sqn 26.04.72; No 892 Sqn (Leuchars; temp. replace XV568) 2.08.72; No 23 MU (mod prog; refinish; prep to i/s) 4.12.72; RN Det Leu (hold, res) 12.06.73; No 892 Sqn (replace XT871) 10.73; No 23 MU (mods) 15.02.74; No 892 Sqn 23.05.74; HSA HOSM (MoD update) 11.11.75; RN Det Leu (prep to i/s; hold, res) 13.05.76; No 23 MU (surface finish) 27.05.76; RN Det Leu (prep to i/s; hold, res) 10.06.76; *014* No 892 Sqn 18.08.76; Cat 3 (flying) accident (keel

Serial	C/no.	

web angle cracked) task completed 03.77; RAF St Athan, RAF ch 27.11.78; SOR RN 11.12.78; *G* No 111 Sqn '79–.

XT864 2475 Ff 5.04.68; del USA 17.07.68; del Yeovilton, RN ch, NASU 22.07.68; *724* No 700P Sqn 3.09.68; *151* No 767 Sqn 7.01.69; Cat 3 (flying) accident (angles joining upper wing surface/fuselage port & stbd cracked; HSA working party commence work 2.11.70, HSA Mod 122 complete 13.11.70, Mod 28 27.11.70); No 767 Sqn; NASU (mod prog) 8.02.71; *151* No 767 Sqn 29.07.71; NASU (prep to i/s for No 892 Sqn) 24.09.71; NASU (prep to i/s for No 892 Sqn) 24.09.71; No 892 Sqn (replace XV567[HC]) 4.10.71; No 23 MU (refinish) 17.01.73; HSA HOSM (mod prog) 6.03.73; No 23 MU (surface finish) 24.01.74; RN Det Leu (mod) 20.02.74; No 892 Sqn (Leuchars) 6.05.74; RN Det Leu (tank repair; mainplane change) 5.11.75; No 892 Sqn 2.02.76; RAF St Athan (surface finish) 2.03.77; *007* No 892 Sqn 4.04.77; RAF St Athan, RAF ch 27.11.78; SOR RN 11.12.78; *J* No 11 Group.

XT865 2502 F-4K11; trials a/c; ff 7.04.68, del USA 5.09.68; del UK, Min Tech 09.68; (not RN ch); Min Tech UK ch (RN loan) 11.11.68; A&AEE *Eagle* trials 06.69; NASU (removal instruments; mods to i/s) 23.10.70; *156* No 767 Sqn (replace XT862) 8.06.71; NASU (mod prog) 21.04.72; *156* No 767 Sqn (replace XT859) 6.07.72; No 23 MU (mod prog) 1.08.72; RN Det Leu 27.11.72; No 892 Sqn (on disembarkation) 18.01.73; No 23 MU (mod prog) 11.10.73; No 892 Sqn (Leuchars) 2.04.74; RN Det Leu (for CNP embarkation; mods) 11.12.74; No 23 MU (surface finish) 31.01.74; RN Det Leu (hold, res) 21.02.75; MoD(PE) (loan, RAE Bedford/HSA arresting gear trials) 20.03.75; RN Det Leu (temp. at Lossiemouth)(res) 21.04.75; No 60 MU Leconfield (repair 3, 4 tanks) 19.06.75; RN Det Leu (Lossiemouth) 23.06.75; No 892 Sqn (replace XV568) 14.07.75; No 60 MU (repair 3, 4 tanks) 10.02 76; No 892 19.02.76; Cat 3 (service) accident (oil canning effect 3, 4 tanks) to No 60 MU 08.76; RN Det Leu (tank repairs) 3.03.77; Cat 3 (flying) accident (stbd keel web cracked, repair completed 25.03.77); No 23 MU (surface finish) 16.06.77; RN Det Leu (res) 6.07.77; Cat 3 (service) accident (left flap-up stop cracked, repair completed 17.05.77); No 892 Sqn 19.08.77; RAF St Athan, RAF ch 27.11.78; SOR RN 11.12.78; *U* No 111 Sqn.

XT866 2526 Ff 9.05.68; del USA 22.10.68; del Yeovilton, NASU, RN ch 11.11.68; *158* No 767 Sqn 3.06.69; (HSA Mod 28 on mainplanes at Yeovilton completed 30.10.70; Mod 122 1. – 3.12.70); NASU (mods) 3.08.71: No 767 Sqn 3.12.71; No 23 MU (mods), to RAF ch 1.08.72; SOR RN 10.08.72; *W* PTF to '78 (dual a/c); No 43 Sqn '78–81; lost 9.07.81 (Leuchars, just after 2400 hrs on approach following instrument problem but probable cause turbulence from 'shepherd' a/c; two major injuries).

XT867 2546 Ff 27.04.68; del USA 8.08.68; del Yeovilton, NASU, RN ch 29.08.68; *152* No 767 Sqn 24.01.69; NASU (mods) 26.04.71; *152* No 767 Sqn; No 23 MU (mods) 1.08.72; RN

Det Leu (custody), to No 892 Sqn on disembarkation 11.11.72; No 23 MU; RN Det Leu (res) 24.10.74; No 892 Sqn; RN Det Leu (custody) 17.09.75; No 23 MU (mods) 3.10.75; RN Det Leu (prep to i/s) 1.06.76; No 892 Sqn 17.08.76; RN Det Leu (res) 30.03.78; RAF St Athan, to RAF ch 20.04:78; SOR RN 16.05.78; *H* No 11 Group.

XT868 2602 Ff 1.05.68; del USA 8.08.68; del Yeovilton, NASU 27.08.68; RN ch 28.08.68; *153* No 767 Sqn 9.01.69; Cat HC (flying) accident (radome and scanner ripped off, engines damage) 10.12.69; NASU (Cat 3 repair) 16.12.69; *151* No 767 Sqn (estab. increase) 2.04.71; NASU 24.03.72; No 23 MU (surface finish; prep to i/s; mod prog) 4.08.72; RN Det Leu (hold, res); No 23 MU (mod prog; refinish; prep to i/s) 18.10.72; RN Det Leu; No 892 Sqn (receipt checks; hold) 29.03.73; No 23 MU (mod prog) 12.11.73; No 892 Sqn (Leuchars) 10.04.74; RN Det Leu (hold) 19.08.76; No 892 Sqn 6.01.77; RAF St Athan (surface finish) 1.02.77; No 892 Sqn 2.03.77; RN Det Leu (hold, res) 16.02.78; Cat J (crashed during flying display RAF Abingdon) 12.05.78; NAIU 22.05.78; scrap to F K Beadle & Son; SOR RN 20.12.78.

XT869 2623 Ff 2.05.68; del USA 2.08.68; del Yeovilton, NASU, RN ch 7.08.68; No 700P Sqn 30.10.68; No 767 Sqn 7.01.69; NASU (MARTSU Cat 3 repair; impact damage t/e spar and flap jack extension when not connected to flap; repair 30.01. – 6.02.70); No 767 Sqn (replace XT683) 18.09.70; NASU (mods); *154* No 767 Sqn 7.07.72; NASU (prep for No 23 MU prog); No 23 MU (mods; refinish; prep to i/s) 22.09.72; RN Det Leu 26.02.73; RN Det Leu (embarkation checks), No 892 Sqn 7.03.73; lost (Cat ZZ; crashed; NAIU Lee for investigation – reclassified Cat 5, to No 71 MU); SOR RN (to instructional and scrap) 3.12.74.

XT870 2646 Ff 14.05.68; del USA 5.11.68; del Yeovilton, NASU, RN ch 11.11.68; No 892 Sqn 17.03.69; NASU (mods) 24.03.70; No 892 Sqn (replace XV565) 5.08.71; HSA HOSM (Mod 459) 13. – 19.06.74; RN Det Leu 26.07.74; MoD(PE) (loan, arrestor gear trials RAE Bedford) 1. – 21.10.74; RN Det Leu 21.10.74; No 23 MU 26.11.74; RN Det Leu (prep to i/s; res) 7.07.75; No 892 Sqn 2.08.76; No 23 MU (surface finish) 29.04.77; *012* No 892 Sqn 16.05.77; RAF St Athan, to RAF ch 27.11.78; SOR RN 11.12.78; No 11 Group.

XT871 2666 Ff 28.05.68; del USA 5.09.68; del Yeovilton, NASU 15.10.68; RN ch 16.11.68; No 892 Sqn 28.03.69; NASU (mods) 2.09.69; No 892 Sqn 6.03.70; NASU (mods) 6.03.70; No 892 Sqn (replace XV590) 16.04.71; NASU; No 892 Sqn; lost '73 (Cat ZZ, ditched operating from *Ark Royal*, technical fault; salvaged for NAIU investigation 12.10.73); SOR RN 8.11.74 (to instructional and scrap)

XT872 2706 Ff 17.06.68; del USA 23.09.68; del Yeovilton, NASU, RN ch 27.09.68; A&AEE/RAE Bedford trials 22.11.68; NASU 31.01.69; *007* No 892 Sqn 2.04.69; NASU (mods) 16.10.69; No 892 Sqn

Serial	C/no.	
		8.12.71; No 23 MU; No 892 Sqn (Leuchars) 14.06.74; No 23 MU 5.09.74; RN Det Leu (res) 9.04.75; Cat 3 (service) accident, No 60 MU (oil canning effect, repairs 2, 3, 4, 5 tanks) 10.09.75; RN Det Leu (res) 21.10.75; No 892 Sqn 6.11.75; Cat 3 (flying) accident (stbd oleo collapsed penetrating mainplane) – to NAIU, RAF St Mawgan (investigation) 9.02.76; No 71 MU, RAF Abingdon (post NAIU investigation) 15.03.76; recat Cat 4 (works, HSA repair) (damaged centre wing section); HSA HOSM (Cat 4 repair) 18.06.76; RN Det Leu (prep to i/s res) 9.05.77; 004 No 892 Sqn 13.06.77; RAF St Athan, RAF ch 27.11.78; SOR RN 11.12.78; T No 111 Sqn '79–.
XT873	2738	Ff 19.11.68; del USA 14.11.68; del RAF (No 23 MU); loan to RN for No 767 Sqn 10.01.69; No 767 Sqn; No 23 MU, return to RAF, SOR RN 17.03.70; No 111 Sqn '79–.
XT874	2775	Ff 29.06.68; del USA 30.09.68; del RAF (No 23 MU); J No 43 Sqn '69–78; E No 111 Sqn '78–.
XT 875	2813	Ff 18.07.68; del USA 22.10.68; del RAF (No 23 MU); loan to RN for No 767 Sqn 27.01.69; No 767 Sqn; No 23 MU, return to RAF, SOR RN 30.07.69; No 11 Group (Kc. '83.
XT876	2856	Ff 19.07.68; del 25.10.68; del RAF (No 23 MU); loan to RN for No 767 Sqn 17.01.69 (collected by NASU); 160 No 767 Sqn; lost (crashed in sea) 10.01.72; Cat 5 (abandoned), RAF ch, SOR RN 02.72.
XV565	2872	Ff 30.08.68; del USA 12.03.69; del from St Louis to NASU, Yeovilton 30.04.69; RN charge 1.05.69; accident; mods HSA completed 9.03.70; No 892 Sqn 16.04.70; lost (ditched, crew recovered) 08.71; SOR RN 1.09.71.
XV566	2896	Ff 3.09.68; del USA 14.01.69; del NASU 26.01.69; RN charge 27.01.69; No 892 Sqn 8.05.69; NASU mod prog 31.10.69; No 892 Sqn 23.03.70; lost (crashed into sea crew not recovered) 3.05.70; SOR RN 15.05.70.
XV567	2922	Ff 20.04.68; del USA 16.06.68; RN charge 15.01.69; A&AEE Eagle trials 06.69; 011 No 892 Sqn; 001 Saratoga trials 10.69; trials RAE Bedford '69; No 892 Sqn to 3.10.71; SOR RN 11.12.78, to RAF; No 43 Sqn.
XV568	2943	Ff 29.04.68; del USA 1.07.68; RN charge 1.04.69; 012 No 892 Sqn; 012 Saratoga trials 10.69; No 892 Sqn to 07.75; SOR RN 11.12.78, to RAF T Leuchars.
XV569	2970	Ff 20.09.68; del USA 14.01.69; RN ch 24.01.69; No 767 Sqn; 013 No 892 Sqn; 013 Saratoga trials 10.69; 013 No 892 Sqn; '73–75; SOR RN 10.08.72, to RAF; X PTF c. 06.85–78; Q Leuchars.
XV570	2995	Ff 3.10.68; del USA 6.01.69; del NASU, RN ch 26.01.69; 014 No 892 Sqn 2.09.69; 014 Saratoga trials 10.69; HSA Brough mod prog 26.11.69; 014 No 892 Sqn 24.03.70; NASU 9.09.71; 014 No 892 Sqn; NASU to RAF Leuchars, RAF ch 4.09.72; SOR RN 22.11.73; Y PTF '73–78.
XV571	3020	Ff 12.11.68; del USA 17.06.69; del RAF (No 23 MU, Aldergrove); A No 43 Sqn c.'69–83.
XV572	3042	Ff 17.10.68; del USA 14.02.69; del RAF (No 23 MU); loan to RN for No 767 Sqn 6.05.69; 156 No 767 Sqn; No 23 MU, return to RAF 24.03.70; N No 43 Sqn '72–83 M c. 83.
XV573	3065	Ff 29.10.68; del USA 24.03.69; del RAF (No 23 MU); L, then C, then L No 43 Sqn '69–76; D Leuchars.
XV574	3087	Ff 20.11.68; del USA 14.02.69; del RAF (No 23 MU); Z No 43 Sqn '69–83.
XV575	3112	Ff 26.11.68; del USA 8.04.69; del RAF (No 23 MU); S No 43 Sqn c. '81–.
XV576	3134	Ff 29.11.68; del USA 2.06.69; del RAF (No 23 MU); D No 43 Sqn '69–83–.
XV577	3155	Ff 4.12.68; del USA 21.04.69; del RAF (No 23 MU); M No 43 Sqn '69–83–.
XV578	3180	Ff 6.12.68; del USA 21.04.69; del RAF (No 23 MU); No 43 Sqn '69–79; lost 28.02.79.
XV579	3204	Ff 6.09.68; del USA 22.11.68; del RAF (No 23 MU); loan to RN for No 767 Sqn 19.06.69; 157 No 767 Sqn; accident, to NASU 24.04.72; 157 No 767 Sqn; No 23 MU, return to RAF 31.07.72; R No 43 Sqn c. '74–83.
XV580	3218	Ff 25.12.68; del USA 12.05.69; del RAF (No 23 MU); Q No 43 Sqn '69–75; lost 18.09.75.
XV581	3235	Ff 4.03.69; del USA 28.04.69; del RAF (No 23 MU); E No 43 Sqn '69–83.
XV582	3253	Ff 11.01.69; del USA 5.05.69; del RAF (Nos 23 MU); initially uncoded, then F No 43 Sqn '69–83.
XV583	3268	Ff 4.03.69; del USA 5.05.69; del RAF (No 23 MU); G No 43 Sqn '69–B c. 83.
XV584	3286	Ff 12.03.69; del USA 11.08.69; del RAF (No 23 MU); F Leuchars, c. 83.
XV585	3302	Ff 28.03.69; del USA 19.05.69; del RAF (No 23 MU); F, H, P No 43 Sqn c. '69–83.
XV586	3317	Ff 11.04.69; del USA 23.06.69; del NASU, RN ch 27.06.69; 011 No 892 Sqn '76; 010 No 892 Sqn '77–78; SOR RN 11.12.78, to RAF; Leuchars.
XV587	3331	Ff 21.04.69; del USA 30.09.69; RN ch 29.10.69; 010 No 892 Sqn c. '77; SOR RN 7.12.78, to RAF G Leuchars c. 83.
XV588	3346	Ff 21.04.69; del USA 22.07.69; RN ch 14.07.69; 010 No 892 Sqn c. '70; SOR RN 31.05.77 (a/c fire, to spares and product).
XV589	3363	Ff 9.05.69; del USA 8.07.69; RN ch 28.07.69; 154 No 767 Sqn '68–69; 006 No 892 Sqn c. '74–; SOR RN 11.12.78, to RAF; P, then O No 111 Sqn '78–80 (among first FG.1s); lost (crashed, RAF Alconbury, radome opened) 3.06.80.
XV590	3394	Ff 12.05.69; del USA 9.07.69; RN ch 28.07.69; 001 No 892 Sqn to 15.04.71; NASU; No 892 Sqn c. '78; SOR RN 11.12.78, to RAF; X Leuchars.
XV591	3409	Ff 3.06.69; del USA 22.07.69; RN ch 14.08.69; 006 No 892 Sqn – '78; SOR RN 11.12.78, to RAF M No 111 Sqn –83.
XV592	3424	Ff 17.06.69; del USA 17.11.69; RN ch 24.11.69; 004 No 892 Sqn c. '73; 005 No 892 Sqn c. '75; SOR RN 7.12.78; L No 111 Sqn '79–83–.

Phantom FGR.2

Serial	C/No.	
XT852	1950	YF-4M1; ff 17.02.67; trials a/c; BAe HOSM, MoD(PE) '81–.
XT853	2020	YF-4M2; trials a/c; BAe HOSM, MoD(PE) '81–.
XT891	2250	F-4M1; first F-4M del USA 20.06.68; first F-4M del UK, RAF (No 23 MU) 20.07.68; No 228 OCU 23.08.68; No 228 OCU/64 Sqn; No 54 Sqn; Z No 228 OCU/64 Sqn '81–83.
XT892	2285	No 6 Sqn '69–; V No 228 OCU/64 Sqn '81–.
XT893	2333	No 228 OCU '69; K No 111 Sqn '74–77; No 228 OCU '81–83.

Serial	C/no.	
XT894	2370	*B*, then *P* No 228 OCU/64 Sqn '78–83.
XT895	2417	*P* No 6 Sqn '74; No 29 Sqn; *T* RAFG '81–83(**I**).
XT896	2456	No 228 OCU '69; *P* No 6 Sqn '69–74; *K* No 19 Sqn '76–; No 228 OCU/64 Sqn –82; No 11 Group '83 (*T*).
XT897	2471	*M* No 228 OCU '81–83
XT898	2485	A&AEE navigation trials '71–72; No 228 OCU/64 Sqn '75; *T* No 2 Sqn '76; No 29 Sqn '79–;*E* No 228 OCU/64 Sqn *c* 83–.
XT899	2507	No 228 OCU '69; *X* No 23 Sqn; No 228 OCU, '82; *X* No 23 Sqn, early '83; *X* No 29 Sqn from 03.83.
XT900	2516	No 14 Sqn '70–75; *O* No 228 OCU '81–83.
XT901	2536	No 228 OCU '69; No 228 OCU/64 Sqn; No 17 Sqn 07.70–72 (among first); *T* No 2 Sqn '72–76; *D* No 228 OCU –83; *Y* No 56 Sqn 03.83–.
XT902	2567	*I* No 228 OCU '81–.
XT903	2592	No 228 OCU 64 Sqn *c.* '82–83; *X* No 11 Group '83–.
XT904	2616	Lost 15.10.71.
XT905	2636	No 54 Sqn, '69; accident 6.05.70; No 17 Sqn, *c.* '75; *H* No 228 OCU/64 Sqn.
XT906	2657	No 31 Sqn '71–; *T* No 2 Sqn *c.* 73–75; *S* No. 228 OCU –83; *Y* No 56 Sqn, *c.* 01.83.
XT907	2665	No 228 OCU/64 Sqn '75–83 (*T* '78–).
XT908	2684	*P* No 6 Sqn '69–74; No 228 OCU/64 Sqn '75–; *Y* No 56 Sqn '80–83.
XT909	2696	No 228 OCU '69–, No 6 Sqn '69–71; No 31 Sqn '71–76; *Y* No 56 Sqn 03.76 (*see* XV470, '489, '497); *K* No 228 OCU/64 Sqn '81–; *M* No 11 Group '83–.
XT910	2709	No 29 Sqn '74–76; No 228 OCU/64 Sqn '76–83.
XT911	2727	No 6 Sqn '69–; RAFG *c.* '81–83 (*K*).
XT912	2742	*K* No 111 Sqn, Coningsby, c. 06.75–; *K* No 23 Sqn, '76 (one of sqn's two dual control a/c, *see* XV396; *see also* '421, '422, '432, '434, '465, '490, '496 which, mainly ex-No 14 Sqn a/c, were No 23 Sqn's first a/c); No 228 OCU/64 Sqn; lost 14.04.82 (collided with XT903 on T-O, Coningsby).
XT913	2754	Lost 14.02.72.
XT914	2771	No 228 OCU '69; No 14 Sqn '70–08.75 (among first del to sqn); RAFG *c.* '81–83.
XV393	2791	No 31 Sqn '71–76; No 228 OCU/64 Sqn '76–83 (*A* '82–).
XV394	2803	No 228 OCU early '69; *P* No 6 Sqn '69–74; *O*, then *C* No 228 OCU/64 Sqn '79–83.
XV395	2822	No 228 OCU early '69; lost 9.07.69.
XV396	2834	No 228 OCU early '69; *C*, then *A* (from 04.76) No 23 Sqn early '76 (CO's mount, *see* XT912); *D* No 228 OCU '82–83.
XV397	2850	No 31 Sqn '71–72; No. 17 Sqn '72–73; lost 1.06.73.
XV398	2864	No 228 OCU/64 Sqn '76– (*H* '82–83).
XV399	2869	No 29 Sqn '79; *L* No 228 OCU/64 Sqn *c* '82; *L* No 56 Sqn, early '83.
XV400	2877	*R* No 6 Sqn '69–74; *I* No 29 Sqn '77–78; No 228 OCU '82; *F* RAFG.
XV401	2885	*A*, then *I* No 41 Sqn '72–77; *B* No 228 OCU/64 Sqn '82–83.
XV402	2893	No 31 Sqn *c.* '71–76; *E* No 2 Sqn *c.* '71–76; *G* No 228 OCU/64 Sqn '82; No 29 Sqn, to Falklands; No 23 Sqn from 03.83.
XV403	2901	No 6 Sqn '69; *A* No 111 Sqn '75; lost 4.08.78.
XV404	2910	No 31 Sqn '71–74; *J* No 111 Sqn 10.74–77; No 29 Sqn '79; *B* No 56 Sqn early '83.
XV405	2919	No 228 OCU/64 Sqn *c.* '74–75; lost 24.11.75.
XV406	2928	Recce pod trials HSA '69 (incl ff of pod at HOSM) and A&AEE '70–71; *D* No 54 Sqn '74; *M* No 111 Sqn '77–78; *A/D* No 29 Sqn *c.* '83.
XV407	2937	*H* No 19 Sqn; *O* No 56 Sqn '83.
XV408	2946	*L* No 6 Sqn '70; No 228 OCU/64 Sqn '74; *N* No 23 Sqn '77–83.
XV409	2955	No 31 Sqn '71–75, *J* No 111 Sqn *c.* 06.75–; No 228 OCU *c.* 82–83.
XV410	2964	A&AEE radio trials '69–70; accident 12.01.78; *H* No 56 Sqn '81; No 228 OCU '82; *E* No 23 Sqn early '83; *E* No 56 Sqn from 03.83;
XV411	2973	No 14 Sqn '70–75 (among first a/c); *S* No 92 Sqn '82–.
XV412	2981	*B* No 41 Sqn '72; *X* No 92 Sqn '77; RAFG '82; *F* UKADR '83.
XV413	2990	*Z* No 92 Sqn '77; No 29 Sqn '80; lost 12.11.80 (in sea 50 miles NE of Cromer; crew killed).
XV414	2999	Wattisham –80; lost 9.12.80 (in sea 10 miles NE of Lowestoft; fuel leak ignited).
XV415	3007	No 31 Sqn '71–76; *P* No 92 Sqn '82–83.
XV416	3017	No 54 Sqn '69–72; *C* No 41 Sqn 07.72; *H* No 111 Sqn '74–75; lost 3.03.75.
XV417	3026	No 14 Sqn '70–74; *E* No 2 Sqn '74–76; lost 23.07.76.
XV418	3036	*C* No 41 Sqn '72–77; No 92 Sqn '78 (as one of first two exp. grey scheme a/c *see* XV478); lost 11.07.80 (crashed Lohne, W. Germany, recovered by No 431 MU).
XV419	3045	No 54 Sqn '73; *G* No 29 Sqn '81–, to Falklands '82; No 29 Sqn from 03.83.
XV420	3053	*D* No 54 Sqn –72; *H* No 29 Sqn '74–77 (among first a/c); *W* No 23 Sqn '82–83.
XV421	3061	*B* No 23 Sqn '75–77; *P*, then *Q* No 228 OCU/64 Sqn '80–83.
XV422	3068	No 31 Sqn '71–76; *E* No 6 Sqn *c.* 09.72; *C* No 23 Sqn '76– (among first a/c); *O* No 92 Sqn '81–82; UKADR.
XV423	3075	*R* No 29 Sqn 12.74–76; *E* No 23 Sqn '80–09.81; *B* No 29 Sqn, to Falklands '82; *D/B* No 56 Sqn 03.83.
XV424	3084	*B* No 6 Sqn '74; *B* No 29 Sqn 06.75; No 56 Sqn; 60th anniversary Alcock & Brown Atlantic Commemorative Flight a/c, for flight 21.06.79, painted in MoD(PE) 'raspberry ripple', *see also* XV486; *I* UKADR *c.* '82.
XV425	3093	No 6 Sqn, '69; *D* No 23 Sqn; *D* No 56 Sqn from 03.83.
XV426	3100	No 31 Sqn '71–76, No 228 OCU/64 Sqn *c.* '82; No 29 Sqn, to Falklands; No 23 Sqn from 03.83.
XV427	3106	No 31 Sqn '71–73; lost 22.08.73, recovered by No 431 MU.
XV428	3115	*H* No 111 Sqn 06.75; RAFG; *I* No 56 Sqn *c.* early '83.
XV429	3124	No 228 OCU, 69; No 6 Sqn '69–; No 54 Sqn –09.76; BAe HOSM, RAF Strike Cmd *c.* '82; *K* UKADR '83.
XV430	3131	*S*, then *R* No 2 Sqn '71–76; *C* No 19 Sqn c. '81–83.
XV431	3140	No 31 Sqn '71–74; lost 11.10.74 (wings folded on T-O from Bruggen, F/L Ray Pilley, pilot, F/L Kevin Toal ejected with a/c almost vertical, saved by zero-zero Mk 7 seats – subject flight safety film *Oversight*).
XV432	3149	*N* No 6 Sqn *c.* '69–; *L* No 54 Sqn, *c.* '72–; *D* No 23 Sqn '76–.
XV433	3158	No 31 Sqn '71–76; *V* No 92 Sqn '81; *F* No 228 OCU '82–.
XV434	3167	*J* No 23 Sqn *c.* '76–77–; *J* No 228 OCU/64 Sqn *c.* '82–83.

Serial	C/no.	
XV435	3174	No 14 Sqn '70–75; *X* RAFG *c.* '82–83.
XV436	3183	No 228 OCU/64 Sqn *c.* '72; *E* No 29 Sqn *c.* '78; lost 5.03.80 (Coningsby, flapless landing, night).
XV437	3195	No 54 Sqn '69, code later *F*; *J* No 56 Sqn *c.* '80–83.
XV438	3201	*A* No 6 Sqn '69–74; *A* No 29 Sqn '74–77; *Y* No 228 OCU/64 Sqn '82–.
XV439	3208	No 14 Sqn '71–74 (among first a/c); *A*, then *D* No 19 Sqn '77–83.
XV440	3214	No 31 Sqn '71–73; lost 25.06.73 (crashed into sea at night off Vliehors, Holland, F/L Hugh Kennedy, pilot, S/L Dave Hodges, killed).
XV441	3220	No 14 Sqn '71–74; lost 21.11.74 (uncontained engine failure, crashed Marsbree, Holland, recovered by No 431 MU).
XV442	3226	*E* No 6 Sqn, '69–; *F*, then *I* No 29 Sqn '74–77; *O* No 92 Sqn; *H* UKADR *c.* '82.
XV460	3231	No 31 Sqn, *c.* '71–76; *W* RAFG *c.* 81–.
XV461	3237	*H* No 29 Sqn *c.* '79; *G* No 56 Sqn, *c.* early '83.
XV462	3243	*U* RAFG *c.* '82–83.
XV463	3249	No 14 Sqn '71–75 (among first a/c); lost 17.12.75.
XV464	3255	No 14 Sqn *c.* '70–75; No 2 Sqn *c.* '76; *B* No 56 Sqn '77–78–; *U* No 228 OCU/64 Sqn *c.* '82; No 29 Sqn to Falklands; No 23 Sqn from 03.83.
XV465	3261	No 31 Sqn *c.* '71–76; *E* No 23 *c.* '76; *Z* RAFG *c.* '81–83; Cat 3 accident 11.81; No 431 MU (repair, at Laarbruch, to fire damage stbd engine bay) 11.81–08.82.
XV466	3265	No 228 OCU; No 6 Sqn '69– (among first a/c); *K* No 56 Sqn *c.* '80; RAFG '82; *E* No 29 Sqn, to Falklands; No 23 Sqn from 03.83.
XV467	3270	*R* No 2 Sqn *c.* early '73–75; *Q* RAFG *c.* '82–.
XV468	3276	No 17 Sqn '71–75 (among first a/c); No 29 Sqn, first Phantom to Falklands; No 23 Sqn from 03.83.
XV469	3282	No 17 Sqn '70; No 31 Sqn *c.* '71–76; *H* No 2 Sqn *c.* '76; *A* No 56 Sqn *c.* '80.
XV470	3288	*H*, later *W* No 2 Sqn '71–74; transferred Nos 14 and 17 Sqns late '74; *C* No 56 Sqn 03.76–77; (one of first four a/c, *see also* XV489, '497, XT909); *W* No 228 OCU/64 Sqn, '82; *G* No 19 Sqn *c.* '83.
XV471	3293	No 17 Sqn '71– (among first a/c); *T* No 41 Sqn *c.* '76; RAFG, '82.
XV472	3298	No 228 OCU/64 Sqn *c.* '75; RAFG *c.* '82–83.
XV473	3304	No 14 Sqn '71– (among first a/c); *L* No 228 OCU/64 Sqn *c.* '82–.
XV474	3309	No 17 Sqn *c.* '70–75; No 2 Sqn *c.* '76; *F* No 56 Sqn *c.* '80; No 29 Sqn, to Falklands; No 23 Sqn from 03.83.
XV475	3314	*D* No 17 Sqn, '71–; RAFG, *c.* '82–.
XV476	3321	No 54 Sqn *c.* 02.70; No 31 Sqn '71–76; *C* No 19 Sqn.
XV477	3329	Lost 21.11.72.
XV478	3336	*O* No 111 Sqn mid-'74–77; No 23 Sqn '78 (one of first two exp. grey-scheme Phantoms, *see* XV418); *F* (then *Q c.* '83) No 56 Sqn early '79–83.
XV479	3344	Lost 12.10.71 (crashed near Karup, Denmark, recovered by No 431 MU).
XV480	3350	No 31 Sqn *c.* '71–76; *J* No 41 Sqn *c.* '73; RAFG *c.* '82–83.
XV481	3355	*H* No 6 Sqn *c.* '72; *E* No 29 Sqn *c.* '75; RAFG *c.* '82–83.
XV482	3361	No 54 Sqn; *E* No 41 Sqn *c.* '72; *U* No 41 Sqn *c.* '75; *L* No 29 Sqn *c.* '77–; *C* No 56 Sqn *c.* 01.03.83.
XV483	3367	No 31 Sqn *c.* '71–72; No 17 Sqn '72–; *U* No 41 Sqn '75; lost 24.07.78, (crashed near Drenke, W. Germany, recovered by No 431 MU).
XV484	3373	No 31 Sqn '71–75; *F* No 23 Sqn '75–77; No 19 Sqn '77–80; No 29 Sqn, to Falklands; No 23 Sqn, from 03.83.
XV485	3377	*W* No 2 Sqn (early period); *K* No 29 Sqn *c.* 06.75–09.76; *P* No 23 Sqn, *c.* 01.83.
XV486	3382	No 14 Sqn '70; No 2 Sqn '72–; No 23 Sqn; Alcock and Brown re-enactment a/c 21.06.79, 'raspberry ripple' finish (*see* XV424); *X* No 228 OCU *c.* '82–83.
XV487	3386	RAFG *c.* '72–; Cat 3 accident 02.73; No 431 MU (repair to fire damaged tail); *K* No 56 Sqn '83.
XV488	3392	No 31 Sqn *c.* '71–76; *R* No 228 OCU–64 Sqn *c.* '79–83.
XV489	3396	No 31 Sqn *c.* '71–76; *F* No 17 Sqn '74, *c.* '70–75; *F* No 56 Sqn *c.* 03.76– (one of first a/c, *see also* XT909 XV470, '497); *V* No 92 Sqn *c.* '77–78; *A* No 23 Sqn early '83; No 56 Sqn '83.
XV490	3401	No 41 Sqn; *M* No 29 Sqn *c.* 06.75–; *G*, then *H* ('79) No 23 Sqn, early '76–03.83; *H* No 56 Sqn, from 03.83.
XV491	3407	No 31 Sqn '71–76; No 29 Sqn; lost 7.07.82 (crashed into sea off Cromer).
XV492	3413	*Q* No 6 Sqn '69–74; *Y* No 41 Sqn *c.* '76; No 228 OCU/64 Sqn *c.* '81–82; *U* No 56 Sqn early '83.
XV493	3420	*F* No 41 Sqn 07.72–74; lost 9.08.74.
XV494	3428	No 17 Sqn '76; BAe HOSM, Strike Cmd '82; *M* No 23 Sqn *c.* 01.83; *M* No 56 Sqn from 03.83.
XV495	3434	*K* No 6 Sqn 09.70–09.72; *L* No 54 Sqn '72–74; *I* No 41 Sqn *c.* '76; *X* No 29 Sqn '78; *L* No 56 Sqn '80–83.
XV496	3442	No 17 Sqn *c.* '70–75; *G* No 41 Sqn *c.* 07.72–; *H* No 23 Sqn early '76; RAFG '82.
XV497	3454	*H* No 41 Sqn 07.72–75; No 17 Sqn *c.* 05.75–01.76; *G* No 56 Sqn 03.76 (one of first four a/c, *see also* XT909, XV470, '489); RAFG '82.
XV498	3466	No 17 Sqn '70–75; RAFG '82; *H* No 23 Sqn early '83.
XV499	3477	*G* No 6 Sqn *c.* '69–74; No 41 Sqn *c.* '73–77; *R* No 92 Sqn *c.* 07.77–; *R* No 228 OCU/64 Sqn *c.* '83–.
XV500	3491	*M* No 56 Sqn '74– (early period); *M* No 111 Sqn *c.* '75–77; *S* No 23 Sqn early '83.
XV501	3507	No 14 Sqn '70–72 (early period); No 31 Sqn *c.* 04.76; *O*, then *T* No 29 Sqn *c.* '79; marked as *B* No 23 for Greenham Common IAT 07.83 No 29 Sqn!

Phantom Losses

Royal Air Force								
1	XV395	FGR.2	9.07.69	20	XV578	FG.1	28.02.79
2	XV479	FGR.2	12.10.71	21	XV436	FGR.2	5.03.80
3	XT904	FGR.2	15.10.71	22	XV589	FG.1	3.06.80
4	XT913	FGR.2	14.02.72	23	XV418	FGR.2	11.07.80
5	XV477	FGR.2	21.11.72	24	XV413	FGR.2	12.11.80
6	XV397	FGR.2	1.06.73	25	XV414	FGR.2	9.12.80
7	XV440	FGR.2	25.06.73	26	XT866	FG.1	9.07.81
8	XV427	FGR.2	22.08.73	27	XT912	FGR.2	14.04.82
9	XV493	FGR.2	9.08.74	28	XV491	FGR.2	7.07.82
10	XV431	FGR.2	11.10.74	RN	XT868	FG.1	12.05.78
11	XV441	FGR.2	21.11.74				
12	XV416	FGR.2	3.03.75	*Royal Navy*			
13	XV580	FG.1	18.09.75	1	XV566	FG.1	3.05.70
14	XV405	FGR.2	24.11.75	2	XT862	FG.1	19.05.71
15	XV463	FGR.2	17.12.75	3	XV565	FG.1	SOR 1.09.71
16	XV417	FGR.2	23.07.76	4	XT876	FG.1	10.01.72
17	XV483	FGR.2	24.07.78	5	XT871	FG.1	SOR 8.11.74
18	XV403	FGR.2	4.08.78	6	XT869	FG.1	SOR 3.12.74
19	XT598	FG.1	23.11.78	7	XV588	FG.1	SOR 31.05.77

Specifications

DIMENSIONS
Span   38 ft 4.9 in (11.706 m)
Wing Area   530 sq ft (49.237 m²)
Aspect ratio   2.82:1
Wing Fold Span   27 ft 6.6 in (8.397 m)
Length   57 ft 7.1 in (17.554 m)
Length, Nose Folded   51 ft 8.6 in (15.573 m)
Height (fin)   16 ft 1.0 in (4.902 m)
Height (canopy)   10 ft 11.7 in (3.345 m)
Height (folded tip)   11 ft 3.6 in (3.444 m)
Stabilator span   16 ft 5.1 in (5.006 m)
Wheelbase   22 ft 11.9 in (7.008 m)
Track   17 ft 10.9 in (5.458 m)

TYRES
Main   30 × 11.5 in Type VIII (762 × 292 mm)
Nose (twin)   18 × 5.7 in Type VII (457 × 145 mm)
Pressure, carrier/land   350 psi/200 psi

FUEL
Internal   1,991 US Gal
External (max)   1,340 US Gal

WEIGHTS (lb/kg)
Empty   30,918 (14,023)
Useful load:
  crew   430 (195)
  fuel, internal   13,240 (6,005)
  4 × AIM-7   1,820 (826)
  miscellaneous   377 (171)   15,867 (7,197)
                                                                  ──────────
Basic T-O Gross   46,785 (21,220)
External fuel tanks
  600 US Gal   3,990 (1,810)
  tank, rack, etc   300 (136)   4,290 (1,946)
                                                                  ──────────
Alternative T-O Gross   51,075 (23,166)
  2 × 370 US Gal   4,921 (2,232)
  tanks, racks, etc   680 (308)   5,601 (2,540)
                                                                  ──────────
Alternative T-O Gross   56,676 (25,706)
Combat Gross (4 × AIM-7; 60% int fuel)   41,489 (18,818)
Landplane T-O Gross   58,000 (26,307)
Landing Gross (4 × AIM-7; 1,200 lb fuel reserve)   34,745 (15,759)

PERFORMANCE
(YF-4M; Spey Mk 201, 4 × AIM-7, 1,200 lbs fuel reserve)
TO over 50 ft (15.24 m) obstacle (basic T-O gross)   2,070 ft (631 m)
Ceiling (combat gross)
  supersonic   54,400 ft (16,581 m)
  subsonic   51,500 ft (15,697 m)
Maximum speed level flight (36,089 ft) (11,000 m)   M 2.2
Acceleration, M .9 to M 2 (36,089 ft) (11,000 m)   3.17 min.
Rate of climb (sea level, combat gross)
  military   13,020 ft/min.
  maximum   45,600 ft/min. (13,899 m/min.)
Approach speed   133 knots
Landing ground roll (landing gross)
  with brake chute   2,350 ft (716 m)
  without brake chute   3,440 ft (1,049 m)

MISSION PROFILES
(YF-4M: Spey Mk 201, 4 × AIM-7, 1,200 lb fuel reserve)

Mission	T-O Gross lb (kg)	Ordnance lb (kg)	Tanks US Gal	Radius nm
TACTICAL				
Hi-Lo-Lo-Hi	52,937 (24,011)	4,718 (2,140)	2 × 370	546
Hi-Lo-Lo-Hi	61,174 (27,747)	4,498 (2,040)	1 × 600	766
			2 × 370	
Hi-Lo-Hi	62,533 (28,363)	11,458 (5,197)	1 × 600	300
Lo-Lo-Lo	62,533 (28,363)	11,458 (5,197)	1 × 600	177
Lo-Lo-Lo	61,174 (27,747)	4,498 (2,040)	1 × 600	357
			2 × 370	
RECONNAISSANCE				
Hi-Lo-Lo-Hi	54,737 (24,827)	pod	2 × 370	665
Lo-Lo, night	54,737 (24,827)	pod/	1 × 370	402
		light	1 × 276	
AIR DEFENCE				
QRA	51,075 (23,166)	—	1 × 600	318
CAP	56,676 (25,706)	—	1 × 600	150
			2 × 370	
INTERCEPT	56,676 (25,706)	—	1 × 600	889
			2 × 370	
				Range
FERRY				
Drop/keep	54,856 (24,881)	—	1 × 600	2,289/
tanks			2 × 370	2,071

NOTES
1. QRA: M 1.8 at 55,000 ft (16,765 m)
2. CAP: 3.26 hours on station
3. Intercept: Area; M 1.5 at 50,000 ft (15,240 m)
4. Ferry: No AIM-7s; Spey Mk 202 range 2,305/2,085 nm

SPEY SPECIFICATIONS
Air flow (sea level, static)	204 lb/sec (92.53 kg/sec)
Turbine stages	2HP, 2LP
Compression stages	5LP, 12HP
Overall pressure ratio	20:1
By-pass ratio	0.62:1

DIMENSIONS
Length	204.9 in (5,204.4 mm)
Maximum diameter	43.0 in (1,092.2 mm)
Intake diameter	32,5 in (825.5 mm)

WEIGHTS (Mk 202)
Dressed	4,060 lb (1,842 kg)
Total basic dry	4,093 lb (1,857 kg)
Installed	4,248 lb (1,927 kg)

PERFORMANCE
Sea level, static conditions

	Mk 201	Mk 202/203
Minimum T-O thrust		
maximum power, reheat	20,095 lb (9,115 kg)	20,515 lb (9,305 kg)
military power, no reheat	12,125 lb (5,500 kg)	12,250 lb (5,556 kg)
36,089 ft (11,000 m)		
Maximum power, reheat	15,960 lb (7,240 kg) (M 2)	12,800 lb (5,805 kg) (M 1.5)

Index